W9-CDX-158

Education Reform and the Limits of Policy

Education Reform and the Limits of Policy

Lessons from Michigan

Michael F. Addonizio
C. Philip Kearney

2012

W.E. Upjohn Institute for Employment Research
Kalamazoo, Michigan

Library of Congress Cataloging-in-Publication Data

Addonizio, Michael.
Education reform and the limits of policy : lessons from Michigan / Michael F. Addonizio, C. Philip Kearney.
p. cm.
Includes bibliographical references and index.
ISBN-13: 978-0-88099-387-6 (pbk. : alk. paper)
ISBN-10: 0-88099-387-1 (pbk. : alk. paper)
ISBN-13: 978-0-88099-389-0 (hardcover : alk. paper)
ISBN-10: 0-88099-389-8 (hardcover : alk. paper)
1. School improvement programs—United States. 2. Educational change—United States. 3. Education and state—United States. 4. Education—Economic aspects—United States. 5. Education and state—Michigan—Case studies. 6. Public schools—Michigan—Case studies. 7. School improvement programs—Michigan—Case studies. 8. Educational change—Michigan—Case studies. I. Kearney, C. Philip. II. Title.
LB2822.82.A33 2012
371.2'07—dc23

2012001332

W.E. Upjohn Institute for Employment Research
300 S. Westnedge Avenue
Kalamazoo, Michigan 49007-4686

Cover design by Alcorn Publication Design.
Index prepared by Diane Worden.
Printed in the United States of America.
Printed on recycled paper.

Contents

Figures

Tables

Acknowledgments

We want to thank all those who played important roles in bringing this book into print. First of all, we are grateful to Kevin Hollenbeck of the W.E. Upjohn Institute for Employment Research, who urged us to embark on the project and, through the Upjohn Institute, provided the sponsorship and support that made possible the printing and publication of this work. We also owe a special thanks to Allison Hewitt Colosky of the Upjohn Institute for her superb editorial work on the manuscript.

Several colleagues generously contributed their time and effort to careful readings of portions of the manuscript; their comments and counsel were invaluable and of great assistance to us in ensuring accuracy of text and improving understandability of content. We need to acknowledge in particular the contributions of Paul Bilelawski in Chapter 3, Ed Roeber in Chapter 4, Elaine Madigan in Chapter 5, and Jeff Mirel in Chapter 7. In addition, several current and former members of the professional staff of the Michigan Department of Education were especially helpful in commenting on other portions of the manuscript and responding to requests for information and confirmation of data, including Bill Bushaw, Paul Stemmer, Joseph Martineau, Jim Griffiths, Steve Viger, Bill Brown, Glenda Rader, and Kim Sidel. Other knowledgeable colleagues provided valuable comment and counsel, including Frank Womer, David Olmstead, Jim Kelly, Ernie Bauer, David Treder, Charlie Greenleaf, and Monte Piliawsky. We are also indebted to Bulent Ozkans, Susanne Krispien, and Julie Smith for their superb research assistance and to Henry Payne and Gary Packingham for permission to reprint their elegant and telling art.

Michael Addonizio owes a special thanks to Wayne State University and its College of Education for granting a sabbatical leave for the 2008–09 academic year, and to the Gerald R. Ford School of Public Policy at the University of Michigan for providing a stimulating venue from which to launch this book project; he is particularly grateful to John Chamberlin and Alan Deardorff for their support and hospitality at the Ford School and to Brian Jacob for his insights into education research and policy analysis.

The assistance and support of all of the above have been invaluable and helped ensure the successful publication of this present work. We, of course, assume full responsibility for any errors of fact or omission.

Finally, we want to acknowledge and thank Joan and Julie for their continuing support and love throughout the long weeks of our effort to bring this present work to completion.

Michael F. Addonizio
C. Philip Kearney

1
Introduction

On April 20, 2006, Michigan Governor Jennifer Granholm signed legislation that set the most demanding high school graduation requirements in the nation. These standards, effective for all students in the 2011 graduating class, require four years of English language arts; four years of mathematics, including algebra II; three years of science; and three years of social studies. Additional requirements in world languages take effect with the class of 2016. These ambitious standards, typically required only for the college bound, were motivated by concerns over Michigan's struggling economy and workforce, concerns brought to public attention by the Lt. Governor's Commission on Higher Education and Economic Growth (the so-called Cherry Commission). The Cherry Commission's 2004 report issues this challenge:

> Michigan's residents, businesses, and governments can either move forward to a future of prosperity and growth fueled by the knowledge and skills of the nation's best-educated population, or they can drift backward to a future characterized by ever-diminishing economic opportunity, decaying cities, and population flight—a stagnant backwater in a dynamic world economy. (Cherry Commission 2004, p. 3)

These standards, prompted by concerns over a state economy that has shrunk steadily since 2001, are the most recent in a series of substantial K–12 education policy reforms dating back to 1990, when the Michigan legislature passed Public Act 25, a sweeping reform that established a state model curriculum, a state accreditation program for all elementary and secondary schools, and formal processes for improving schools and publishing school reports on a regular basis.

The pace of Michigan's education reform accelerated dramatically during Governor John Engler's first term, 1991–94, with new legislation on teacher tenure, charter schools, interdistrict school choice, and, most notably, comprehensive tax reform and a complete overhaul of K–12 school finance. Passage of these sweeping reforms was aided by a generally robust state economy and some measure of bipartisan cooperation in the legislature. The cumulative impact of these reforms eventually came to be nothing less than a new landscape for public schools in Michigan, with more centralized and less stable funding, volatile district enrollments, and, with charter schools, the advent of nonunionized teachers.

But the pace of education reform slowed dramatically during Engler's third term in 1999–2002 as policymakers, recognizing the apparent limits of many of the measures they so quickly had enacted, began to evaluate and fine-tune their dramatic innovations. Constraints were placed on charter school growth, school choice options were broadened to allow cross-county student movement, and local district options for enhanced operating funds were curtailed. However, the bulk of the Engler-era reforms remained essentially unchanged during the administration of Governor Granholm, perhaps owing to popular support for the charter and choice initiatives and a faltering state economy that has generated little new revenue with which to facilitate further school finance reforms. However, while choice and charters continue to enjoy popular support, a growing number of educators, parents, and other school advocates have expressed concern over the state's dwindling financial support, measured in real terms, for most school districts in Michigan.

CONCURRENT NATIONAL REFORMS

With the notable exception of the state's dwindling financial support for public schools, Michigan's K–12 education reforms have paralleled recent nationwide trends. Here we need to distinguish between nationwide reform movements and reforms advanced under federal legislation. While some reforms, such as school choice and charter schools, become nationwide movements as they are adopted in state after state, fewer initiatives of comparable scope are instituted by the U.S. Congress. The U.S. Constitution makes no mention of education, leaving such matters "to the States . . . or to the people."[1] Indeed, it was not until 1958, following the Soviet Union's launch of the satellite Sputnik, that Congress entered the education policy arena in any substantial way, with passage of the National Defense Education Act, a federal financial aid program designed to improve education in mathematics, science, and foreign languages. The next important piece of federal education legislation was passed a few years later as part of President Lyndon Johnson's War on Poverty, with the educational centerpiece being the 1965 Elementary and Secondary Education Act (ESEA). This act signaled for the first time a broadly conceived federal program of financial assistance to the nation's elementary and secondary schools, with its central thrust being the provision of funds to local school districts to design and implement new compensatory education programs for low-income children.

A few short years later, concern over the performance of public schools rose appreciably across the nation following the 1983 publication of *A Nation at Risk* (National Commission on Excellence in Education 1983), a controversial report highly critical of U.S. public schools. Despite its faulty conclusion that the stagflation plaguing the U.S. economy at that time was attributable to poor performance by our public schools (our economy prospered in the 1990s without dramatic school improvement), the report ignited a flurry of education policy reforms across the states. These reforms—which included teacher certification tests, early childhood education initiatives, high school graduation requirements, and more statewide standardized student testing—emphasized student and school performance, in contrast to the concerns of equity and access that had dominated school policy debates in the 1970s. Public schools were now expected to be adequate or even excellent, not just equal.

This debate over public school performance and the accompanying cries for accountability have risen several more decibels since the 2001 reauthorization of ESEA, commonly known as the No Child Left Behind Act (NCLB). Under NCLB, schools and districts that fail to make "adequate yearly progress" for two consecutive years are subject to a set of reforms and sanctions designed to improve school performance. As a school continues to fall short of adequate yearly progress, the scope of the required remedial measures widens to include offer of transfer to children who wish to leave the school, the provision of supplementary educational services outside the normal school day, the replacement of school staff, and the conversion of the school to charter status.

Further, the school accountability movement, with its emphasis on educational outcomes, has changed the focus of school finance policy analysis and litigation from equity and the relative spending levels of local school districts to the more fundamental matter of student achievement. That is, school funding should now address adequacy as well as equity. More specifically, a state's school finance system should provide all schools with resources sufficient to support high levels of achievement by all students, regardless of their social or economic background. This concept of educational adequacy, which received its first explicit judicial expression in a notable 1989 Kentucky case (*Rose v. Council for Better Education* 1989), has been applied by courts in more than a dozen states to declare school finance systems unconstitutional and has prompted school finance reforms in other states as well, including Michigan.

This confluence of reform efforts has led to the proliferation of a vast array of new and revised education policies at both state and national levels, policies aimed at producing a veritable renaissance in American public education. As the problems abound, the policies keep pace, but the answers and solutions—for a variety of reasons—continue to come hard. If we have learned anything over these past years, we have learned that there are definite limits to policy, limits to implementing even well-constructed reforms, and limits to what reforms can accomplish. Yet we soldier on, experiencing both victories and defeats, and ever striving to better understand and overcome the constraints and limits we face in attempting to fashion and effect substantive reforms in our nation's public schools. While there is no doubt that an abundance of newly enacted education policies abounds across the state and across the nation, more fundamental questions remain. What is the nature of these reforms? What do they hope to accomplish? How successful have they been?

In this book, we attempt to provide some answers to these questions by examining a set of major education policy reforms undertaken in Michigan and across the country over the past 20 or more years, a time of unprecedented educational innovation in the United States. These innovations include finance reform, state assessment of student performance, a series of school accountability measures, charter schools, schools of choice, and, for Detroit, a bevy of oft-conflicting policies and reform efforts that have belabored but seldom helped its public schools.

In the pages that follow, we examine the decidedly mixed outcomes and effects of this large array of reform policies and programs. Each chapter addresses a specific policy area, outlining reform activity across the nation with an emphasis on Michigan's efforts as well as on one or two states that led these changes.

In Chapter 2, we examine the seemingly endless controversy over money and schools: Does more money make schools better? We then look at the financing of Michigan's public schools, setting out a brief history of past attempts at reform prior to the enactment of Proposal A in 1994–95 and its promise of increased equity for both taxpayers and students, as well as an adequate and stable revenue source to support quality programs in the schools. We review the factors that led to the reform, the principal components of the reform, and the consequences or effects of the reform, with a particular focus on its fiscal equity effects. But we also include in our discussion the closely related issue of adequacy, for in addition to the question of justice and fairness in the state's distribution of resources, we ask whether the resources are adequate to provide a quality education for all Michigan students, and whether they are supported by a stable revenue stream.

In Chapter 3, we describe and comment on past and particularly more recent efforts to develop a state accountability system for the schools of Michigan, so that, in the words of the U.S. Congress, no child is being left behind, and that all children, all schools, and all school districts are making adequate yearly progress in bringing all students to acceptable levels of academic proficiency by the federally mandated target date of 2013–14. We examine in some detail the nature of Michigan's accountability program, initially entitled EducationYes! and subsequently MI-SAS and later MI-SAAS, and how it meets—or fails to meet—the federal directives of NCLB and its requirements for adequate yearly progress.

In Chapter 4, we address an important corollary to the building of accountability systems, the 40-year effort to develop and implement both a state assessment program, the Michigan Educational Assessment Program (MEAP), and the National Assessment of Educational Progress Program (NAEP). Both efforts are aimed at rigorous measurement of the academic achievement of the students in our public schools, and the public reporting of that information to the citizenry, often to the chagrin of school people. Our examination includes an in-depth look at educational achievement in Michigan over the past four or more years using data from the MEAP and the NAEP, high school graduation rates, and other evidence. In this examination, we also compare Michigan's performance to that of other states as well as the more demanding standards of the NAEP program, and comment on the substantially lower performance levels reported for Michigan by the NAEP.

In Chapter 5, we introduce the issue of school choice and the increasing attention that policymakers, in Michigan and across the nation, are paying to parents' desires to choose the type and the setting of the school their children will attend. In Michigan, this increasing attention to school choice led initially to the legislature's 1993 establishment and the rapid growth of charter schools, or public school academies, of which there are now some 240 enrolling over 100,000 Michigan pupils. These charter schools are fast becoming a significant force in Michigan public education, but also a force reflecting both successes and failures, and somewhat mixed hopes for the future.

In Chapter 6, we further develop this issue by turning to the second of Michigan's school choice reforms. In 1996, the legislature enhanced parental and student choice with its enactment of the schools of choice program, allowing students to leave their home districts to enroll in neighboring districts with public funding following automatically. Again, we see both benefits and costs—benefits to students who matriculate and to the school districts that receive them, but significant costs and few benefits to the school districts that lose students to their neighboring districts. We also address a serious and increasing problem brought on by the reform, namely, the danger of further segmentation and the "creaming" of more able students from "losing" districts such as Detroit and Benton Harbor.

In Chapter 7, we turn our lens on Detroit Public Schools and its sad history of continuing failure, going from being one of the nation's more prestigious, big city, urban school districts of the 1940s, 1950s, and 1960s, to literally one of the worst in the country by 2011. The picture we present of Detroit Public Schools is one marked by general socioeconomic decline, unrelenting political conflict, fiscal mismanagement, revolving-door leadership, and broken promises. It is a sad but instructive story, particularly with respect to the future of big city, urban education in the United States. We portray a public school system in Detroit that is evolving from a district-based system to a hybrid consisting of traditional district schools, recently subject to dramatically increased state oversight, a diverse and growing array of charter schools, and increased private and philanthropic activity.

We conclude our treatise in Chapter 8 with a discussion of what has been accomplished and learned during this period of dramatic change in American public education. Then, on the basis of these lessons, we pose our thoughts and ideas about the years ahead. We believe now is an opportune time for taking stock of our state's K–12 educational system, and we hope this book will enhance our understanding of the limits of our current state policies as a means of improving outcomes in our public schools. Such understanding is essential as, in the words of the Cherry Commission (2004, p. 3), we "move forward to a future of prosperity and growth fueled by knowledge and skills," or become "a stagnant backwater in a dynamic world economy."

Note

1. The 10th amendment states, "The powers not delegated to the United States by the Constitution, nor prohibited by it to the States, are reserved to the States respectively, or to the people."

2
A Fiscal and Educational System under Stress

As the opening days of school approached in the fall of 2011, Michigan and its public schools in particular faced an uncertain future. While the national economy struggled to show some signs of lasting recovery from the Great Recession of 2008 and 2009, the state's economy continued its unremitting decline. For the fiscal year beginning October 1, 2011, Governor Rick Snyder and the legislature eliminated a $2 billion budget deficit, partly through draconian cuts in education at the K–12 and postsecondary levels. As a consequence of the state's deteriorating revenues and passage of a substantial business tax cut, Michigan's local school districts sustained an unprecedented cut in state aid for school year 2010–11, compounding a shortfall in their local revenues. As of this writing, more than 40 districts in Michigan are in deficit, and many more across the state face the prospect of a budget deficit or severe spending cuts in the year to come.

In this chapter we turn first to the question of whether money makes a difference. We look next at the financing of Michigan's public schools, offering a brief history of past attempts at reform prior to the advent of Proposal A in 1994–95 and its promise of equity for both taxpayers and students, as well as an adequate and stable revenue source to support quality programs in the schools. We review briefly the factors that led to the reform, the principal components of the reform, and the consequences or effects of the reform, with a particular focus on its fiscal equity effects. Our discussion includes the closely related issue of adequacy. For not only are justice and fairness of the state's distribution of resources among schools and school districts called into question, but also whether the resources are adequate to provide a quality education for all Michigan students, and whether they are supported by a stable revenue stream.

MONEY AND SCHOOLS: FACTS, MYTHS, AND RECENT HISTORY IN PUBLIC SCHOOL FINANCE

Does more money make schools better? No other question has attracted more attention and generated more controversy among education researchers over the last 40 years. The two sides in this long-running debate are nicely summed up by noted economist Eric Hanushek and a highly regarded team of scholars from the University of Chicago:

> Schools as a whole demonstrate an inability to use available resources effectively. There is little reason to believe that an additional dollar put into a school will improve student achievement. (Hanushek 1981, p. 37)

> The general conclusion of the meta-analysis presented in this article is that school resources are systematically related to student achievement and that these relations are large enough to be educationally important. Global resource variables such as [per pupil expenditures] show strong and consistent relations with achievement . . . Instead of reform without the possibility of enhanced resources, policymakers should advocate reform which incorporates high standards, continuing assessment, and adequate resources. (Greenwald, Hedges, and Laine 1996, pp. 384, 386)

This debate has raged since the publication of the well-known Coleman Report (Coleman et al. 1966), which found that school resources had a surprisingly small effect on measured student achievement (specifically, reading scores). This report, undoubtedly one of the most influential in the history of U.S. education and social policy making, has inspired a mountain of research seeking to estimate the relationship between school resources and student learning. This line of research has drawn heightened interest since the publication of *A Nation at Risk* (National Commission on Excellence in Education 1983)—a controversial report that was highly critical of U.S. public schools and ignited a flurry of educational policy reforms at the state and federal levels.[1]

Most of the studies of school resources and student achievement have modeled standardized test scores, aggregated to the school or district level, as a function of student and family background characteristics (e.g., parental education level and family income), peer effects, and school resources. In many of these studies, the effects of such school resources as per pupil expenditures, pupil-teacher ratios, and teacher characteristics—generally, degree level and years of teaching experience—have been found to be small and inconsistent (Hanushek 1986). More recently, however, researchers have found evidence that school resources do matter and that increased spending *can* raise student achievement (Ferguson and Ladd 1996; Krueger 2003). In particular, researchers have constructed more valid measures of teacher quality (e.g., certification test scores, college course work, competitiveness of undergraduate college, and impact on student achievement test scores) and have found significant teacher effects on student achievement (Ehrenberg and Brewer 1994; Ferguson and Ladd 1996; Rivkin, Hanushek, and Kain 2005).

School Accountability and Educational Adequacy

The debate about money and schools has risen several decibels since the advent of the school accountability movement in the early 1990s and the 2002 reauthorization of the federal No Child Left Behind Act (NCLB). Under NCLB, schools and districts that fail to make "adequate yearly progress" (AYP) for two consecutive years are subject to a set of reforms and sanctions designed to raise student achievement. These interventions become more substantial as a school continues to fall short of AYP requirements, including the offer of transfer to children in failing schools, the provision of supplementary educational services outside the normal school day, the replacement of school staff, and the conversion of the school to charter status. Sanctions may also be imposed on failing school districts, including the withholding of funds, replacement of district staff, and the reorganization or dissolution of the district. As schools are held more accountable for the measured achievement of their students, questions of school resource levels and efficiency receive new emphasis.

The role of the courts

The school accountability movement, with its emphasis on educational outcomes, has moved the focus of school finance litigation from *equity* to *adequacy*; that is, from comparisons of per pupil property wealth and school spending levels across local districts to the more fundamental matter of student achievement. In so-called adequacy lawsuits, plaintiffs allege that their state's constitution obliges the legislature to provide *all* students, regardless of background or degree of socioeconomic disadvantage, with an education that ensures their achievement at high levels, generally defined by a passing score on a standardized achievement test. Moreover, plaintiffs seek a *court-ordered funding level* determined by a "costing-out" study in which a plaintiff's expert or court-appointed master identifies the educational programs and services required for state achievement goals and calculates their dollar costs.

This legal strategy, first applied in the groundbreaking Kentucky case *Rose v. Council for Better Education* (1989), has proved to be a winning one, with plaintiffs' success rates substantially exceeding their winning percentages in earlier "equity" lawsuits dating from the landmark 1971 *Serrano v. Priest* decision of the California Supreme Court. The use of these costing-out studies by many state courts has generated fierce controversy among both legal scholars and school finance experts. Some in the legal community see the courts' enforcement of these studies as judicial usurpation of the legislature's powers of the purse, while some economists challenge the validity of the studies themselves.[2] Nevertheless, despite legitimate concerns over whether these judicial excursions into school finance policy making are founded on an ephemeral link between school spending and school quality and violate basic principles of separation of powers, plaintiffs will continue to file these adequacy lawsuits given their success to date.

Money and Schools: Lessons Learned

The long-running debate over school funding has generated more heat than light, but some useful conclusions have emerged. First, while more money is clearly no guarantee of school improvement, real improvement is much less likely without it. That is, money is necessary but not sufficient for school quality. Second, figuring out *how* to spend money so as to improve student learning is the right question, one that is more daunting than many school advocates care to admit. But careful research has been helpful here. Princeton economist Alan Krueger has identified several education initiatives that are well supported by research evidence: fully funding Head Start and Early Head Start; increasing the school year by 30–40 days, especially in inner-city areas; lowering class size in schools with large concentrations of low-income students; and improving the quality of teachers, especially in low-income areas, through merit-pay and other incentive programs (Krueger 2003). Obviously, these and other reforms cost money. As Harvard researcher Timothy Hacsi (2003, p. 203) observes, "We need to know which [reforms] have the most impact on what kind of student, and we need to know how various reform possibilities interact. To have the kind of quality schooling many of us *claim* we want for all children, we will need to spend more money than we do now" (emphasis in the original).

In theory, then, schools can be improved by spending more money wisely, and some reliable research evidence is available to guide these spending decisions. At the same time, however, it is clear that school funding decisions, as to both overall level and particular spending categories, are driven mostly by politics, not science. University of California at Berkeley Professor Norton Grubb cites political and historical forces that shape school spending decisions: " . . . public education (like most public activities) is driven by conventional interest group politics—a struggle for scarce resources based on the power of interest groups rather than on the rightness of the cause. The constituency for jobs is often more powerful than that for improved educational performance, and so battles over the level and distribution of spending (on teachers, for example) rather than over the promotion of learning often dominate educational politics . . . " (Grubb 2009, p. 33).

As for the historical inertia of public school spending, Grubb observes that "most revenues (more than 80 percent of total expenditures) are locked up in salaries and benefits covered by contracts and cannot be changed at all in the short run; even in the long run, changes cannot take place without bitter political battles (especially battles with unions)" (p. 35).

To sum up, money is necessary but not sufficient for improving our public schools. It must be used wisely to support education programs that are based on sound evidence. Moreover, the funding of public schools is essentially a political process in which schools compete with other programs and priorities for limited tax dollars, and the most effective uses of school resources are themselves often compromised by competing and frequently hidden agendas. In light of all this, it is not surprising that school funding levels and school performance are not consistently aligned. Some schools determine how to use resources effectively given their people's talents and needs while other schools squander their money. As a result, a consistent link between money and school quality remains elusive.

FINANCING MICHIGAN'S PUBLIC SCHOOLS

State aid for local public schools in Michigan dates back to the establishment of statehood in 1837. In those early years, the proceeds of the state's Primary School Fund were apportioned among schools according to the number of pupils in each township, and the townships were authorized to levy local taxes to support their schools. Schooling was "free" for residents but only for three months each year. Beyond that, a tuition fee was charged to parents.[3]

Prior to 1973–74, Michigan distributed general aid to local schools through a foundation aid system that guaranteed a minimum expenditure per pupil in every district. However, by 1973 Michigan's highest spending district tripled the per pupil expenditure of the state's lowest spender. Facing disparities of this magnitude, as well as a court challenge of the constitutionality of the school funding system, the Michigan legislature replaced the foundation formula with a guaranteed tax base (GTB) system, effective with the 1973–74 fiscal year (*Milliken v. Green* 1972, 1973). In that first year, more than 90 percent of Michigan's school districts received GTB aid, assuring all of them equal revenue per pupil for equal tax effort. However, by 1993–94, this percentage had fallen to approximately two-thirds, and the ratio of per pupil spending between the highest—and lowest—spending districts had risen to the levels of the early 1970s (Wassmer and Fisher 1996, p. 92). Further, school property tax rates had risen to politically unpopular levels in many localities, with 122 school districts within four mills of the state's constitutional 50-mill limit (Citizens Research Council of Michigan 1992).[4] Unhappiness with the local property tax received its most dramatic expression in the Kalkaska School District, where voters' repeated rejections of a millage renewal resulted in the closing of public schools on March 15, 1993, after a mere 135 days of class!

A Brief History of Attempted Reforms

Taxpayers and legislators had hoped the 1973 statutory change to a GTB formula would substantially eliminate school spending disparities between property-rich and property-poor districts and reduce the overall reliance on the property tax for school funding (Caesar, McKerr, and Phelps 1978). These hopes were never fulfilled, however, and reform efforts continued. Indeed, from 1972 to 1989 Michigan voters were presented with no fewer than nine opportunities, either statutorily or constitutionally, to reduce property taxes and change the way schools are financed. All of these proposals were soundly defeated (Public Sector Consultants 1992).

Prelude to reform[5]

In Michigan's 1990 gubernatorial campaign, Republican candidate (and soon-to-be-governor) John Engler promised a hefty cut in property taxes if elected. Once elected he launched an initiative petition drive to place on the November 1992 ballot a proposed constitutional amendment—known as Proposal C—aimed at providing an across-the-board cut in local property taxes, accompanied by a cap on future increases in assessments (Citizens Research Council of Michigan 1992). The legislature, through its own action, also placed a plan on the ballot. Proposal A would limit annual assessment increases on homestead property to the lesser of 5 percent or the inflation rate. Both proposals were soundly defeated by the voters, bringing the total number of consecutive failed reform attempts to 11.[6]

The voters' rejection of proposals A and C of 1992 was followed by one more ill-fated reform effort: a constitutional amendment that would provide both property tax relief and school finance reform. Following extensive bipartisan deliberations in the Michigan House before and after the November 1992 elections, and an ensuing round of marathon negotiations between lawmakers and Governor Engler, both houses of the legislature garnered the two-thirds votes necessary to place yet another reform proposal before the Michigan voters. However, on

June 2, 1993, voters defeated Proposal A by a 55–45 percent margin.[7] Reformers were now batting a pathetic 0 for 12.

The Breakthrough: Senate Bill 1

Despite the voters' rejections of Proposal C in November 1992 and Proposal A in June 1993, Governor Engler and Republican leaders in the Senate remained committed to seeing a property tax reduction enacted during the governor's first term. Accordingly, in mid-July 1993, they introduced SB 1, a relatively modest property tax relief plan that would have lowered assessment ratios over several years. It was at this point that State Senator Debbie Stabenow, an avowed Democratic gubernatorial candidate, stepped to center stage and challenged the governor and the Republican majority by introducing a most radical amendment: the total elimination of the local property tax as a source of funding for school operations.

Whether it was a bold stroke by Senator Stabenow to break the 20-year logjam on school finance reform (as she later claimed), or a somewhat foolhardy bluff aimed at forcing Governor Engler and Senate Republicans to moderate their proposal (as others argued and political

Reprinted with permission.

cartoonist Gary Packingham vividly illustrated), the result was startling. The governor and Senate Republicans leapt to the challenge, and in a quick 29–5 postmidnight vote on July 21, 1993, adopted SB 1 as amended. The next day, the House, on a 69–35 vote, quickly followed suit. So in one fell swoop, the legislature had eliminated entirely local property taxes for school operations—about two-thirds of the schools' total operating funds! In mid-August, the governor signed SB 1 into law, becoming Public Act 145 of 1993.

Public Act 145 reduced K–12 operating revenue by more than $6.5 billion. Additional revenue losses of $180 million accrued to other local governments that had relied on local school millage to fund economic development projects. Moreover, full replacement of this revenue by state taxes was prohibited by the Michigan Constitution. Specifically, the state is prohibited from collecting total tax revenues in excess of a fixed proportion of total state personal income.[8] Consequently, it was clear to the governor and the legislature that any new revenue structure would necessarily combine state taxes allowable under the constitutional limit with a partial restoration of local property taxes.

Following extensive negotiations among Governor Engler and legislative leaders, the Michigan legislature capped a marathon 26-hour session by passing a compromise reform package on Christmas Eve morning in 1993. The package offered two alternative revenue plans, each calling for partial restoration of the local property tax. One plan featured a constitutional amendment to raise Michigan's sales tax rate from 4 to 6 percent, while the alternative statutory plan would raise the Michigan personal income tax rate from 4.6 to 6 percent.[9] Both plans included a state tax on all property.[10] On March 15, 1994, Michigan voters approved the constitutional amendment, Proposal A, by a resounding 69–31 percent margin. The 20-year reform drought was over.

The Foundation Formula

A proposal crafted by a bipartisan 14-member House task force formed the basis of the new school funding program.[11] The new legislation took Michigan from a GTB aid formula back to a foundation program as the core of school funding. Unlike the pre-1974 foundation, however, Proposal A imposed strict limitations on local district options for revenue enhancement. With these reforms, the state had essentially removed the school tax and spending decision from local district voters and claimed it for itself.

Detailed explanations of the workings of the new school aid program are published elsewhere (e.g., Addonizio, Kearney, and Prince 1995; Kearney and Addonizio 2002; Addonizio and Drake 2005) and are briefly summarized here. The new law provided that every district have a foundation of at least $4,200 per pupil. In addition to establishing a minimum local foundation allowance, the legislation set a statewide basic foundation allowance at $5,000 per pupil for 1994–95. The maximum (or "hold harmless") level of state-guaranteed foundation revenue per pupil was set at $6,500. Thus, districts spending less than $3,950 per pupil in 1993–94 were increased to $4,200 for 1994–95, and districts between $3,950 and $6,500 in 1993–94 received increases ranging from $160 and $250 according to a sliding scale with increases inversely related to prior year spending. The 52 districts spending more than $6,500 in 1993–94 were allowed to levy additional hold harmless millage to realize a $160 increase in 1994–95.

The basic foundation allowance was recalculated annually according to indices of revenue and enrollment growth through the 1997–98 fiscal year. Districts spending more than the basic allowance received per pupil increases equal to the annual dollar increase in the basic allowance, while districts below the basic allowance received increases up to twice that amount. Beginning in 1998–99, the legislature jettisoned the indexing formula and directly determined annual changes in the basic allowance. By 1999–2000, all Michigan districts had been raised to at least this basic level and, under current law, now receive equal annual increases in per pupil funding. In this way, current interdistrict differences in per pupil spending, while much lower than they had been under the prereform regime, are locked in by statute. This "range-preserving effect" is illustrated in Figure 2.1, which compares the foundation grants in four local districts and the state basic allowance.

Because their local foundation allowances have exceeded the state basic allowance since the inception of the foundation program in 1994–95, Grand Rapids, Ypsilanti, and Bloomfield Hills have each received annual revenue increases per pupil equal to the dollar increase in the state basic allowance.[12] Onaway, on the other hand, had a 1994–95 local foundation allowance that was below the state basic level. Accordingly, this district received annual per pupil increases equal to twice the

Figure 2.1 Foundation Growth, 1993–94 Pre–Proposal A Foundation Base through 2008–09 ($)

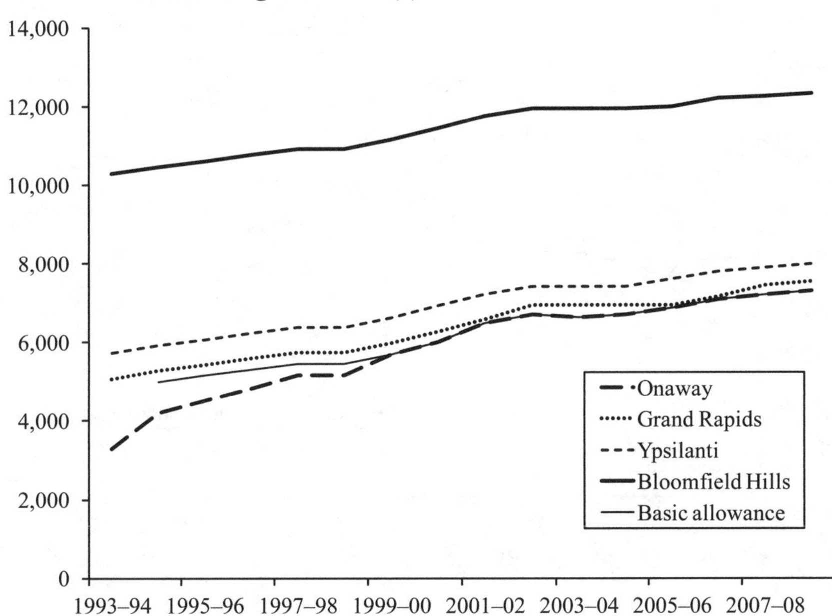

SOURCE: MDE Bulletin 1014, various years.

increases in the state basic allowance until 1999–2000, when Onaway caught up with the state allowance level. At that point, Onaway's annual foundation increases were equal to the increases in the basic allowance and the local allowances of every district above the state basic level, hence, the range-preserving effect.

In 2007–08, the legislature reset the basic foundation level to the maximum or hold harmless level and reinstituted the earlier foundation formula whereby districts below the basic level receive twice the annual dollar increase of those districts above the basic level. Essentially, this adjustment is designed to eventually equalize the foundation allowances of all but Michigan's 52 hold harmless districts and reduce the disparity between these districts and the rest of the state. To date, this potentially significant adjustment has had little effect due to the lack of new foundation aid. The annual foundation levels since the inception of Proposal A are depicted in Figure 2.2.

Figure 2.2 Per Pupil Foundation Levels, 1994–95 through 2008–09 ($)

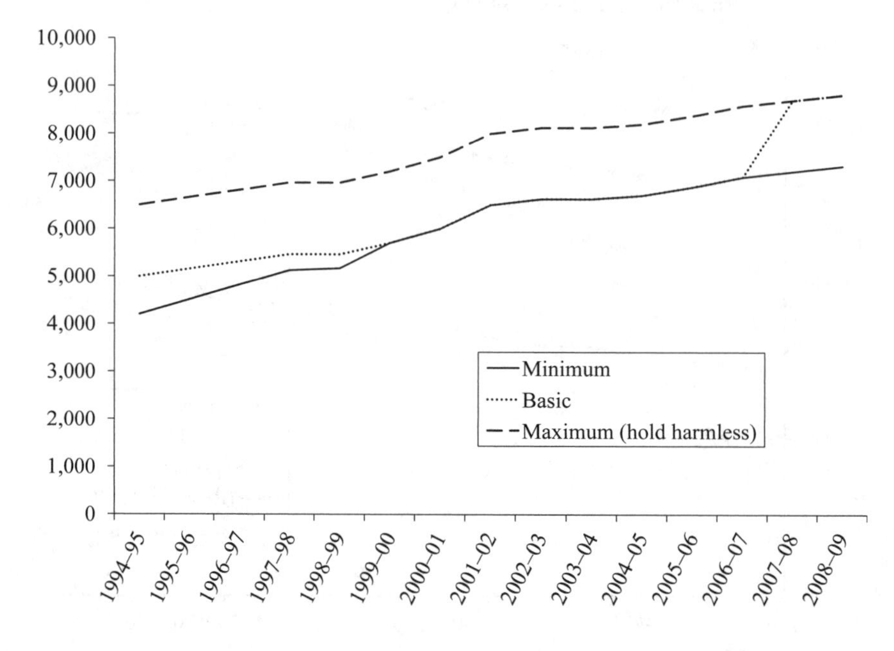

SOURCE: MDE Bulletin 1014, various years.

Now in its fifteenth year, Michigan's foundation formula has "leveled up" the distribution of general per pupil revenue across local districts, as shown in Figures 2.1 and 2.2. Interdistrict disparities in general per pupil revenue have been reduced, and the formula adjustment adopted in 2007–08 could dramatically reduce existing disparities, potentially equalizing per pupil foundation levels for all but Michigan's 52 hold harmless districts. The adequacy of formula funding, however, is another matter. The rate of growth in the benchmark state basic allowance has varied due to state policy decisions, litigation over state funding for special education, state and local revenue collections, and fluctuations in statewide K–12 enrollments. Following three consecutive annual increases, the basic allowance saw no increase in 1998–99, when the state substantially increased payments to districts for special education in response to the 1997 decision of the Michigan Supreme Court in *Durant et al. v. State of Michigan.*[13]

For the period 1994–95 through 2002–03, the basic allowance rose at a compound annual rate of just under 3 percent, exceeding the average annual inflation rate of 2.52 percent over this period as measured by the Detroit Consumer Price Index (CPI). More importantly, these increases in the basic per pupil allowance were appropriated by the legislature during a period of steadily rising enrollments (see Figure 2.3). Statewide K–12 enrollment peaked at just over 1.75 million in 2002–03. Enrollments then began a steady decline, falling to just over 1.66 million in 2007–08, the lowest level in 14 years. Despite this steady enrollment decline statewide, however, Michigan's deteriorating economy and revenue collections have constrained growth in the basic allowance since 2002–03. Annual growth in the basic allowance averaged a mere 1.4 percent between 2002–03 and 2008–09, well below the rise in the Detroit CPI and despite the decline in statewide enrollments.

Figure 2.3 State K–12 Membership History

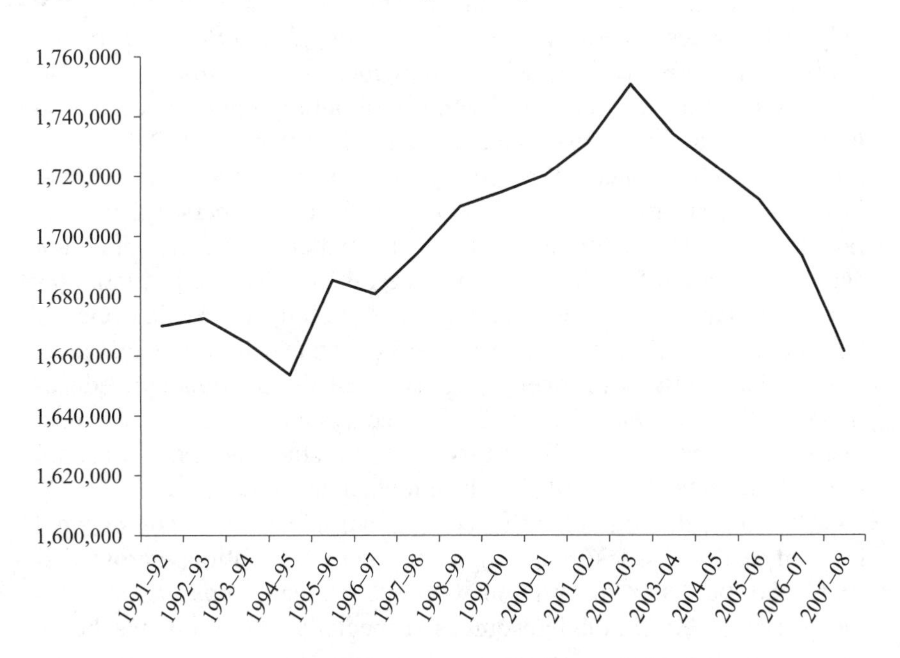

SOURCE: MDE Bulletin 1014, various years.

Aggregate Funding Levels

The resource levels and financial condition of a school district are often described in terms of the district's per pupil funding level. For example, in Michigan much attention is paid, understandably, to each district's foundation allowance. By itself, however, this statistic gives a very incomplete picture of a local school system. Consider, for example, a district whose per pupil revenue rises 2 percent in a year, while its enrollment falls 3 percent over the same period. Despite the increase in per pupil revenue, such a district would sustain a 1 percent revenue loss, necessitating spending cuts, withdrawals from fund balance, or some combination in order to avoid an operating budget deficit. Such scenarios have been commonplace in Michigan this decade, as unprecedented enrollment shifts have resulted from the workings of the state's interdistrict choice and charter school initiatives and population loss stemming from economic and demographic trends.

Consequently, state school finance systems must be concerned not only with issues of equity—that is, ensuring that differences in per pupil funding are not excessive across local communities—but also with issues of the adequacy and stability of public school funding. The issues are related but separable and qualitatively different. Put simply, revenue stability concerns the ability of a tax system to maintain revenue yield year after year as economic activity and personal income fluctuate over the economic cycle. Policymakers and educators want some assurance that sufficient aggregate revenue will be available for our public schools as the economy goes through its inevitable cycles of boom and bust. Alongside this issue of aggregate school revenue level are district- and school-level concerns about the *adequacy* of educational resources. That is, does the finance system provide every local district with resources sufficient to enable all students in every school to meet the state's standards of educational achievement?

Certainly, the attainment of educational adequacy is complicated by a myriad of issues, including enrollment fluctuations across districts, the incidence of children with exceptional needs, variation in the prices of educational resources (especially classroom teachers), family and community influences on student learning, changing educational standards, and the efficiency with which schools employ their resources. Nevertheless, this issue has gained considerable traction in school finance debates since the early 1990s, when states began to adopt school accountability programs, which the federal government tacitly endorsed with the 2001 reauthorization of the Title I legislation. commonly known as the No Child Left Behind Act.

Under NCLB, schools and districts that fail to make AYP toward their respective state achievement goals for two consecutive years are subject to a set of reforms and sanctions designed to improve student achievement. As we noted at the outset of this chapter, the scope of these reforms and sanctions widens as a school or district continues to fall short of AYP requirements. Schools may be subject to student transfers, the replacement of staff, or conversion to charter school status, while districts may sustain funding reductions, staff replacement, or reorganization. This sharp focus on measured student achievement and school accountability has prompted more than 30 states to undertake "education adequacy studies," which seek to determine, or at least approximate, the amount of funding needed to provide all students with a reasonable opportunity to meet state achievement goals.[14]

No such study has been undertaken in Michigan, despite growing concern on the part of educators, parents, and some policymakers over the deteriorating financial condition of many of our public schools and declining levels of real state support. A history of Michigan's aggregate school funding levels is depicted in Figure 2.4. The top line represents nominal dollars while the bottom depicts constant (1979) dollars, discounted using the Detroit CPI.[15] Our discussion will focus on constant dollars. Over the seven-year period from fiscal year 1978–79 through FY 1985–86, total real state and local revenue for public schools rose a mere 2.5 percent, an average annual compounded growth rate of less than 0.4 percent. This period was notable for the severe "double dip" recession spanning the period from 1979 to 1983. In the eight years preceding Michigan's Proposal A reforms, FY 1986–87 through FY 1993–94, total real revenue grew 19.7 percent, for an average annual growth rate of 2.27 percent. In the eight years following Proposal A, FY 1994–95 through FY 2002–03, total real revenue grew only 14.0 percent, or an average annual growth rate of 1.66 percent.[16]

Financing schools as jobs disappear

Aggregate revenue growth has slowed dramatically in recent years, with total real state and local revenue actually falling by 7.6 percent

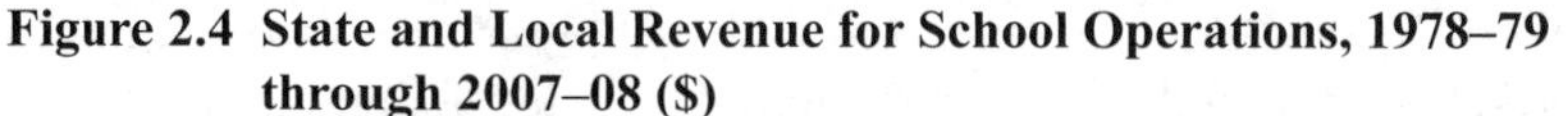

Figure 2.4 State and Local Revenue for School Operations, 1978–79 through 2007–08 ($)

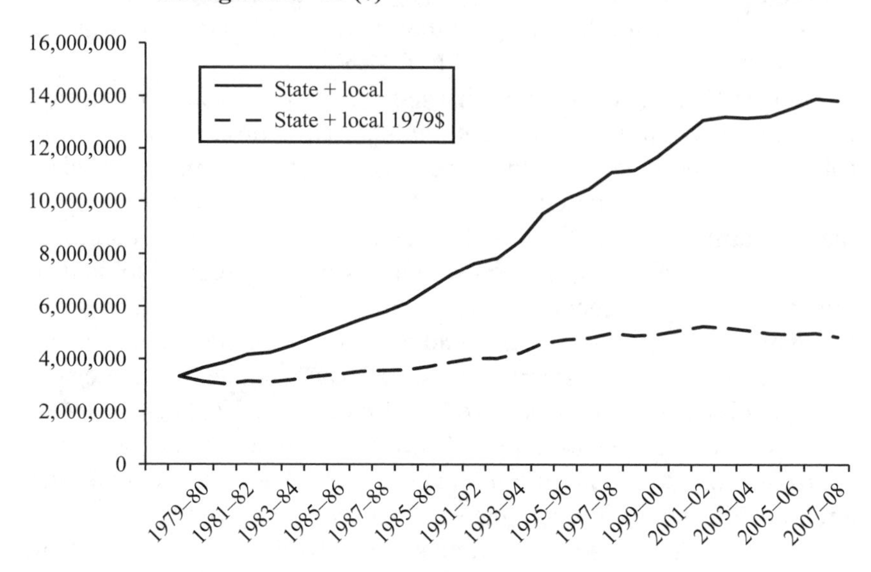

SOURCE: Authors' calculations and MDE Bulletin 1011, various years.

between 2001–02 and 2007–08, an average annual loss of just over 1.1 percent. Indeed, in recent years Michigan public schools have experienced fiscal pressures of a magnitude not seen in the state since the early 1980s. For districts beset by dramatic enrollment declines, revenue losses are unprecedented. Some examples of urban school districts sustaining dramatic enrollment losses are given in Table 2.1.

This loss of real revenue for schools is attributable to two major factors. First, changes in Michigan's tax system enacted since the adoption of Proposal A have eroded the tax base and reduced school funding. These changes included the lowering of the state personal income tax, sales and use tax changes, changes in the state and local property tax, and economic development incentives. Drake (2002) estimated the cumulative revenue loss for schools resulting from these changes in our tax laws at nearly $2 billion between 1994 and 2002.[17] Second, public school funding has suffered as Michigan's manufacturing economy has slumped and collapsed. One telling indicator of this collapse is Michi-

Table 2.1 District Enrollment and Revenue Losses

District	1997–98 Enrollment	2002–03 Enrollment	2007–08 Enrollment	5-year loss	10-year loss	5-year loss (%)	10-year loss (%)
Detroit	176,432	163,702	106,164	12,730	70,268	7.2	39.8
Flint	25,395	21,593	15,664	3,802	9,731	15.0	38.3
Pontiac	12,802	11,529	8,149	1,273	4,653	9.9	36.3
Saginaw	12,891	12,141	9,559	750	3,332	5.8	25.8
Grand Rapids	27,521	25,882	20,276	1,639	7,245	6.0	26.3
Lansing	19,268	17,808	15,452	1,460	3,816	7.6	19.8
Benton Harbor	5,810	5,146	3,751	664	2,059	11.4	35.4
Battle Creek	8,607	8,011	6,569	596	2,038	6.9	23.7
Marquette	4,510	3,765	3,295	745	1,215	16.5	26.9
Muskegon	7,140	6,655	5,665	485	1,475	6.8	20.7

SOURCE: MDE Bulletin 1014, various years.

gan's declining employment level. The state's job figures since 1999 are given in Figure 2.5.

Between May 2000 and July 2009, the Michigan economy shed 880,000 jobs, including an astounding loss of 386,000 jobs during the last 12 months of this long decline. Well over half of these losses were well-paid manufacturing jobs. As a result, 2009 was the worst year of real loss in gross domestic product (GDP) in our decade-long slide. And while the steep job loss abated somewhat in 2010, Michigan's unemployment rate continues to exceed the national rate by a wide margin.

In Figure 2.6, we compare the Michigan and U.S. unemployment rates during the state's "lost decade." The unemployment rate is the percentage of people in the labor force (i.e., people working or actively looking for work) who cannot find work. This means, of course, that this statistic understates the unemployment problem because it overlooks the "discouraged workers," who have given up their job search.

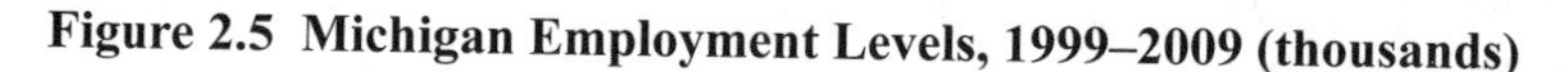

Figure 2.5 Michigan Employment Levels, 1999–2009 (thousands)

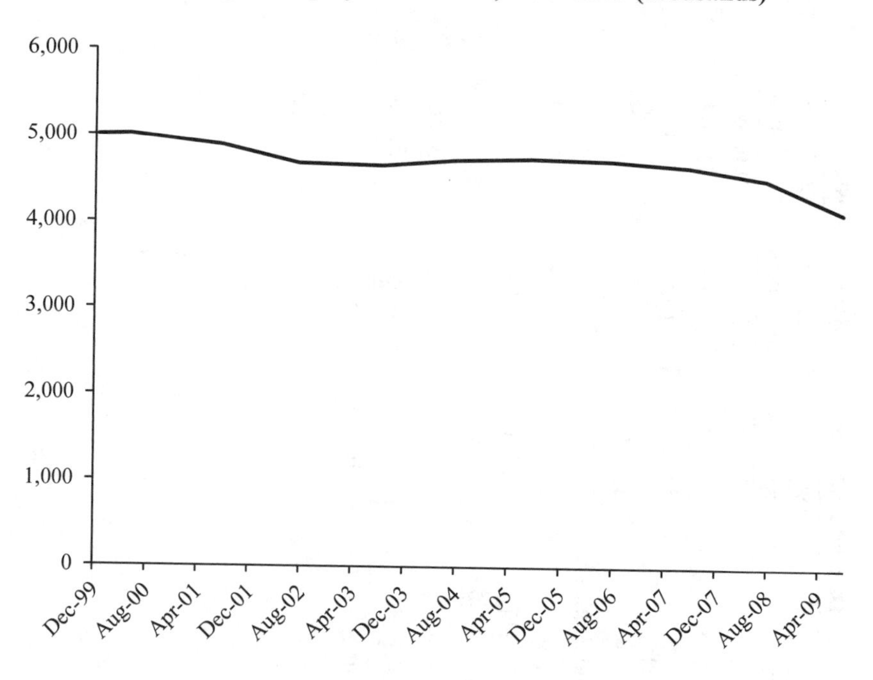

SOURCE: Bureau of Labor Statistics, U.S. Department of Labor.

Figure 2.6 U.S. and Michigan Unemployment Rates, 2000–09 (%)

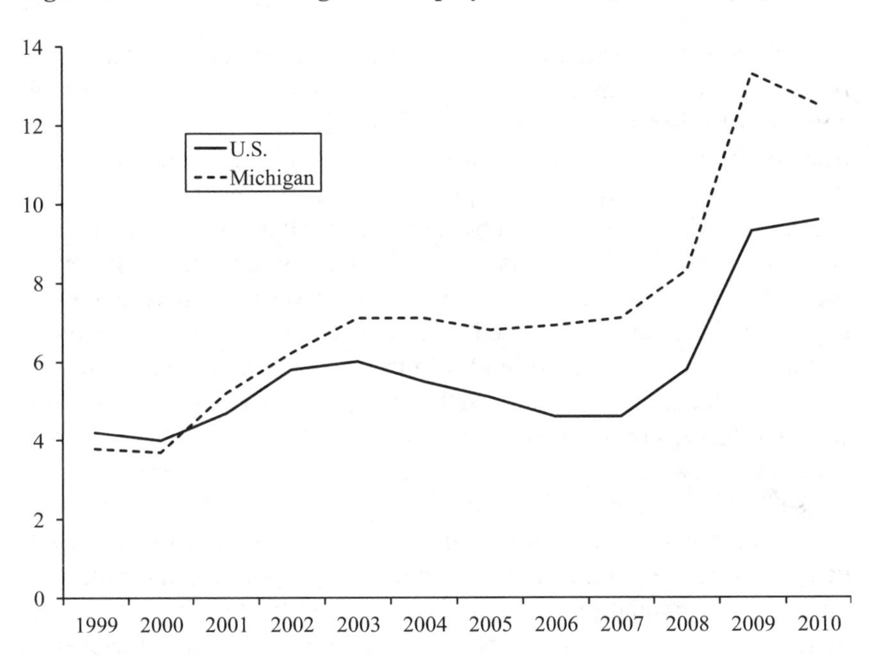

SOURCE: Bureau of Labor Statistics, U.S. Department of Labor.

Keeping this limitation in mind, we can see that Michigan's unemployment rate tends to move in the same direction as the national rate but is more volatile, peaking at 13.3 percent in 2009, a full four percentage points above the national rate. And although Michigan's rate dropped to 12.5 percent in 2010 while the national rate continued to rise, Michigan's economy continues to struggle and the short-term outlook remains gloomy. Some manufacturing may return, but most of Michigan's new jobs will be lower paid (O'Conner 2009). Decreased wages, along with tighter credit, will mean lower sales and income tax revenues for the state, while lower real estate values will depress property tax collections for the state and local governments. Finally, the state can expect fewer taxpayers to fund state and local treasuries. About 376,000 residents have left the state since 2000, and the exodus is expected to continue in the coming years as other states, less tied to auto manufacturing, rebound more quickly from the great recession.

Fund Balances

As we noted earlier, a school district's financial condition cannot be neatly summed up in a single statistic. For example, per pupil revenue, an oft-cited figure in school finance discussions, may conceal the true condition of a district if not supplemented by data on enrollment trends. A district with high per pupil revenue may well find itself in a precarious financial position if beset by substantial enrollment declines. A more revealing indicator is a school district's fund balance; that is, the district's savings account or financial reserves (the proverbial rainy day fund). Generally expressed as a percentage of a district's annual operating expenditures, the fund balance indicates a district's ability to maintain educational programs in the event that operating revenue falls, whether through reductions in per pupil state aid, enrollment loss, or a precipitous rise in costs, such as health care, pension, or energy costs. These funds have been particularly important for school districts in recent years as state "executive orders" have reduced school aid in midyear, after budgets have been adopted, contracts signed, and programs initiated. The availability of a fund balance to offset such midyear cuts in state support allows districts to maintain programs and services to year's end, thus avoiding disruptive layoffs and program cancellations. Since the 1994 finance reforms, which essentially eliminated local millage increases, fund balance has played a more important role in K–12 school finance. Statewide aggregate fund balances for traditional districts and public school academies (PSAs) are given in Figure 2.7 for the years 1993–94 through 2007–08.

As the figure shows, fund balances of Michigan school districts began rising immediately following the Proposal A reforms and reached record levels in 1998 and 1999. The substantial increase in fund balances in 1998 was partly attributable to the state settlement of *Durant et al. v. State of Michigan* (1997).[18] More importantly, however, school leaders understood that the Proposal A reforms compelled districts to retain larger fund balances than those of the pre–Proposal A era. First, implementing legislation virtually eliminated the authority of local districts to ask voters for additional operating millage. Second, this legislation also established a state aid payment schedule that called for 11 equal monthly allocations to the districts, with no payment in September. In order to limit borrowing costs, districts try to build fund balances

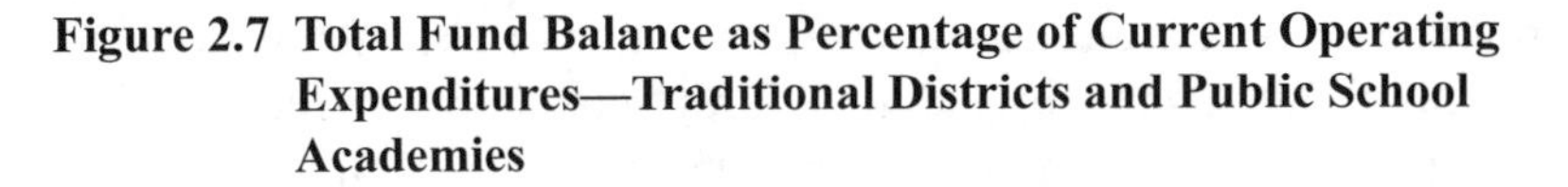

Figure 2.7 Total Fund Balance as Percentage of Current Operating Expenditures—Traditional Districts and Public School Academies

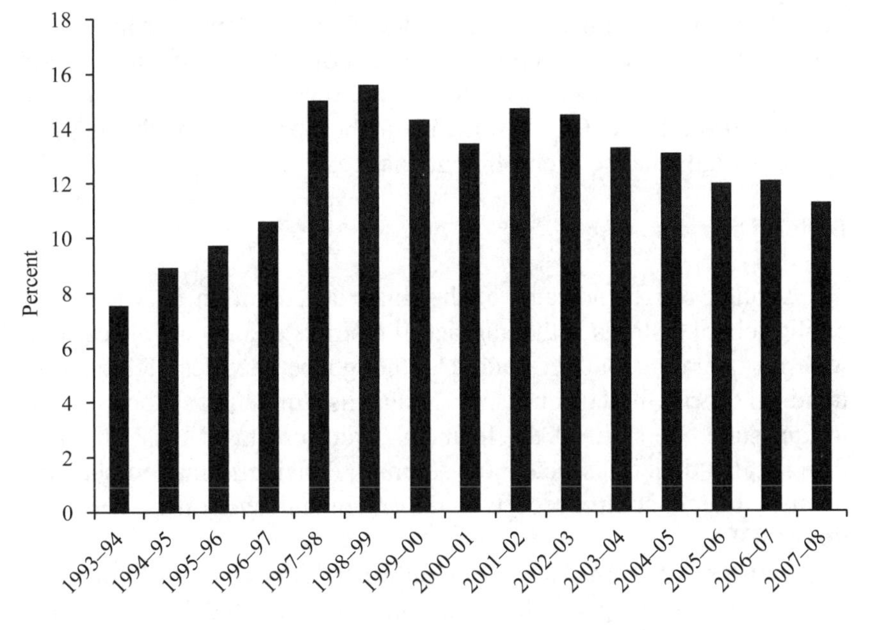

SOURCE: MDE, Michigan School Business Officials, and authors' calculations.

in advance of their fall school opening. Finally, school districts now rely on the state for about 80 percent of their operating funding, making them much more vulnerable to the vagaries of state revenue collections, appropriations, and payment schedules. Prudent financial management under such uncertain circumstances requires bigger bank balances to absorb state funding cuts and lower borrowing costs. Indeed, the Michigan School Business Officials Web site recommends a fund balance of between 15 and 20 percent for local districts.[19]

As Figure 2.7 reveals, district fund balances have fallen steadily since 2002, as districts have sought to protect their educational programs in the face of declining state support. At the same time, however, while some districts have drawn down their fund balances to maintain academic programs, others have done the reverse, cutting back on school programs in order to preserve fund balances as protection against the possibility of more draconian aid reductions in the future. Even a substantial fund balance, by itself, is hardly conclusive evidence of an educationally thriving school district. On the contrary, high balances may reflect the pessimism of local educational leaders over the state's ability or willingness to support their schools. And fund balances are undoubtedly smaller today as schools enter the 2011–12 academic year. Addonizio and Drake (2005) find that the best predictor of changes in a district's fund balance is enrollment change.

Deficit Districts

Another rough indicator of the financial condition of Michigan's public school districts is the number of districts ending each fiscal year with an operating budget deficit. Although perhaps less telling than trends in district fund balances, the annual lists of deficit school districts trigger state oversight of the financial management of these districts. Specifically, deficit districts must submit a deficit elimination plan and monthly budget control reports to the Michigan Department of Education (MDE).

A history of the number of deficit districts is given in Figure 2.8. Separate totals are given for traditional districts and PSAs. Several observations can be made on these data. First, although the rise in the number of traditional deficit districts reflects the declining enrollments and revenues experienced by some districts since the advent of Michigan's current economic slide in 2001, these recent deficit district counts are much lower than those experienced during the 1979–83 recession. Second, the numbers for PSAs are particularly difficult to interpret; many are quite small and comparatively new. The spike in deficit PSAs in 1996–97 may well reflect an abundance of new schools facing relatively large start-up costs, which must often be covered with operating revenue since PSAs cannot levy property taxes for either capital or operating expenses.

Ultimately, the number of deficit districts provides only limited insight into the financial condition of Michigan public schools. Certainly, districts in deficit are experiencing serious financial stress, but a balanced operating budget is no proof of financial health. Rather, it may well reflect sound management of declining resources. The books are balanced through reductions in educational programs and other oper-

Figure 2.8 History of Deficit Districts

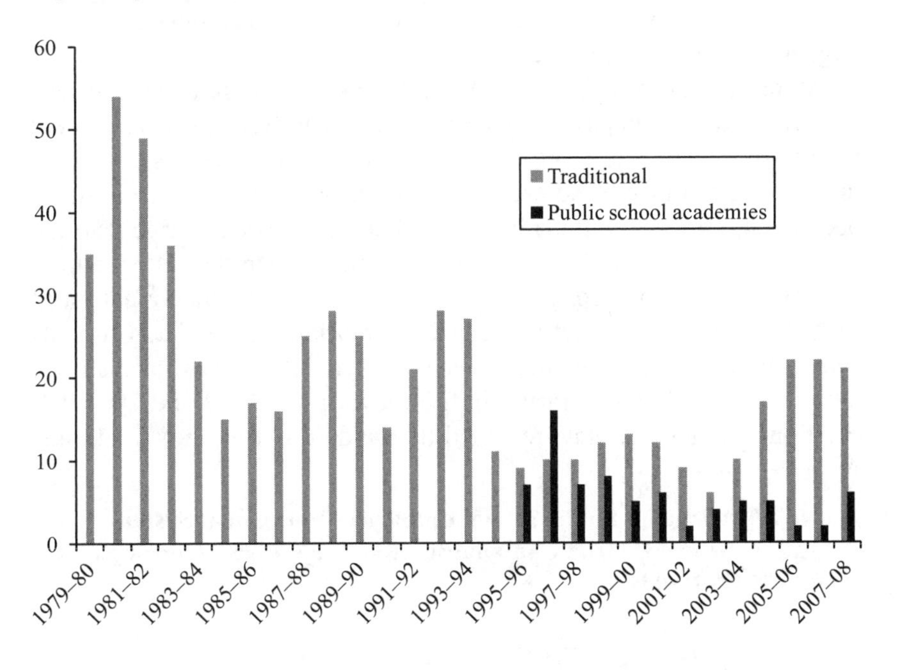

SOURCE: MDE and authors' calculations.

ating expenditures, but the educational costs of these cutbacks, while rarely estimated, may be substantial.

Financing the Retirement System: A Looming Crisis

Among the major changes in K–12 finance ushered in with Proposal A was a reassignment of responsibility for funding the school retirement system. Prior to the implementation of Proposal A in 1995, state government and local school districts shared the cost of the employer portion of contributions to the Michigan Public School Employees Retirement System (MPSERS). These contributions, expressed as a percentage of employee payroll, prefunded the actuarial costs of the defined benefit plan of public school employees and covered the costs of retiree health benefits on a pay-as-you-go basis.[20] After Proposal A, full responsibility for retirement costs was assigned to local districts. So, just as local school districts essentially lost their authority to raise operating revenue on their own, they were given additional financial responsibility for a large and rapidly rising cost.

After falling from 1996–97 through 1998–99, retirement costs as a percentage of current payroll have risen significantly, from 10.77 percent in 1998–99 to 16.5 percent in 2008–09. This rate history is presented in Figure 2.9. Indeed, the escalation in contribution rates would have been even more precipitous had it not been for an accounting "sleight of hand" executed in 1997 and again in 2007, when the state, following several years of strong investment earnings, reset the valuation of MPSERS assets to market value. These "mark to market" adjustments substantially reduced required pension payments by school districts, but provided only temporary relief. Following the 1997 and 2007 calculation changes, the state resumed its standard five-year "smoothing"

Figure 2.9 Michigan Public School Employees Retirement System School District Contribution Rates, FY 1995–96 through FY 2008–09

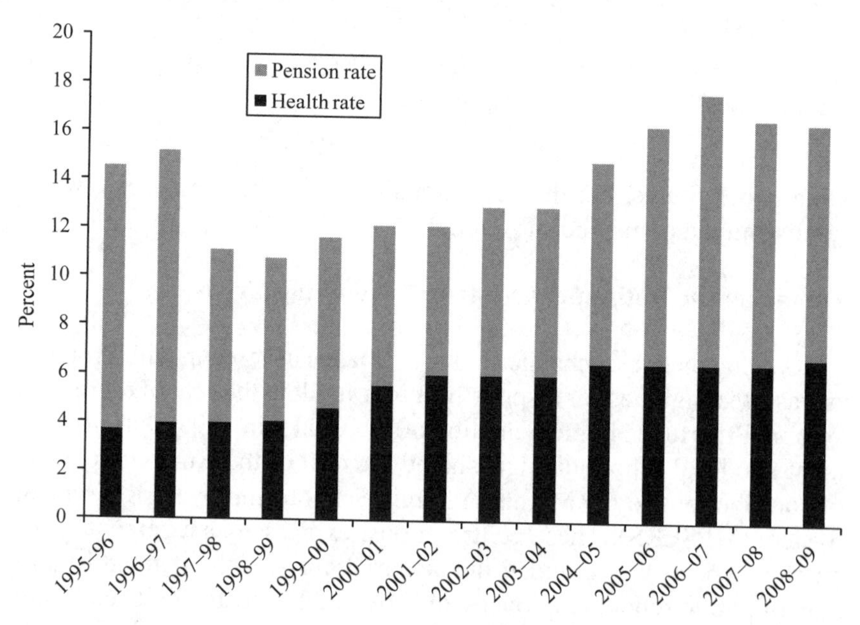

SOURCE: Michigan Public School Employees Retirement System.

calculation of valuation assets, a practice designed to attenuate annual fluctuations in the contribution percentage. And the schools' pension and health care costs will continue to climb faster than their revenues in the foreseeable future. According to the Citizens Research Council of Michigan (2004), the schools' combined contribution rate will rise to about 32 percent of payroll by 2020.

Impact on school district budgets

In the absence of reforms designed to curb the district's spiraling retirement costs, the outlook for K–12 education budgets is bleak indeed. As noted earlier, increases in the state foundation grant have been very modest in recent years. Indeed, since 2003, much of these increases have been claimed by rising pension and health care obligations. The result, of course, is mounting pressure on school districts' instructional budgets. Contribution costs from MPSERS expressed in per pupil terms are presented in Figure 2.10.

Measured in per pupil terms, school district retirement costs have nearly doubled over this nine-year period, rising from $538 in 1998–1999 to $992 in 2007–08. Over this same period, the state basic foundation allowance rose $1,742. By this measure, fully 26 percent of the foundation increase has been consumed by rising retirement costs. And while future annual increases in the foundation allowance are far from certain, particularly in the near term, school district retirement costs are projected to rise steadily (Citizens Research Council of Michigan 2004).

Capital Funding

In recent years, there has been growing concern over the conditions of public school facilities and the ability or willingness of states and local districts to ensure that all children have access to adequate school buildings in the United States (Plummer 2006). A series of reports reveal a substantial and growing deficit in our elementary and secondary school capital stock across the nation. For example, a study by the National Center for Education Statistics (NCES) in 2000 finds that three-quarters of schools in the United States reported that repairs, renovations, and modernizations were required to bring their school buildings up to good

Figure 2.10 Michigan Public School Employees Retirement System Costs per Pupil, FY 1998–99 through FY 2007–08 ($)

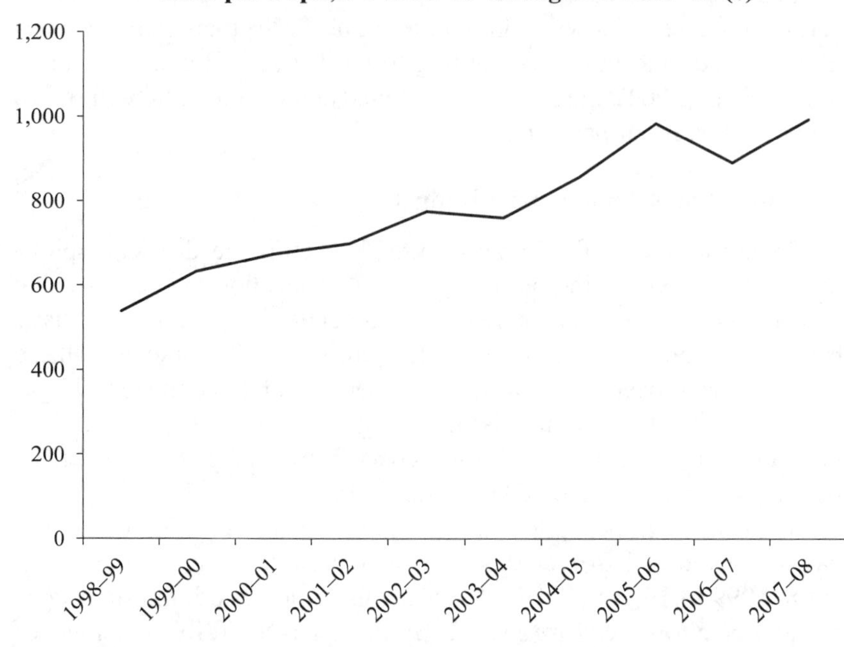

SOURCE: Michigan Public School Employees Retirement System, MDE, and authors' calculations.

condition. And in recent years, school finance litigation across the states has cited inequities in school facilities when challenging the constitutionality of school funding systems (Plummer 2006). The problem of financing school capital expenditures is particularly acute in Michigan. In a 2005 study, the Citizens Research Council of Michigan and the Educational Policy Center estimate the cost of unmet capital needs in Michigan public schools at $8.9 billion, with about one-fourth of this need found in five low-income, central-city school districts: 1) Battle Creek, 2) Detroit, 3) Flint, 4) Muskegon, and 5) Saginaw (Arsen et al. 2005).[21]

It is no coincidence that the greatest unmet capital needs are in our state's most property-poor districts. Michigan is 1 of only 12 states that provide no aid to local school districts for capital projects (Duncombe and Wang 2009).[22] The state did provide aid to partially equalize local district capital millage until 1980, when this aid program fell victim to state budget cuts, and has given no such grant support since then. And this issue was not addressed by the Proposal A reforms of 1994. Consequently, school districts are obliged to fund capital projects from local resources: cash reserves, building and site sinking funds, or, most commonly, the sale of long-term general obligation bonds. In the case of sinking funds or bond sales, the local district must rely exclusively on local property taxes to directly finance their school construction projects or cover debt service payments. In the absence of any equalization aid from the state, property-poor districts face exceptionally high tax burdens when servicing bonds.

The sole form of assistance from the state is provided through the School Bond Loan Program, wherein eligible districts can borrow from the state to help make principal and interest payments on their bonds. This state assistance, however, does not become available until a district's taxpayers are levying fully 13 mills to service their bonds, and because these funds must be paid back to the state, eligible districts must continue to levy this 13-mill rate until the loan is repaid. Taxpayers in Detroit, for example, will be paying 13 mills annually for capital spending over a period of no less than 25 years as a result of local voters' passage of a $1.5 billion bond issue in 1994. This debt was extended in November 2009 with voter approval of another bond issue for school rebuilding in Detroit.

The inequity in Michigan school capital funding cannot be overstated. Duncombe and Wang (2009), using two different measures of funding inequality, rank Michigan 39th and 40th, respectively, among 48 states. Their analysis fails to capture another important dimension of Michigan's capital spending problem: property-rich districts are able to finance new school buildings while levying relatively modest millage rates *and then add to their enrollments and operating revenue through Michigan's "schools of choice" program.* Conversely, property-poor districts with inferior school facilities are drained of enrollments and operating revenue as their resident students are lured away by the new facilities in neighboring districts. These compounding inequities render our school capital funding system indefensible. Standard formulas for state participation in school capital funding are well known, since the great majority of states employ them. Michigan needs to join the mainstream and provide every child with a decent public school.

SUMMARY AND CONCLUSIONS

Michigan's major school finance reforms began dramatically in 1993 with the elimination of local property taxes for school operations, and culminated in 1994 with voter approval of a constitutional amendment (Proposal A) that increased the state sales tax and earmarked the added revenue for the schools. These and other reforms, including the replacement of a guaranteed tax base aid formula with a foundation formula, succeeded in reducing both property tax burdens and differences among districts in per pupil funding. For a time, the changes were applauded by both taxpayers and educators alike.

The promise of Proposal A, however, has come and gone. In recent years, public schools in Michigan have experienced fiscal pressures of a magnitude not seen in the state in more than 40 years. One source of fiscal pressure was the 1999 passage of a series of rate cuts in the individual income tax and business taxes. These tax cuts, passed during a period of robust economic growth, were partially offset by increases in the cigarette tax and the expansion of state lottery games. Nevertheless, the tax cuts had two important effects on the state's ability to support public services, including education. First, the cuts made the state's tax structure more regressive, with effective tax rates rising for low-income households and falling for high-income households. Second, they opened a structural gap between state revenues and state spending. This gap will not be closed by a return to a "full employment" economy—it can be closed only by budget cuts, tax increases, or some combination of the two.

A more potent source of fiscal pressure, however, has been the unrelenting decline in the Michigan economy. Between May 2000 and July 2009, the Michigan economy shed 880,000 jobs, including an astonishing 386,000 jobs during the last 12 months of this period. More than half of these losses were well-paid manufacturing jobs. The impact of this economic decline on state tax collections and K–12 support has been severe. Real, inflation-adjusted aggregate revenue for our public schools fell by 7.6 percent between 2001–02 and 2007–08. Urban districts, beset by severe enrollment declines, have been particularly hard hit. District fund balances, which had been built up in the late 1990s, have steadily declined since 2002, while district retirement costs have spiraled upward.

The Impending Financial Storm

As this book is being written and schools approach the midpoint of their 2010–11 fiscal year, school administrators confront mounting financial pressures unprecedented in their professional experience. A $165 cut in per pupil foundation funding imposed in FY 2009–10 essentially remains in effect, as the regular FY 2010–11 appropriation restored a mere $11 per pupil for this year and last. This legislation also raised the districts' retirement rate from 16.94 percent to 19.41 percent of payroll, costing schools an additional $255 million. And while a supplemental appropriation reinstated the remaining $154 per pupil to district foundation allowances along with additional payments ranging from $23 to $46, these are but one-time payouts of federal stimulus funds.

All evidence points to further school revenue losses in the coming year, as Governor Rick Snyder and the new legislature face a projected $1.6 billion general fund budget deficit and federal stimulus funding runs out. In the face of these looming cutbacks in school funding and rising pension costs, many districts will continue to reduce their spending, possibly managing to cut costs through sharing or privatizing some services, but also eliminating programs and allowing class sizes to continue their upward drift. As districts continue to draw down fund balances in order to limit teacher layoffs and service cutbacks, they will jeopardize their credit ratings and their ability to absorb state funding cuts in future years, and more districts will fall into deficit.

This scenario of unrelenting contraction will continue to unfold until the state provides the public schools with additional tax revenues. This will require more than economic recovery for the state. A structural overhaul of our state and local tax system is needed to adequately fund our public schools. While Michigan's economy has contracted in recent years, tax revenues have shrunk much more rapidly; broad-based tax rate reductions and selective tax abatements, combined with an antiquated sales tax that leaves our growing service sector largely untouched, have eroded funding for education at all levels (Ballard

2010). Whether our state leaders can summon the political will to repair these structural flaws in our tax system remains an open question.

Money and Schools: A Final Word

Although experience has shown that money and school performance are not perfectly or even closely correlated, the steady erosion of the financial position of Michigan's public schools since 2001–02 has undoubtedly impaired the quality of educational programs across the state. Money is not the solution to all problems that plague our poorly performing schools, including many of our urban schools that suffer from unstable leadership, conflicting political agendas of those in authority, and ineffective staff. In these situations, money is often wasted, and any influx of new funding would accomplish little in the absence of effective leadership, shared vision, collaboration, and other organizational attributes that money can't buy. Further, we understand that an organization can often take advantage of a funding reduction to eliminate inefficient programs and practices, even those previously considered "sacred cows," and adopt needed reforms.

At the same time, however, the unrelenting cutbacks in real funding levels of the sort experienced by many Michigan school districts over the last six years, particularly the massive revenue losses sustained by some of Michigan's poorest inner-city districts, can only endanger their educational mission. Moreover, Michigan's precipitous economic decline has seriously impaired the well-being of families and children, along with the ability of state and local government to support them through programs in areas such as housing, health, income support, and social services. We must understand that families and children are themselves vital school resources and that "nonschool" policies and circumstances impacting their welfare will inevitably impact educational outcomes as well.

Notes

1. Much of the controversy stems from the report's flawed analysis of the economic impact of school quality. Specifically, the report attributed the stagnant productivity of the U.S. economy in the early 1980s in large part to poor school quality as evidenced by low student scores on standardized achievement tests. As we now know, however, neither the economic recovery of the mid-1980s nor the unprecedented economic growth of the 1994–2001 period can be explained by changes in our public schools or rising test scores. Changes in the macro economy occur much too suddenly to be explained by the quality of such a slow-to-change institution as our public schools. Poor planning and investment decisions in the private and public sectors, rising international trade and political factors were responsible for the deep recession examined in the report (Murnane 1988).
2. For an analysis of the role of the courts in school finance litigation, see, for example, Eastman (2007). For a stinging critique of the scientific validity of the costing-out studies, see Hanushek (2007).
3. For a brief description of public school governance and finance in these early years, see Thomas (1968).
4. A mill in Michigan is equivalent to a maximum of a dollar in tax paid per $2,000 of market value.
5. This section draws upon Addonizio, Kearney, and Prince (1995, pp. 237–240).
6. Concurrently, and for the prior three years dating back to the end of Governor Blanchard's administration, two grassroots efforts also had been under way. One, called KIDS, was an unsuccessful petition drive aimed at strengthening the education clause of the Michigan Constitution. The second, known as the Olmstead/Kearney (or "O/K") Plan, was an initiative petition drive aimed at providing school finance reform through statutory change.
7. If it had been adopted by the voters, Proposal A of 1993 would have rolled back school property tax rates to 18 mills and established that rate by charter, provided for the district levying the full 18 mills a $4,800 per pupil foundation grant indexed to revenue growth, included in the $4,800 grant all existing state retirement and categorical payments to districts, provided a local option of an additional 9 mills equalized at $100 per pupil per mill, and raised the state sales tax from 4 percent to 6 percent.
8. Article IX, Section 26 reads, in part, "The revenue limit shall be equal to the product of the ratio of Total State Revenues in fiscal year 1978–79 divided by the Personal Income of Michigan in calendar year 1977 multiplied by the Personal Income of Michigan in either the prior calendar year or the average of Personal Income of Michigan in the previous three calendar years, whichever is greater." The applicable ratio is 0.0949, or 9.49 percent.
9. For more detail on the alternative revenue plans, see Addonizio, Kearney, and Prince (1995).
10. The idea of a state property tax for public school operations was not new. It had been proposed in 1969 by a Governor's Commission on Educational Reform.

11. The members of the task force, known as "Team 14" and consisting of 7 Democrats and 7 Republicans, were James Agee, Maxine Berman, Robert Brackenridge, William Bryant, Willis Bullard, Barbara Dobb, Robert Emerson, Don Gilmer, Lynn Jondahl, William Keith, Susan Grimes Munsell, James O'Neill, Glenn Oxender, and Ted Wallace.
12. Of course, the basic allowance may decline or remain unchanged from year to year, depending on the state's revenue collections and appropriations decisions. For example, the basic allowance remained at $6,700 for fiscal years 2002–03, 2003–04, and 2004–05.
13. In that decision, the Supreme Court held that special education programs are a state mandate and that the state had failed to fund such programs at the levels required by the state constitution. The court ordered the state to pay approximately $212 million in damages to the 84 plaintiff districts. Recognizing that nonplaintiff districts may have had equivalent claims for state compensation of mandated school costs, the legislature approved payments for both plaintiff districts and the approximately 500 eligible nonplaintiff local and intermediate districts. Plaintiffs were paid in full on April 15, 1998, while payments to nonplaintiffs were made over an extended time period. Total restitution exceeded $840 million.
14. Some of these studies were ordered by the courts as part of school funding lawsuits (e.g., Arizona, Arkansas, New York, Ohio, and Wyoming), while others have been initiated by state legislatures or sponsored by school organizations in anticipation of litigation (Rebell 2006).
15. FY 1978–79 is chosen as the base year because it was the first year for which the so-called Headlee Amendment was in effect. Adopted by Michigan voters in 1978, this substantial tax limitation amendment to Article IX of the Michigan Constitution imposed new constraints on K–12 funding. Specifically, Section 31 of the amendment requires millage rate reductions in districts where property assessments rise faster than the rate of inflation. Such "rollbacks" were commonplace following passage of the amendment.
16. Revenue growth slowed over this period despite the remarkable 12.4 percent increase in aggregate nominal school funding appropriated by the legislature for 1994–95, the first year of the Proposal A reforms. This generous increase was clearly intended as a sweetener to bolster public support for the reforms.
17. The biggest school revenue loss, nearly $700 million, came from the phased reduction of Michigan's income tax rate from 4.4 percent to 3.9 percent. When enacting these cuts, the legislature protected the School Aid Fund (SAF) from revenue loss by increasing the percentage of income tax revenue earmarked for SAF. This meant, however, that the General Fund, General Purpose (GFGP) fund would absorb the loss, resulting in less GFGP support for public schools.
18. In that decision, the Michigan Supreme Court held that the state had failed to fund special education at the level required by the state constitution and ordered the state to pay approximately $212 million in damages to 84 plaintiff districts. Recognizing that nonplaintiff districts undoubtedly had equivalent claims against the state, the legislature approved payments for plaintiffs and nonplaintiffs alike, with total payments exceeding $840 million.

19. http://www.msbo.org/pdf/2004/FundBalInfo.pdf (accessed October 3, 2009).
20. The Michigan Constitution requires that pension benefits be prefunded and that any unfunded liability be amortized. No such requirement exists for health benefits and prefunding of health benefits is not standard practice (Citizens Research Council 2004).
21. While this estimate of unmet school facility need is substantial, the authors point out that if these capital expenditures were financed through the sale of 30-year bonds at 5 percent interest, the state's annual school spending would rise by less than five percent (Arsen et al. 2005).
22. The other states are Idaho, Illinois, Indiana, Iowa, Louisiana, Nebraska, Nevada, North Dakota, Oklahoma, South Dakota, and West Virginia (Duncombe and Wang 2009).

3
Holding Schools Accountable

For both Michigan and the entire nation, No Child Left Behind (NCLB), the landmark federal legislation adopted with great fanfare in January of 2002, is the *sine qua non* of school accountability programs—at least until it is amended by the Congress in a forthcoming reauthorization. To fully appreciate the act's current import for public education in Michigan and the nation, one must first venture back a bit into the history of both U.S. and Michigan education, and look briefly at the act's many antecedents, for NCLB did not arrive *de novo* in 2002 on the public education scene. It is, in many important ways, the product of a broad array of progenitors stretching back to at least the late 1950s, and as far as Michigan is concerned, even back to the early nineteenth century.

For our present purposes, the signal historical event might well have been the launch of Sputnik in 1957 and the immediate events that followed, beginning with the passage of the National Defense Education Act (NDEA) in 1958. The adoption of the NDEA was a response to the fear that Russian schools had become superior to America's public schools in mathematics and science, that something had to be done immediately to regain that superiority, and that a program of federal aid was an absolute necessity if our schools were to regain their advanced educational position. At the federal level, the NDEA was soon followed in 1965 by the adoption of the Elementary and Secondary Education Act (ESEA), signaling the creation for the first time of a broadly conceived federal program of financial assistance to the nation's elementary and secondary schools, unprecedented in size and scope. The adoption of the ESEA also marked the beginning of a bevy of public and private educational reform efforts at the national level, at the state level, and at local school district and school levels, eventually culminating in the adoption of NCLB in 2002.

It is to NCLB and EducationYES!, the parallel accountability effort in Michigan, that we give our major attention in this chapter. But to do this well, to fully understand NCLB and EducationYES! (as well as its present successor, MI-SAAS), we must first attend to two tasks we identified in our opening paragraph. We need to trace briefly the historical roots of EducationYES!—roots that for Michigan education stretch back over the 140-year period that predates the launch of Sputnik in 1957. Second, we need to set NCLB and EducationYES! into the larger framework of what has become a 50-year multicomponent and nationwide effort to reform and improve American education. Only then can we move on to address and fully appreciate the events of the immediate past. In order to cover this total span of some 200 years in a somewhat coherent manner, we arbitrarily have divided those years into three overlapping periods: 1) 1805–1900—the territorial years and early years of statehood; 2) 1900–50—the first half of the twentieth century; and 3) 1950 to the present—the period that will command our major attention.

However, before we begin, it is best to offer an opening statement or description of what we mean by the term *accountability*. Common dictionary entries define accountability as "being responsible, answerable, capable of being explained."[1] But perhaps a better and more publicly accepted understanding of the term, particularly as it is applied to public education, comes from educational historian Raymond Callahan, who equates the term accountability with the term *efficiency*. In his 1964 seminal work, *Education and the Cult of Efficiency,* Callahan identifies efficiency as the maxim often claimed to be the basic premise of American manufacturing, namely, "the finest product at the lowest cost" (p. 234). He further notes that, in his view, it is a premise where the emphasis all too often was placed more on lowest cost rather than finest product. Callahan's opinion on the matter, as far as public education is concerned, is perhaps best epitomized in a comment one still often hears from contemporary educational reformers of a conservative bent, namely, "there will be more money for education when there is more education for the money" (Doyle and Levine 1985, p. 113). As Callahan observes, referring to an October 1958 article in *Fortune* magazine, "the schools were [seen as] no different from General Motors for their job was to 'optimize the number of students and to minimize the input of man-hours and capital'" (p. 254).

It was well into the third time period—the late 1950s to the present— before the emphasis began to shift appreciably and give increasing weight to the second half of the efficiency maxim, the finest product.

But we get ahead of ourselves. We turn now to take a brief look at the initial period of time: 1805–1900—the territorial years and early years of statehood. Then we move on to an even briefer look at the second time period: 1900–1950—the first half of the twentieth century. Finally we take a more extended look at the third period—the late 1950s to the present. As we noted earlier, this last period will command our major attention.

1805–1900—THE TERRITORIAL YEARS AND EARLY YEARS OF STATEHOOD

Public education in Michigan first arrived on the scene in 1817, when the territorial legislature authorized a general school system, organizing public education in the form of a primary school and an academy. But it was another 20 years and the granting of statehood in 1837 before any concrete steps were taken, starting with the establishment of the Office of State Superintendent of Public Instruction. During the next two years, the state legislature adopted a spate of legislation, including the establishment of school districts in each township, a requirement that school districts hold school for at least three months, and the provision of minimal funding of these schools afforded both by means of a Primary School Fund and the legislature's granting of local authority to levy taxes to support these schools. This period also saw the establishment of the University of Michigan, and shortly thereafter the establishment of "branches" of the university, the veritable forerunners of Michigan's present day high schools. This led, in 1848, to the actual establishment in Detroit of Michigan's first public high school.

Thirty-one years later, in 1869, the legislature solidified the state's responsibility for providing some modicum of education by adopting a law requiring all public schools to be free and open without charge to the pupils of the district, followed in 1871 by the adoption of a compulsory education law requiring that all children between the ages of 8 and 14 attend school at least 12 weeks each year. We might argue that these two statutes constituted Michigan's first calls for accountability in education—on the one hand, holding the state accountable for the provision of free and open public education, albeit for only three months, and on the other hand, holding parents accountable for ensuring that their children attend school, again, albeit for only three months. Recalling Callahan's comments about American manufacturing's basic maxim, the 1871 Michigan legislature, to its credit, appears to have paid some minimal attention to both sides of the maxim, the lowest cost and the finest product.[2]

School Accreditation

In terms of accountability, the 1870s were somewhat remarkable in that the decade witnessed two important events that would hold significant consequences for future accountability programs in Michigan as well as in some of the neighboring states. The first of these—and the more important, at least in terms of accountability—was the University of Michigan's official establishment of its high school accreditation program in 1871, generally considered the first of its kind in the United States (Williams 1998, pp. 17–19). Under this program, the university began to grant "accreditation" to secondary schools providing preparation for university study, provided university faculty members judged them of high quality on the basis of site visits. Graduates of these accredited secondary schools were then eligible for admission to the University of Michigan on the basis of their diplomas rather than having to undergo an entrance examination.

The University of Michigan's program eventually led, in 1895, to the founding of the North Central Association Commission on Accreditation and School Improvement (NCA CASI). The University of Michigan accreditation program, as we shall see in a later section, also was the forerunner of both the Michigan Accreditation Program (MAP I), established by the Michigan Department of Education (MDE) in 1988, and Michigan's present state accountability program—EducationYes!, established in 2002. In this instance, there appears to be little question but that the ostensible concern of the early—and even later—proponents of school accreditation was more on the finest product side of the aforementioned maxim. The accreditation of a school by the university as well as by the NCA CASI in surrounding states came to be seen as an assurance to parents and to the public that the school indeed was providing the finest product.

The Kalamazoo Case

The second significant event of that period was the 1875 ruling by the Michigan Supreme Court in the now famous Kalamazoo case, namely, that the state had a right to levy taxes to support a complete system of public education, including high schools and universities (Johns, Morphet, and Alexander 1983, p. 5). In effect, the ruling became a precedent used by the plaintiffs' attorneys to establish a basis for the public funding of the Kalamazoo High School, as well as prompting many Michigan townships to follow suit. The state had now assumed responsibility—or accountability—for the provision of "open and free" public education through the high school years. Coupling this event with the immediately prior establishment of the University of Michigan Accreditation Program, it appears that the finest product side of the maxim had indeed become a paramount concern. However, as the years passed, and judging from Michigan's—and several other states'—long and contentious history with school finance reform, many enduring arguments arose over the meaning of free. One has to ask whether equal if not increasing emphasis was being placed on the lowest cost rather than the finest product side of the equation. In truth, what Michigan and a good many other states have witnessed over the years is something of a back and forth movement, a waxing and a waning, with the balance scales at one point in time tipping toward finest product and at another point toward lowest cost.

Before we leave this period, it is fitting to say a bit more about Michigan's influence on school accreditation generally, an influence that, as we noted above, went far beyond the boundaries of Michigan, for the university's school accreditation program was extended not only to secondary schools within the state but to others as well. By 1899, students in some 187 high schools in 15 different states were eligible, by diploma alone, for admission to the University of Michigan (Williams 1998). The Michigan Plan, as it came to be known, gathered supporters in other states and regions and eventually led in 1895 to the aforementioned meeting in Chicago at Northwestern University and the founding of the NCA CASI. Today, NCA CASI accredits schools and districts in 19 states, the Navajo Nation, and the Department of Defense Dependents Schools worldwide (NCA 2009).[3] Thus, the decision some 138 years ago by the University of Michigan to initiate a program of high school accreditation had far-reaching effects and, we argue, effects that were for the most part intended to address the finest product side of the equation—even if, as we shall see, serious questions arose at later times about the effectiveness of school accreditation.

1900–50: THE FIRST HALF OF THE TWENTIETH CENTURY

In terms of meaningful accountability programs in American public education, the 50-year period from 1900 to 1950 might best be summed up in two descriptive terms—*Scientific Management* (Taylor 1911) and the *Cult of Efficiency* (Callahan 1964). Beginning in the early 1900s, American business, through the writings of Frederick Taylor, discovered the efficiency expert and rapidly adopted Taylor's new system of industrial management that fast became known as scientific management, or the "Taylor system." Callahan vividly recounts the many efforts to adapt Taylor's principles and introduce them into American education in the early years of the twentieth century.

This is the period that saw the rise of a group of educators who became known as "efficiency experts" or "engineers," and the introduction into the schools of a myriad of efficiency measures. These measures included the development of new achievement tests in language arts and mathematics; scales for rating the efficiency of teachers; surveys of school systems undertaken by outside experts, usually professors of administration from the colleges and schools of education; and the platoon schools that were first developed and implemented in Gary, Indiana. It was the period of records and reports, of educational cost accounting, of the educational balance sheet and child accounting.

As Callahan (1964) points out, " . . . no reasonable man can deny the advisability of applying certain business practices where they are appropriate to the work of the schools" (p. 177). But he also reminds us that these practices are at best a means to an end: providing "the best possible education for all of our children" (p. 177). During this period, the balance indeed had tipped heavily toward the lowest cost side of the equation. As Callahan notes, "When efficiency and economy are sought as ends in themselves, as they were in education in the age of efficiency . . . the education of children is bound to suffer. The same thing is true regarding certain business values. A concern about the wise expenditure of funds and the avoidance of waste is as desirable in education as it is in business. But a 'wise' expenditure of funds depends on the outcomes which are expected or, in business terms, the quality of the product desired" (pp. 177–178).

Schools in Michigan and throughout the nation were not immune to this somewhat inordinate preoccupation with the "cult of efficiency." But, beginning in the late 1950s and early 1960s, because of rising public concerns about the quality of America's schools, events soon led toward righting the balance and the placing of increased weight on the finest product side of the equation. It is to this period we now turn.

THE LATE 1950s TO THE PRESENT

Growing Calls for Information on Performance

In the previous section we recounted the University of Michigan's establishment of the nation's first high school accreditation program in 1871. The Michigan Plan, as it came to be known, soon gathered supporters in other states and regions and led to the founding of the NCA CASI in 1895. For the most part, both the Michigan Plan and NCA CASI appeared to address the finest product side of Callahan's equation, as the many proponents of accreditation staunchly claimed up through the 1950s and early 1960s.

However, in the mid-1960s doubts and concerns began to creep in, centered largely on accreditation's seemingly restricted focus on the "inputs" of schooling, with scant attention being paid to the "outputs" of schooling. Critics began to cite numerous examples of accredited high schools—particularly in Detroit and other urban districts—falling far short in their attention to or success with the finest product side of the equation. Serious and growing concerns were raised—by parents, legislators, and the general public—about the quality of schooling and, in many instances, the apparent failure of accredited high schools to provide their graduates (or nongraduates for that matter) with the most basic of skills in academic areas such as reading, writing, mathematics, science, and social studies.

But accreditation wasn't the only culprit, perhaps just one of the more visible targets. There arose a growing concern and dissatisfaction with American public education, particularly with the American high school. This discontent was being voiced in the media, in educational and secular journals, in public reports, and in any number of published books and monographs, which led to increasing calls for reforms aimed primarily at the finest product side of Callahan's maxim. Still there were substantial disagreements among the many voices calling for the reform of the American high school (Angus and Mirel 1999). On one side, there were those who supported the views of James B. Conant, the former president of Harvard University. Conant strongly favored a strengthening of the comprehensive high school and its central theme of curricular differentiation, providing students of different abilities with a wide range of courses and programs attuned to their interests and abilities (Conant 1959a,b; 1961). On the other side, there was a sizable group of advocates who championed the views of scholars such as Arthur Bestor (1985) and saw curricular differentiation as the crux of the problem. From this group came the call for state legislatures across the nation to adopt rigorous and demanding high school graduation requirements, to do away with what Powell, Farrar, and Cohen (1985) called "the shopping mall high school." Central to all of these arguments was the apparent lack of meaningful and readily available information on the academic performance of students. This shortfall very soon became the focal point of the critics' dissatisfactions—in effect, there arose a mounting cry for information about the finest product side.

It was during this time—the early 1960s—that efforts got under way at the federal level to address these demands for information on student achievement through the creation and development of the National Assessment of Educational Progress (NAEP), soon to become known as the Nation's Report Card. It also was at this same time that Michigan, in the persons of the superintendent of public instruction and staff members in the education department's newly formed Bureau of Research, began to lose faith in input-oriented school accreditation and turned their attention instead toward the outcome side, the finest product side, toward creating a system to annually gather and report information on the academic performance of students in Michigan's public schools. In a series of policy briefs, bureau staff outlined what they saw as the problem and offered their suggested solution, namely, the creation of a statewide educational assessment program, beginning with reading and mathematics at grades 4 and 7. In a series of three public memoranda, Ira Polley, the then state superintendent of public instruction, transmitted the staff proposal to the Michigan State Board of Education (SBE). In April of 1969, the SBE responded by directing Polley "to prepare and submit appropriate legislation for the periodic assessment of educational progress in the public elementary and secondary schools of Michigan" (Kearney, Crowson, and Wilbur 1970, p. 16). Thus was born the Michigan Educational Assessment Program (MEAP), one of, if not the, nation's first statewide assessment programs, soon to be followed by similar programs in a growing number of other states. In the next chapter, we discuss at some length the creation, implementation, and further development of the program over the past 40 years. But we leave the MEAP for now, and instead shift our focus to Michigan's broader effort to establish a statewide accountability program, an effort that followed rather immediately on the establishment of the MEAP.

John Porter's Six-Step Accountability Model

In October of 1969, John Porter replaced Ira Polley as the Michigan Superintendent of Public Instruction. Polley had been a strong voice in support of the development and implementation of the MEAP, the new state educational assessment program that was just getting under way. Initial fears were that the assessment program, with the loss of one its strongest supporters, might now "wither on the vine." But if Polley was a strong supporter of the MEAP, John Porter became an ardent supporter not only of the MEAP but also of the more wide-ranging concept of educational accountability. The finest product side of the equation had truly come to the fore. In Porter's view, accountability had two essential dimensions. He saw the first dimension as access to information about performance—which the MEAP would provide—and the second dimension as the ability to change those factors thought responsible for unsatisfactory performance—an ability yet to be realized. Porter summed up his view of educational accountability in these words: ". . . the guarantee that all students without respect to race, income, or social class will acquire the minimum school skills necessary to take full advantage of the choices that accrue upon successful completion of public schooling, or we in education will describe the reasons why" (Kearney 1971, p. 5).

As 1970 dawned, Porter moved quickly to begin development and implementation of a six-step process that came to be known as the Michigan Accountability Model. The six steps included the assessment program as step three, but added five other steps to the process:

1) identification of common goals,
2) development of performance objectives,
3) assessment of needs,
4) analysis of delivery systems,
5) evaluation of programs, and
6) recommendations for improvement.

These six steps were not in themselves novel, and one could reasonably argue that, whether intuitively or consciously, they generally made up the problem solving and planning activities in which teachers, administrators, and other educators regularly engaged. At the time, what was novel was Porter's effort to gain commitment of a state's entire educational system to a program of coordinated improvement, to what was one of the nation's first state accountability systems. The extent to which the six-step program was successful is of course debatable, particularly with respect to the final three steps in the process. It is much easier to judge the success of the first three steps, even though their initial development and implementation appeared to be backward, or chronologically reversed—logically, one would conclude that steps one and two should have preceded step three. But step three—assessment—came first, well before the state had formally identified its common goals, and before it had developed performance objectives based on those common goals. For Porter and the Bureau of Research staff, this did not seem an insurmountable problem. They felt that steps one and two could be undertaken, completed, and then step three could be appropriately "tweaked," that is, the necessary modifications could be made in the assessment measures themselves. But we leave to the next chapter judgments on the success of the approach of tweaking step three of the model, and turn now to visit briefly the development of steps one and two.

In early 1970, the SBE, at Porter's behest, appointed an advisory task force composed of Michigan educators, parents, students, and other lay citizens, and gave the task force the charge of identifying and delineating what they felt should be the common goals of a state educational system capable of meeting the growing and changing needs of contemporary society. In June of 1970, the task force presented its recommendations to the SBE, which reviewed the recommendations and made revisions and additions. As a result, 30,000 copies of a document entitled "The Common Goals of Michigan Education: Tentative" were printed and distributed to educators and citizens throughout the state. Twenty-six public meetings were held across Michigan to elicit the opinions and concerns of local educators and lay citizens regarding the common goals. Subsequently, the SBE, after reviewing the opinions and concerns and revising the goals, formally adopted the document in 1971 and distributed it broadly throughout the state (MDE 1971).

In effect, two of the six steps were now in place—step one and step three. At this point in our narrative, one might now raise some appropriate questions: What has become of the "Common Goals of Michigan Education" first adopted 40 years ago in 1971? What effects have the goals had on Michigan education? What direction did they provide to subsequent reform efforts? The simple answer is, "not much." For the most part, the document has faded from view, and any remaining copies likely are gathering dust on bookshelves or are lost in filing cabinets.[4] But that may be unfairly dismissive. One could argue that the Common Goals did indeed serve a useful purpose. They demonstrated that the MDE, in its attempt to introduce sweeping reforms into Michigan education, intended to move in a logical and systematic fashion to build a genuine accountability system. To most it would seem to make good sense to establish goals, then translate them into specific performance objectives, then develop the instruments to measure the attainment of those objectives, and so on. At a minimum, the state of Michigan was able to demonstrate that it had identified its common educational goals (the nation didn't do this until 1990), and *ex post*, it could demonstrate connections between the goals and the actual performance objectives that later were developed.

Over the next several years, the MDE did indeed develop a comprehensive set of performance objectives and, in turn, a new and improved set of assessment measures directly tied to those objectives. A recounting of those efforts—which underlay the state's movement from norm-referenced to objective-referenced tests in the MEAP, from group measures to individually reliable measures, from broad to increasing specificity in the performance objectives, from generalities to the establishment of grade-level expectations and benchmarks—are also best left to the next chapter, where we deal at length with the history of the MEAP over the past 40 years.

One could reasonably argue that Porter's accountability model has led to the annual production of a considerable amount of useful information on the academic performance of Michigan's public school students. Nonetheless, this still leaves questions about what happened with steps four, five, and six of the Michigan Accountability Model. What became of them? What guidance and direction did they provide to Michigan's ongoing efforts at reform? How useful were they as tools to help improve Michigan education? In this instance, one would have to argue that nothing specific came out of those three steps, which, like the "Common Goals," soon faded from view. Yet, in another sense, one also could argue that they were subsumed under larger efforts arising out of the state legislative reform mandates of the 1980s and the 1990s, and the even larger array of national reform activities and congressional mandates set in motion by the advent of the Reagan Administration and the National Commission on Excellence in Education's publication of *A Nation at Risk* in April of 1983. For it was the release of this report that served as the catalyst for generating renewed attention and action, at both state and national levels, to the problems and perceived shortcomings of America's public schools.

There are any number of excellent overviews of the multiple nationwide and statewide reform efforts that have transpired since the 1983 release of *A Nation at Risk*—accounts that are much more comprehensive and much more detailed than any account we could provide within the limits of this current chapter.[5] Consequently, rather than attempt to offer an extended review of these many and diverse efforts, we provide here only a brief and somewhat cursory review of that broad range of national and state-level activity. We trust that this brief review will help set the stage for the arrival of NCLB on the national scene in 2002, and concurrently EducationYES! on the Michigan scene.

A Nation at Risk—Catalyst for Nationwide Education Reform

In the mid-1980s, then secretary of education Terrel Bell created an 18-member National Commission on Excellence in Education. The commission's report, entitled *A Nation at Risk*, did its job extremely well, capturing the nation's attention with its eye-catching if not alarmist opening statement: ". . . the educational foundations of our society are presently being eroded by a rising tide of mediocrity that threatens our very future as a Nation and a people . . . If an unfriendly power had attempted to impose on America the mediocre educational performance that exists today, we might well have viewed it as an act of war" (National Commission on Excellence 1983, p. 7).

The publication of *A Nation at Risk* helped jump-start what many have called the first wave of national (and state) reform—concentrating in general on such activities as strengthening requirements for high school graduation, developing minimal competency tests at both district and state levels, and advocating and initiating merit-pay programs for teachers. Several more reform waves were to follow, brought on by follow-up gubernatorial actions at the state level as well as by further significant executive and congressional actions at the federal level. In Michigan, the state board's response was to adopt its 1984 "Blueprint for Action," calling for high school graduation requirements, school improvement plans, and a new state school accreditation system—the Michigan Accreditation Program (MAP I), which first became operational in 1988.

At the federal level, in 1989, at the behest of the National Governors Association, newly elected President George H.W. Bush and the nation's governors came together in a two-day educational summit in Charlottesville, Virginia. The outcome of the Charlottesville Education Summit was an agreement to develop a set of National Education Goals—to wit, "an ambitious, realistic set of performance goals."

> By performance goals we mean goals that will, if achieved, guarantee that we are internationally competitive, such as goals related to: the readiness of children to start school; the performance of students on international achievement tests, especially in mathematics and science; the reduction of the dropout rate and the improvement of academic performance, especially among at risk students; the

> functional literacy of adult Americans; the level of training necessary to guarantee a competitive workforce; the supply of qualified teachers and up-to-date technology; and the establishment of safe, disciplined and drug free schools. (*New York Times* 1989)

Referring back to Callahan's maxim, it appeared that President Bush and the nation's governors were now placing increasing emphasis on the finest product. Subsequently, in his 1990 State of the Union address, President Bush announced the establishment of six National Educational Goals—six goals that, for the most part, directly reflected the language set forth above (Executive Office of the President 1990). Some months later, in the fall of 1990, agreement was reached with the Congress on the establishment of a 14-member bipartisan National Educational goals panel. In 1991, at the urging of Secretary of Education Lamar Alexander, the Congress took the next step and established the National Council on Education Standards and Testing (Ravitch 1995a). The goals panel and the six national goals themselves (now increased to eight) subsequently were formally established in law in 1994 during the Clinton Administration under the Goals 2000: Educate America Act (Public Law 1994). This act was intended to lay the groundwork for the development of state and national standards in education (Ravitch 1995b). However, this effort failed to get off the ground, due in large part to concerns about federal intrusion into the long-held traditions of state and local control of education (an effort that was given new life in 2009 by action of the nation's governors and education chiefs; see Chapter 4 in this volume).

From these somewhat jumbled beginnings there followed any number of ensuing federal actions and activities aimed at the reform of American education, actions also aimed at complementing if not pushing further the reforms already under way in a number of states and local school districts, including Michigan. Of particular note was the movement or approach that became known as systemic school reform. The chief authors and advocates of this approach were Marshall Smith and Jennifer O'Day. They proposed a design for a systemic state structure that would be based on clear and challenging standards for student learning—standards for the finest product, if you will. State policies would be tied to the standards and reinforce one another in providing guidance to schools and teachers about student instruction. These policies in turn would provide a structure of coherent state leadership, while at the same time giving schools the flexibility to develop learning strategies best suited to their students. In effect, systemic education reform was intended to combine the "waves" of school reform into a long-term improvement effort that would provide coherence and direction in state reform efforts and put substance and content into the restructuring movement (Smith and O'Day 1990). It is not a huge leap from these beginnings to the reasoning behind the subsequent call by the U.S. Department of Education for each state to develop its own State Accountability Plan—a call that became the prime requirement undergirding each state's implementation of NCLB.

The Demise of the Traditional Approach to Accreditation

Before we turn toward 2001 and the development of NCLB, and the parallel development in Michigan of EducationYES!, let us return for a moment to the mid-1980s and the University of Michigan accreditation program, and its counterpart NCA program, which operated until 1992 under the auspices of the university. For while the state superintendent and the SBE, by their actions in initiating the MEAP in 1968, had turned their backs on the university's and the NCA's accreditation programs, those programs did not immediately go away. The University of Michigan program, as well as the NCA program, began in modest ways to incorporate into their ongoing plans attention to student performance and student outcomes. Beginning in 1985 the university and its school of education assigned both programs to its newly formed Bureau of Accreditation and School Improvement Studies. In the bureau, the programs took on a somewhat rejuvenated life, focusing more attention on the outcomes side of the coin, and employing new information technologies in the collection, analysis, and reporting of accreditation-related data to the schools and the public (Bureau of Accreditation and School Improvement Studies 1988). But the life of the University of Michigan program was fast coming to an end, and it finally gave up the ghost in 1993 upon recognizing that its program would soon become duplicative of the efforts of the SBE.

Public Act 25—A New Accountability Framework for Michigan

Complementing the spate of educational reform efforts at the national level briefly described above, state policymakers in Michigan set out on a somewhat parallel path. By the late 1980s, the state legislature was expressing growing interest in educational accountability, so much so that in 1990 they passed Public Act 25, requiring the creation of a new accountability framework under which Michigan's schools would operate. We say new in deference to the original accountability framework established in 1970 under John Porter's six-step process described earlier. But by the mid-1980s, as we noted earlier, and with the exception of steps two and three—i.e., the performance objectives and the assessment—the six-step process pretty much had fallen into disuse.

The new legislation adopted in 1990 called for an accountability framework consisting of four principal components: 1) school improvement, 2) a core curriculum, 3) accreditation, and 4) an annual education report. Under the *school improvement* component, schools were required to develop school improvement plans, establish school improvement teams, and measure progress toward the achievement of the plans' objectives. Under component two, the state established a model core curriculum and proposed, but did not mandate, specific learning outcomes for all students. While the schools were encouraged to align their curricula with the model core curriculum, they were not required to do so. Rather, the legislation only required a district to notify its residents if the curriculum was not aligned. The SBE and the MDE developed the third component, accreditation, which became known as MAP II. Modeled on the beginning work done under MAP I, the new MAP II generally followed traditional approaches to accreditation—schools were to be evaluated on the basis of their curricula, their staffing, their facilities, and whether they met the requirements of the school improvement process. The final component of Public Act 25 required all schools to publish an annual education report informing their residents on how the schools were doing on student achievement, parent participation, accreditation status, and other factors relating to school improvement efforts. The law also required each school to hold a public meeting to review its annual report.

Even given these somewhat demanding mandates, policy analysts at one of the major state universities argued that the Public Act 25 legislation suffered from a critical fault, namely, " . . . the absence of any mechanism for assessing whether the school improvement process defined by the law was effective. Did schools that participated in mandated school improvement activities improve or not? Answering this question required a mechanism for assessing performance of students, schools and school districts" (Education Policy Center 2000).

The Michigan legislature moved to rectify this shortcoming in 1995 by requiring that the accreditation component of the Public Act 25 framework include information on student performance on the MEAP. This amendment placed the MEAP at the heart of standards-based accountability in Michigan (Education Policy Center 2000). But even this amendment did not rejuvenate the state's accreditation program (MAP II). The assessment data, of course, were there, but a number of troubling questions arose on how to restructure the MAP II program, and build a MAP III program in a way that would accommodate the MEAP data. How would cut scores be set?[6] How would they be used to determine a school's accreditation status? Would any information other than the MEAP data enter into accreditation decisions? How would accreditation decisions be reported both to the schools and to the public? Questions such as these led to a series of ongoing discussions among senior staff in the MDE about how the department and the state board should respond. One such response, reportedly advocated by a senior staff member, proposed adopting a simple approach to accreditation, namely, establishing a single MEAP cut score. Any school at or above the cut score would be accredited; any school below the score would not.

The state board never voted on that proposal, or at the time seriously considered any other alternatives. The board was having its own problems with Governor John Engler, who was challenging the authority of the board on several fronts by issuing a number of executive orders transferring major functions of the board and the MDE to other departments of state government. Included in these executive orders was the transfer of the MEAP to the Treasury Department. Aside from the governor's growing dissatisfaction with the state board, the ostensible rationale behind the transfer was that the Treasury Department administered the Michigan Merit Scholarship Program.[7] Thus you had the MDE responsible for MAP III, and while required to use the MEAP data to make accreditation decisions, the MEAP program itself now was lodged in a different department of state government. To further compound the problem, by executive order, the governor also created the Center for Educational Performance and Information and made it responsible for handling the MEAP data and related performance information on the schools. The state board and the MDE still had the accreditation responsibility, but were left without the MEAP and without control over the data lode that it produced.

At the same time the pressures for information on academic performance continued to rise, principally from the business community if not from the general public. The education community also became increasingly concerned about how the MEAP data would be used in making accreditation decisions and how those decisions would be shared with the public.

EducationYES!—The Beginnings

So MAP III, one might say, was limping along, looking for the answers to such questions, when in early 2001 the SBE appointed Tom Watkins as Michigan's new Superintendent of Public Instruction. Watkins was not the traditional schoolman; rather, he brought to the role a diverse background with substantial leadership experiences in the for-profit, nonprofit, and public sectors—including senior-level staff and executive positions in Michigan state government. He also had spent time in the early 1990s as "special assistant for school initiatives" to David Adamany, the president of Wayne State University. It was during that period that Watkins played a key role in creating Michigan's first charter school—he was not completely bereft of experience in public education.

One of Watkins's first senior staff appointments was of Bill Bushaw as deputy superintendent and chief academic officer. Bushaw, at the time of his appointment, was the executive director of Michigan's NCA program of accreditation and school improvement. He had shepherded that program's spin-off from the University of Michigan in 1993 and its establishment as an independent and self-funded entity, installing it as an increasingly important player in Michigan public education.

Bushaw, in early conversations with Watkins, suggested that there was a more thoughtful way to go about responding to Public Act 25, to build a quality accreditation program using more than just the MEAP tests. Watkins gave Bushaw the green light, and Bushaw set out to fashion a design for a new state accreditation and accountability program. Watkins and Bushaw also wanted to do it in a way that would not require opening up Public Act 25 to further amendment.

Bushaw visited contemporaries in North Carolina, California, and Florida and talked with persons in those state education agencies who were building or had built state accountability programs, seeking advice and counsel based on their experiences. He also was interested in learning more about efforts under way in the assessment field to develop "growth models," and he was particularly interested in the work of William Sanders (Sanders, Saxton, and Horn 1997) and his value-added assessment system. Bushaw believed that growth or value-added accountability models could be an important element in the new Michigan system. Such models presumably would permit measuring the annual academic growth of individual students or groups of students, in effect measuring what portion of a year's academic growth they were achieving for each year of instruction.

By late fall, working with fellow staff member Paul Bielawski and measurement consultant John Wick, Bushaw had produced an early draft of EducationYES! He shared this initial draft with the state board, seeking its review and comment. The board received the draft favorably, and offered comments and suggestions for revision. In December of 2001, Bushaw presented a revised and more comprehensive proposal to the state board. The board responded by giving the go-ahead for further development of EducationYES! and for public hearings on the proposal to be held in January 2002. Following the public hearings, Bushaw presented a further revision of the EducationYES! proposal to the SBE for its review. In March of 2002, the SBE formally approved the revised proposal.

As originally conceived, the design behind the achievement portion of EducationYES! was simple but elegant. At its heart, the design called for developing and reporting three separate measures of academic performance: 1) achievement status, 2) achievement change, and 3) achievement growth. Achievement status, drawing on the MEAP, would measure and report how well a school was doing in educating its students in designated subjects at designated grade levels in any given year. Specifically, it would report how many students had achieved proficiency in designated subjects.[8] To ensure stability and reliability of the achievement status score, it would be based on a mean of three years of comparable MEAP data.

Achievement change would measure and report this same information over time, for example, how a school was doing from one year to the next in reading achievement for all of its fourth graders. To ensure stability and reliability of the achievement change score, it would be based on a mean of five years of comparable MEAP data. This also was the score that would be linked into the federal requirement for adequate yearly progress (AYP) under NCLB. But more about that later.

Achievement growth, again drawing on the MEAP data and using an aforementioned growth or value-added model, would measure and report a score depicting how an individual student, or group of students, was progressing over time from grade level to grade level in, for example, mathematics. In effect, achievement growth would report on the extent to which the school was adding value each year for each student going through the system.

These three hard measures would then be complemented but not outweighed by a cluster of softer measures called performance indicators. The design behind this portion of EducationYES! was not so simple or elegant, and later led to serious problems in measurement and reporting. The performance indicators themselves were intended to measure and report on a school's performance in 11 areas, which constituted a potpourri of indicators grouped into three clusters.

The first cluster, indicators of engagement, covered three areas: 1) performance management systems, 2) continuous improvement, and 3) curriculum alignment. The second cluster, indicators of instructional quality, covered four areas: 1) teacher quality and professional development, 2) extended learning opportunities, 3) arts education and humanities for all students, and 4) advanced course work. The third cluster, indicators of learning opportunities, covered four areas: 1) family involvement, 2) student attendance and dropout rate, 3) four-year education and employment plan, and 4) school facilities. This hodgepodge of three clusters and 11 areas carried some serious measurement problems. How, one might ask, could you develop a single valid and reliable score out of this veritable mess? In effect, this design put the department into the catch-22 situation we describe below.[9]

All four scores—the three achievement scores and the performance indicators score—were to be weighted. The three achievement scores—each of which was weighted at 22.33 percent—would thus constitute 67 percent of a school's total or composite score; the performance indicators score would count for the remaining 33 percent of the school's composite total score. All four scores—plus the composite total score—would use a score scale of 0 to 100. The scores on each of the four components would be calculated and reported using the scaled score plus a label, that is, a grade of A, B, C, D, or F. These four scores would then be combined into a composite total score for the school, again expressed on a 0 to 100 scale along with a grade of A, B, C, D, or F.

Thus, a given school, say, in 4th grade reading, would receive three scores and letter grades for achievement—status, change, and growth—plus a score and letter grade for performance indicators. This same school might receive additional scores and letter grades, for example, in 7th grade mathematics—and perhaps in other academic areas at other grade levels. The designers assumed that all of these independent scores and letter grades could in turn be combined into a single composite total score and letter grade for the entire school. A school's composite score and letter grades then were to be used in determining the school's status in terms of AYP under NCLB, as well as the school's Michigan accreditation status—summary accredited, accredited, interim accredited, or nonaccredited. For each school, all of this information, summarized and appropriately formatted, would then constitute its Michigan school report card—released not only to the school and district but also to parents, the legislature, the news media, and the general public. The annual release of the school report cards would ensure that each school and local district would become publicly accountable for its performance. The reader might conclude that the annual report card would provide a lot of information, but a lot of information not all that easy to absorb and understand.

As we noted above, the design appeared at first glance to be simple but elegant—at least as far as the achievement measures were concerned. Unfortunately, while a general design was there, the measurement methodologies, as well as the processes and procedures needed to accomplish all of this, were neither spelled out nor available. A substantial number of problems and questions remained to be addressed, including how to set the cut scores; how to determine A, B, C, D, or F grades for the achievement measures and the performance indicators; how to calculate the composite total score for a school; how to determine a school's accreditation status; and how to measure and report growth or added value.

The performance indicators in particular presented serious problems. They were not to be objectively scored but rather self-reported. The design called for gathering data in each of the 11 areas but only calculating and reporting scores for the three clusters, plus a single total score and grade for the entire gamut of performance indicators. As originally conceived, it appears that the total performance indicators score and grade would serve in part to compensate for low achievement scores—one might say a sort of get out of jail free card.

But the most pressing problem facing the state board was how to align EducationYES!, the state's accountability program, with the demanding requirements of NCLB, the federal government's newly adopted accountability program, and particularly its requirement of AYP. And the timing, depending on one's view, was either favorable or unfavorable, for the two programs had appeared almost concurrently on the educational scene. The Congress adopted the new federal legislation in January of 2002, the same month that the SBE was holding public hearings on the draft proposal of EducationYES!

EducationYES!—The Accreditation Advisory Committee

In March of 2002, following the public hearings, the SBE approved the basic design of EducationYES! While the basic design set forth the general framework of EducationYES!, as we indicate above there was much work to do before the design could be fully fleshed out. With Watkins providing the organizational support, Bushaw, along with Bielawski and Wick, immediately undertook the task of refining and completing the design. To assist them in the task, at Watkins's urging, the SBE in April of 2002 established a broad-based, five-member advisory committee.[10] The board charged the committee with developing recommendations in three areas:

1) initial distribution of schools in grade categories, i.e., assigning the cut scores for the achievement measures;

2) measuring school performance indicators, i.e., assigning the cluster scores and the total score for the indicators; and
3) alignment of EducationYES! with federal legislation, i.e., developing a score to meet the NCLB AYP requirement.

The committee began its work in May 2002 and submitted its final report and recommendations to the state board a year later in April 2003—having met as a working group a total of 22 days over that time period, plus providing interim reports to the state board on five different occasions (SBE 2003a). The written report of the committee is a bit complex and somewhat involved, and deals with a number of areas with which the reader may either be unfamiliar or have little interest—for example, the linear transformation of MEAP scores to a 0 to 100 scale. Accordingly, in what follows we try to avoid complex language and explanations and stick to a plain-English telling of the story.[11]

Assigning cut scores

The committee turned its immediate attention to its first charge, namely, setting cut scores for assigning "proficiency" levels and letter grades of A, B, C, D, and F based on the achievement status scores.[12] In effect, the committee had been asked by the state board to make judgments about "proficiency" designations and the letter grades to be assigned to different levels of performance on the individual assessments, and for aggregate or composite performance overall. If done correctly, that alone would be a sizable task. There were 11 separate sets of scores in the achievement status category. At the elementary school level, there were reading and mathematics. At the middle school level, there were reading, mathematics, science, and social studies. At the 11th grade level, there were reading, writing, mathematics, science, and social studies.

Apparently in the early staff thinking behind EducationYES!, there was some talk of arbitrarily setting the cut scores, for example, by "grading on the curve," where *x* percent would get A's, *y* percent would get B's, and so on, irrespective of the actual scores. There also was talk of either a single person or a small group making these judgments, keeping it simple, so to speak. The accreditation advisory committee, however, in pursuing its charge, insisted that these judgments be made through a formal standard-setting process to ensure the integrity of the cut scores and letter grades. For that reason the committee asked department staff to convene a standard-setting panel broadly representative of classroom teachers, administrators, parents, and members of the business community. That panel met on two separate occasions to examine actual score profiles, and based on that examination offer its recommendations on cut scores and letter grades to the committee for its review. The committee reviewed and subsequently accepted the panel's recommendations, and in turn recommended their approval to the SBE. The cut scores and letter grades, once approved by the SBE, were then used in the first public reporting of EducationYES! results.[13]

In dealing with the achievement status scores, a related concern of the committee was how to address the "masking" of the variance in the scores that resulted from using a simple mean or average score for a grade or school. For example, a school might have a relatively high mean or average score on 4th grade reading, apparently signifying it was doing quite well, yet have a number of very low scores hidden, or masked, under that mean or average score. To address this, the committee recommended putting more weight on the scores of low achievers in calculating achievement status, thereby encouraging schools to place priority on improving the achievement of students who attained the lowest scores on the MEAP assessments. It was felt that a local school's attention to these low achievers would have a salutary effect leading to improvement in their performance, while at the same time ultimately raising the total achievement status score for a subject, grade level, and school.

For the achievement change category there were, of course, the same 11 scores as used in the achievement status category—and a change score had to be calculated for each. The achievement change score, as noted above, would measure and report change over time, for example, how a school was doing from one year to the next in reading achievement for its fourth graders. This was the score to be linked with AYP required under NCLB. As we discuss further in the next section, the NCLB goal is to have all students in all subject matter areas attain 100 percent proficiency by the 2013–14 school year. The achievement change score in EducationYES! determines if student achievement in a school is improving at a rate fast enough to attain this goal. To accomplish this end, the committee developed and recommended an achievement change score that involved a calculation based on two trend lines or slopes, an actual score slope for the school against a target score slope linked to the goal of 100 percent proficiency by 2013–14. Calculating a school's improvement rate in achievement from one year to the next, averaging three years of those improvement rates, and plotting those as a trend line would produce the school's actual score slope, i.e., from any given year to the next. Then plotting the school's actual score slope against its target score slope would indicate whether the school was on, above, or below target. The percentage by which the school was above or below target dictated the school's achievement change score.

The committee took upon itself the task of determining what these achievement change cut scores and grades ought to be. A grade of A was awarded to a school whose actual score slope was 125 percent above its target score slope; a B was awarded to a school whose actual score slope was between 75 and 125 percent of the target score slope; a C went to a school whose actual score slope was between 25 and 75 percent of the target score slope; a D was given to a school whose actual slope lay between 25 percent of the target score slope and 25 percent of the target below zero; and finally, an F was given to a school whose actual score slope was more than 25 percent of target below zero. As we indicated above, the achievement change score was closely linked to the AYP requirement under NCLB; we shall have more to say about that in a later section. The SBE accepted the committee's recommendations and used the achievement change cut scores as the basis for determining letter grades and, more importantly, whether a school had made AYP. These letter grades and AYP status also were included in the first public release of EducationYES! results.

It was in the achievement growth category that the advisory committee ran into a major problem—the committee was not able to calculate achievement growth scores for any number of reasons, not the least of which was the lack of measures and scores at adjacent grade levels. Without scores at adjacent grade levels, one could not build a cross-grade scale and thus follow the progress of a student's scores, say, in mathematics, as he or she proceeded through the grades. Put simply, the calculation of achievement growth would have to await the implementation of MEAP testing at all grade levels from three to eight, which would not be accomplished until at least 2004–05. Furthermore, because under EducationYES! as designed, one needed an average of three years to ensure reliability and add stability to the scores, it would be sometime after the 2005–06 MEAP administration before achievement growth scores could be reported in a valid and reliable manner. Another problem arose from the many different grade-level configurations found in Michigan's schools, making it virtually impossible in many cases to attribute growth to a single school. For example, in those instances where a group of children might be tested in a middle school at grade seven with some having matriculated to grade seven from grade six in two or more different elementary schools, which schools would get the growth score? At the time, there also was the difficulty of linking students' scores from grade four to grades seven and eight. There were a number of other problems, chiefly psychometric, that had to be resolved before Michigan could confidently and safely utilize an achievement growth score—and some of these problems continued to plague the program up through the school year 2010–11. As of the 2008–09 school year, EducationYES! had yet to employ an achievement growth score, although there was an attempt to add such a score in 2009–10. While the inclusion in EducationYES! of an achievement growth score would seem to be highly desirable, the promise—at least at the time of this writing—still outpaces the reality. The notion of a growth, or value-added, score is an attractive one, and a good many promises have been made and are being made by their proponents. Still, at the present time the measurement community is of mixed views on the validity and reliability of these scores, and there is much debate about the desirability of their use.[14]

The Performance Indicators

As mentioned earlier, the three clusters and 11 areas included in the performance indicators were a veritable potpourri—a hodgepodge that posed both serious construct and measurement problems. As the accreditation advisory committee began its work, a separate group was still in the process of developing the performance indicators. Unfortunately, as the committee noted in its final report, the development of the performance indicators " . . . proceeded on a separate track relatively immune from feedback offered by the Accreditation Advisory Committee. The performance indicators were developed by teams of intermediate and local educators largely in isolation from the work of the committee" (SBE 2003a, p. 16).

On reviewing and examining the work of these teams, the advisory committee identified four serious problems with the performance indicators. First, since the data were to be self-reported, there likely would be little variation in the scores. Second, as a result of little variation in the scores, the great majority of schools likely would score very high on the measures, leading to a distribution highly skewed to the right. Third, based on a pilot study, there indeed was strong reason to believe that a full-scale implementation would not produce valid and reliable measures on which to assign cut scores and grades; most schools would end up with high scores on the three cluster areas—in effect three A's on the clusters and an A on the total score. Fourth, the committee argued that rather than measures of performance, the performance indicators more properly fell into the category of measures of program policies.

While the committee lauded the SBE and the MDE on their desire to include performance indicator data in addition to the MEAP data in EducationYES!, it also pointed out the substantial difficulties of developing and incorporating into the program a valid and reliable set of performance indicator measures, and particularly measures from which cut scores and letter grades could be drawn. It judged that the proposed performance indicators fell far short of the mark. Contrary to what the MDE claimed, the indicators did not provide a snapshot of school performance, nor were they research based (SBE 2003a, p. 17). Nevertheless, the SBE and the MDE went forward with the performance indicators as an integral part of EducationYES!, and their use continued through school year 2007–08.

In short, the performance indicators truly were, and at least through the 2007–08 school year continued to be, a hodgepodge apparently designed to provide a get out of jail free card for schools experiencing low scores on the MEAP achievement measures. The Accreditation Advisory Committee concluded that if performance indicator measures were to continue to be included in EducationYES!, then the state board and the MDE would be well advised to go back to the drawing board and undertake a serious development effort that would produce a set of valid and reliable measures from which cut scores and grades could be drawn (SBE 2003a, p. 17).[15]

The third charge that the SBE gave to the Michigan Accreditation Advisory Committee was the alignment of EducationYES! with NCLB. The central mandate of NCLB is that each state develop and implement an annual state accountability plan for all of its schools, complete with state-adopted content standards in the subject areas that are offered. In addition, the state is required annually to assess each student's progress toward meeting those subject matter content standards and, concurrently, meeting NCLB's ultimate goal of having all students in all designated subject matter areas attain 100 percent proficiency by the 2013–14 school year.[16] Alignment of a state's accountability plan with the program requirements of NCLB was a major challenge that faced all 50 states. For Michigan, which had the beginnings of a state accountability plan in Public Act 25 and MAP III, and a plan much further developed as a result of its initial design work on EducationYES!, it became the challenge of how to move forward on the development of EducationYES! while simultaneously aligning it with the requirements of NCLB. How best to accomplish this, as we noted above, was the third charge given to the accreditation advisory committee, and it is to this third charge—or, as one might say, how to effect a "shotgun marriage" of EducationYES! and NCLB—that we now turn.

EducationYES! and NCLB

As noted earlier, EducationYES! had its many progenitors—MAP III, MAP II, MAP I, the six-step accountability process of the early 1970s, the MEAP, and before that the University of Michigan and NCA school accreditation programs. EducationYES! also was a direct result of rising concerns among parents, the legislature, the business community, and the general public about the quality of the schooling being provided to Michigan's children and young people.

As recounted in the prior section, the Michigan legislature in 1990 had moved to adopt Public Act 25 as an engine of reform, later amending it in 1995 to bring it closer to becoming an engine of accountability by requiring that accreditation, one of the four main elements of Public Act 25, begin using the MEAP scores to provide a measure of the effectiveness of the Public Act 25 reforms. Concurrently, in response to the act's call for a model curriculum, Michigan also was developing and adopting new content standards and corresponding grade level expectations in the subject matter areas offered in the model curriculum. These new standards and grade level expectations were then used to guide both the revision of existing MEAP tests and the development of new MEAP tests to cover additional subject areas and grade levels. Based on this work, Michigan, as it undertook the initial development of EducationYES!, was well on its way to building a full-fledged MEAP-based state accountability plan, and in doing that it also was moving ever farther toward the finest product side of Callahan's maxim.

Running on a parallel reform track was a multiplicity of federal reform efforts, including efforts under Title I to implement systemic reform, complete with the establishment of new content standards and performance standards, and measures of school effectiveness in attaining those standards. In 1994, as a part of the reauthorization of ESEA, the Congress added to Title I the requirement that the states gather and report information on the yearly progress of Title I recipients in designated academic areas. Thus was born the notion of AYP, which became the hallmark of NCLB, and in many cases the bane of those who worked in the schools.

With the adoption of NCLB in early 2002, not only was AYP applicable to Title I schools, it also became applicable to non–Title I schools. Specifically, AYP required that a school must be on track to have all its students academically proficient in reading and mathematics by school year 2013–14. As part and parcel of the AYP requirement, NCLB mandated that during the first year, 2002–03, annual statewide assessments had to be administered in reading and mathematics in grade spans 3–5, 6–9, and 10–12. Comparable tests in science were to begin in school year 2007–08. By school year 2005–06 the states had to begin administering annual, statewide assessments in reading and mathematics in grades 3–8, assessments aligned with the state's own academic standards. At the high school level, the requirement was at least one other test in these subjects at grades 10–12. These assessments had to be able to deliver individual student scores, as well as group scores at grade, school, and district levels. The scores also had to be broken down and reported by four student subgroupings: major racial/ethnic groups, students with disabilities, limited English proficient students, and economically disadvantaged students. Some have argued that this requirement has been NCLB's greatest contribution, "turning the spotlight . . . on the achievement of demographic subgroups whose underperformance used to lie hidden within school district and state averages" (ETS 2009, p. 1).[17]

For Michigan, meeting these measurement requirements was not a problem of great moment; the MEAP already was structured to meet such requirements, even if new assessments in the three required subject areas would have to be developed at certain grade levels. Assuming resources would be made available, all of this could be accomplished by school year 2005–06. As we noted earlier, EducationYES!, incorporating the recommendations of the accreditation advisory committee, already had settled on an achievement change score to measure whether a school was meeting the AYP requirement.

The major problem that remained was how to marry the two systems. Could a school be accredited under EducationYES! if it had not made AYP? How would a school or district administrator meaningfully and reasonably explain such an outcome to the school's constituency, or to the general public? What status would the state give to a school that made AYP but failed accreditation? How could an administrator explain that sort of outcome? In short, could the state marry the two systems in a valid, meaningful, and understandable way? Fortunately, there seemed to be an available and acceptable, if not totally satisfactory, resolution for this problem.

The accreditation advisory committee, the MDE, and the SBE settled on a solution suggested by Sandy Kress, an Austin, Texas, attorney who had been an education adviser to George W. Bush during his tenure as the Governor of Texas. Upon Governor Bush's election to the presidency in 2000, and in his championship of NCLB, the president called on Sandy Kress once again and asked him to visit with and advise the several states on a way to handle the problem of marrying the results of a state's accreditation system with a state's results under AYP. Kress's solution, adopted for use in EducationYES!, is summarized in Table 3.1.

In interpreting Table 3.1, the reader is reminded that the achievement change score used in EducationYES! is expressed both as a scaled score and as a letter grade of A, B, C, D, or F (see p. 67). The first column lists the composite scaled scores and their positions as cut points between letter grades, the second column lists the letter grades given to schools that did not make AYP, and the third column lists the grades given to schools that did make AYP. Thus, as one can see, a school not making AYP could not receive a letter grade higher than B, even if it

Table 3.1 Unified Accountability for Michigan Schools

EducationYES! composite score	Does not make AYP	Makes AYP
90–100	B (iv)	A
80–89	B (iv)	B (iv)
70–79	C (iii)	C (iii)
60–69	D/Alert (ii)	C (iii)
50–59	Unaccredited (i)	D/Alert (ii)

NOTE: (i) – (iv) indicate the priorities that the MDE would use in making decisions about intervention and assistance.

received a grade of A on the EducationYES! composite score. A school receiving an A on the composite score and also making AYP would receive an A. The minor roman numerals in parentheses simply indicate the priorities that the MDE would use in making decisions about what assistance and intervention actions it would take to help Title I schools receiving the corresponding letter grades or accreditation status. As with the NCLB sanctions, the assistance and intervention actions were limited to Title I schools.

Thus, with its recommendation of using Kress's solution for how to marry the two systems, the accreditation advisory committee had fulfilled its three charges. There were a number of other concerns that the advisory committee expressed about the initial design of EducationYES!, as well as committee suggestions for further development of the program. For the reader who is interested, these can be found in the committee's final written report to the state board (SBE 2003a). For a description of EducationYES! as it has operated over the succeeding five years—2003–2004 through 2009–2010—the interested reader may want to look at one or more of the summary bulletins issued by the MDE and made available periodically to local schools and districts (SBE 2003b; MDE 2006a, 2008a).

Before we leave this discussion, we should note two other NCLB requirements included in and reported under EducationYES! First, there was the requirement that each of the aforementioned subgroups make AYP. Based on composite district scores, the failure of any one of the subgroups to make AYP acted as a "trip wire," resulting in placing the district in the "Does not make AYP" category. Second, there was the NCLB requirement that the state choose an additional indicator of making or not making AYP. Michigan chose to use school attendance as its additional indicator for its elementary and middle school grades. Michigan set its initial attendance target at 85 percent. Schools at or above 85 percent were assumed to be meeting the AYP requirement. At the high school level, this requirement called for Michigan to use the graduation rate as the additional indicator. In this case, the expectation was not 100 percent by school year 2013–14, but rather that growth toward higher targets would be encouraged. Michigan used 80 percent as its beginning target in 2002–03, resetting it to 85 percent in 2005–08, and to 90 percent in 2008–09.

Michigan released its first results on AYP for the 2001–02 school year in early 2003. Some 2,489 schools—89 percent—had made AYP. As can be seen from Table 3.2, unfortunately, these numbers did not hold up for long. In the following year, the percentage of schools making AYP dropped to 76 percent, bounced up a bit in the following years, and came in at 86 percent in 2009–10. Still, 509 schools—some 14 percent of all public schools—failed to make AYP.[18]

Without a doubt, there is considerably more that could and perhaps should be said about NCLB itself—including the host of other implementation problems Michigan and its sister states still face: the flexibility (or lack thereof) provided by the U.S. Department of Education in implementation of NCLB, and the effectiveness of the law

Table 3.2 Michigan Schools Making AYP, School Years 2001–02 through 2009–10

School year	Yes	Yes (%)	No	No (%)	Total schools
2001–02	2,489	89.3	297	10.7	2,786
2002–03	2,415	75.6	781	24.4	3,196
2003–04	2,746	77.9	791	22.4	3,527
2004–05	3,134	88.5	408	11.5	3,542
2005–06	3,058	85.4	524	14.6	3,582
2006–07	3,153	82.9	648	17.1	3,801
2007–08	3,003	79.8	758	20.2	3,761
2008–09	3,143	85.6	528	14.4	3,671
2009–10	3,188	86.2	509	13.8	3,697

SOURCE: MDE.

in improving American education. More importantly, NCLB itself may be subject to major revisions depending on what the Congress may or may not do in the pending reauthorization of ESEA and its component Title I and NCLB programs. The substance of the reauthorization also likely will be strongly influenced by Secretary of Education Arne Duncan's Race to the Top program (see p. 250 in Chapter 8 of this volume). There is a plethora of references—journal articles, reports, and books—available for the person interested in pursuing the reauthorization issue further.[19] For our present purposes, we limit ourselves to a short recounting of recent developments in Michigan that very likely may lead to substantial revisions in EducationYES!

From EducationYES! to MI-SAS and on to MI-SAAS

As of this writing, it appears that Michigan may soon be saying good-bye to the somewhat beguiling title of EducationYES! for its state accountability program and replacing it with the more plainspoken titles of Michigan's State Accreditation System—MI-SAS (MDE 2009), or more likely, Michigan's School Accreditation and Accountability System—MI-SAAS (Flanagan 2010). And the new titles apparently may not be the only changes.

The 2009 MDE paper proposes major revisions to EducationYES!, the first of which is to reduce the categories of accreditation to three: 1) accredited, 2) interim status, and 3) unaccredited. The second change, and some would argue not an improvement, is to eliminate the letter grade designations—no more A, B, C, D, or F. The third is to remove the performance indicators from the scoring scheme and include them as one of eight compliance items to be answered with a simple yes/no to the question of whether the school submitted them as a part of its annual reporting to the MDE—so it's goodbye to the performance indicators as a "get out of jail free card" for those schools and districts scoring low on the academic achievement measures. We applaud the MDE on this proposed change. The other seven compliance items will address questions of whether

1) all teachers are certified,
2) the school published its annual improvement plan,
3) the school offered the required curricula,

4) the school published a fully compliant annual report,
5) the school annually tested literacy and mathematics in grades 1–5,
6) the high school six-year graduation rate is 80 percent or above, and whether
7) the school participated in NAEP, if it was selected to do so.

If the answer is no to any one question in two consecutive years, the accreditation status would be lowered one level.

The fourth change, and an arguable improvement if such a measure can be proved valid and reliable, is to add an achievement growth measure to the program. Achievement growth was the third achievement measure built into the original design of EducationYES! but never realized for reasons pointed out earlier (see pp. 67–68).[20] The achievement growth measure proposed under the revisions, called performance level change, would enable schools to show that while some of their students may not yet be proficient, their achievement scores are improving from year to year. Such scores would fall into a range from "improvement" to "significant improvement." In effect, implementing the proposed performance level change scores would represent an attempt to implement the value-added or growth model contemplated in the initial design of EducationYES! The performance level change score also would substitute for the achievement change measure in determining AYP.

Under the proposed revisions, the results of the MEAP would still form the bedrock upon which state accreditation decisions are made. A school would be designated as accredited if the school had no more than one subject below 60 percent proficient and no subjects below 35 percent. A school would be designated interim status, but still considered state accredited, if two or more subjects were lower than 60 percent but not lower than 35 percent. Any school that had one or more subjects lower than 35 percent would be unaccredited.[21]

As far as the interface between MI-SAS and NCLB is concerned, the same three accreditation categories are to be used, namely, accredited, interim status, and unaccredited. A school would be state accredited if it met Michigan accreditation standards and AYP. A school would receive interim status if it met all Michigan accreditation standards but did not make AYP, or if it met Michigan accreditation standards for interim status whether or not it made AYP. If a school did not meet Michigan accreditation standards and irrespective of whether or not it made AYP, it would be unaccredited. Thus, even though a school did not make AYP, it still could be state accredited by Michigan standards in the category interim status. The critical difference under the proposed changes is that AYP no longer would be the controlling factor vis-à-vis state accreditation. It, of course, would be a controlling factor vis-à-vis federal requirements and sanctions.

In the summer of 2010, the state superintendent proposed to the SBE four further changes to MI-SAS, plus the change of name to Michigan's State Accreditation and Accountability System—MI-SAAS. The proposed changes arise from new guidelines issued by the Department of Education as well as the legislature's recent adoption of reform legislation in response to the Secretary of Education's Race to the Top program. The four proposed changes to MI-SAS are

1) schools in the lowest 5 percent in the state proficiency ranking are automatically unaccredited,
2) schools in the lowest 6–20 percent are automatically interim accredited,
3) schools in the lowest 5 percent for the School Improvement Grant or the School Reform Office are automatically unaccredited, and
4) to be fully accredited, schools must assess at least 95 percent of students in every subject tested.

As of this writing, all of these changes—those proposed originally in MI-SAS and those now proposed in MI-SAAS, including the new title—are only proposed changes. All must go through a public review process, seeking input from the schools, the districts, and the public, as well as an approval process by the SBE and the House and Senate Education Committees. If all goes well, the proposed target for implementation would be school year 2011–12. The changes, if enacted, would strengthen and streamline the Michigan accountability system. They would also enhance the state's ability to deliver valid and reliable information on how Michigan's public schools and school districts are progressing in the academic performance of students, on the schools' and districts' progress—or lack thereof—in attaining 100 percent proficiency for all students, and on the districts' compliance with related federal and state legislative mandates.

WHAT WILL THE FUTURE BRING?

The building of state accountability programs in Michigan has been a long and sometimes arduous journey, beginning with local control reigning supreme and largely unchallenged from the late nineteenth century through the mid-twentieth century, to the dawn of the 1970s and state imposition of a mandatory annual assessment of achievement in reading and mathematics for all students in grades 4 and 7, to coupling state assessment with efforts to build a six-step accountability process, to the expansion of state assessment to additional grades and subject areas shortly thereafter, to the transfer from the University of Michigan to the MDE of what had become a largely nonaccountable school accreditation process, to the relatively ineffectual mandates of Public Act 25 as initially adopted, to the building of a new state accountability program in EducationYES! and its almost immediate but difficult marriage to NCLB and AYP, to the smoothing out of that marriage, to the prospects of implementing an enhanced state accountability program in MI-SAAS, and now to providing individual data on the performance of teachers and administrators.[22] During this process Michigan has accommodated a host of new and sometimes old or rehashed ideas and proposals for reform.

In reflecting on the past 40–50 years of efforts to build a state accountability program for Michigan's public schools, on where Michigan now is with respect to accountability, and on where it might be headed in the near future, a number of questions come to mind. What good has come, or will come, of all of this? How effective have these policy reforms been? Is Michigan education today better as a result? Are students better off—learning more and succeeding in greater numbers? Has the shift of decision-making responsibility from the local school district to state government to the federal government had positive results for students? Have the increased intrusion of the federal government into public education, the growing involvement of state government in public education, the state's tightening of academic requirements, and the public reporting of results all been for the better? Has the casting aside of the long-cherished principle of subsidiarity—leaving decision-making responsibility to those closest to the action—helped or hindered the goal of providing "the finest product" for Michigan children and young people? Undoubtedly honest and straightforward answers to these questions would lead to the conclusion that in many if not all cases the jury is still out. Certainly many good things have happened and improvements have come about, but there also have been stumbles and grumbles. It is safe to say that while still generally supportive of its public schools, the Michigan public—as well as the American public—is not fully satisfied with overall school performance. The policies adopted have had their limits, both in their crafting and in their implementation.

Beyond these general questions, we argue that there are four specific questions that demand immediate attention. First, what happens if Michigan—or any other state—fails to meet the NCLB and AYP goal of 100 percent proficiency by school year 2013–14 based on its own standards, i.e., those measured by the MEAP or, for any other state, its state assessment programs? EducationYES! and NCLB are now in their eighth year. It is just three short years until 2013–14, the school year the final bill comes due, so to speak. As of this writing, at the end of the 2010–11 school year, 528 of Michigan's public schools—some 14 percent—have yet to make AYP. And even with marked increase in the number of schools making AYP over the last two school years (now at 3,188), and the consequent decrease in the number and percentage of schools not making AYP, the trajectory is not all that promising. With the exception of the two most recent years for which data are available, the success rate has been on a downward trend, dropping from a high of 89 percent in 2004–05 to a low of 80 percent in 2007–08 (see Table 3.2). While the 2008–09 and 2009–10 bounce upward to 86 percent is welcome, will it hold? Apparently it will not, given the SBE's recent decision to raise cut scores on the MEAP and the very real drop in scores that is sure to follow (see Chapter 4). Should Michigan just soldier on and bend every effort to raise student academic performance to meet these new and more demanding proficiency levels?

Second, what happens if Michigan—or any other state—meets the goal based on its own standards, but does not meet the goal based on national standards, i.e., those measured by the NAEP, the Nation's

Report Card? Unfortunately, in the case of Michigan, the latter outcome also is highly likely, irrespective of whether the goal of 100 percent proficiency is or is not reached based on MEAP standards. Indeed, at the present time, using the MEAP standards for 4th grade reading and math, 74 and 75 percent of Michigan students, respectively, attained proficiency in 2009–10. However, using the NAEP standards, those figures fall to 30 and 31 percent, respectively. At grade 8, the comparable figures for reading and math are 83 percent and 70 percent using the Michigan MEAP standards. But again, using the NAEP standards those scores drop to 31 and 34 percent, respectively. These are pretty drastic differences and should be cause for considerable concern.

With the recent release of first-time results on the NAEP Trial Urban District Assessment, the situation in the Detroit Public Schools is even worse and the concerns even greater. The Trial NAEP scores for Detroit for grade 4 and grade 8 math and reading are abominable. Only a paltry 5 percent of 4th graders achieved proficiency in reading and only 7 percent in math. At grade 8 the corresponding figures were 3 percent and 4 percent. Instead of these students achieving the goal of 100 percent proficiency by 2013–14, it appears more likely that Detroit will have upward of 95 percent of its students not proficient, at least as measured by the NAEP.

Addressing these differences—particularly MEAP versus NAEP—quickly gets us into a dispute over state versus national standards. Is the question of what should be taught in the public schools one that should be reserved to the separate states? After all, under the 10th Amendment, education is a matter left to the states. Or is it more properly also a national and federal concern? Under Section 8 of Article I of the U.S. Constitution, the Congress has the authority, if not the responsibility, to provide for the general welfare and common defense of the nation. In addressing the state versus national standards question, we very quickly become involved in questions of federalism. To what extent should a state tolerate federal intrusion into basic questions on the goals or purposes of public education? To what extent does the federal government—or a national entity—have a proper role in this? Who should set the standards for Michigan's or any other state's students? Should we look to and be satisfied with a set of nationwide standards, such as those currently being developed under the auspices of the National Governors Association and the Council of Chief State School Officers?[23]

Third, how will the recent resurgence of past arguments for curricular differentiation play out against current arguments for rigorous and demanding high school graduation requirements? Should our public schools, particularly our high schools, attend to and reflect the theme of curricular differentiation, providing students of different abilities with a wide range of courses and programs attuned to their interests and abilities, as Conant (1959a,b; 1961) argues? Or should our public schools eschew curricular differentiation and continue to heed the call for rigorous and demanding high school graduation requirements as Bestor (1985) and his colleagues argue and as Michigan recently has opted to do?[24] There already is some evidence that nationwide the pendulum may be moving back toward Conant's view, based on the recent advocacy of campaigns such as A Broader, Bolder Approach to Education (2009), championed by the likes of education notables such as Diane Ravitch, Helen Ladd, Tom Payzant, Richard Rothstein, Christopher Cross, and others. Should Michigan and other states, as that group suggests, begin to move beyond attention "not only to basic academic skills and cognitive growth narrowly defined, but to the development of the whole person . . . [to] physical health, character, social development and non-academic skills . . ." (A Bolder, Better Approach to Education 2009, p. 2)? Should the states add a substantial array of qualitative measures to the quantitative measures already firmly ensconced in their state accountability programs?

Fourth, what will be the outcome for Michigan and the other 49 states of the pending reauthorization of ESEA and likely changes in the requirements of NCLB and AYP? President Obama, according to his recent announcements, supports the overall goal of NCLB but with reservations (Obama '08 2008). As noted earlier, President Obama's education secretary, Arne Duncan, in his Race to the Top program, is calling for increased rigor and accountability in federal education programs. But what the Congress will do in the reauthorization of NCLB, and when it will do it, remains anyone's guess given the present economic crises facing the nation, and more importantly, given the Republican party's return to power in the House of Representatives as a result of 2010 Congressional elections. It likely will not be business as usual. Will any revision be quite modest? Or will we witness substantial changes in the law and its requirements? Will the Congress heed the advice offered in a respected scholar's recent examination of the law? "Rather than abandoning some of the more useful components of NCLB, we should maintain and improve them, but we need to drop the fiction that all children will be proficient and that all teachers will be highly qualified by the 2013–14 school year" (Vinovskis 2009, p. 234).

Can our state and federal accountability programs deliver on the promise of academic success for all students? Will they? At the present time, we ourselves find no clear-cut answers to these questions. But we do hold modest hopes that programs such as NCLB and EducationYES!; MI-SAAS, if it comes about; and the new state-mandated educator evaluations, despite all their shortcomings, eventually may begin to deliver on what they promise, namely, to increase academic success for all students. Echoing the words of John Porter, they just may help provide ". . . the guarantee that all students without respect to race, income, or social class will acquire the minimum school skills necessary to take full advantage of the choices that accrue upon successful completion of public schooling, or we in education will describe the reasons why" (Kearney 1971, p. 5).

Notes

1. See, for example, *The American Heritage Dictionary, Second College Edition*. Houghton-Mifflin, 1985.
2. For a brief account of this early period, see Chapter 2 in Thomas (1968).
3. Since 2006, NCA CASI is an accreditation division of AdvancED, which is also the parent organization of the Southern Association of Colleges and Schools Council on Accreditation and School Improvement and the National Study of School Evaluation.
4. It is worth noting that a second edition of the Common Goals was published in the early 1980s, and that much later the Michigan Curriculum Framework, published in 1997, contained an overarching set of goals.
5. For a detailed recounting of federal activity during this period, see Vinovskis (2009). For a sample of reform activity at national, state, and local levels during the same period, see Finn and Walberg (1994). *S*ee also Gross and Gross (1985) and Toch (1991).
6. A cut score is a score that separates test takers into various categories, such as a passing score and a failing score, a proficient score and a nonproficient score, or gradations of proficiency, e.g., basic, proficient, advanced.
7. Under this program, a student's scores on the 11th grade MEAP, if high enough, made the student eligible to receive a $2,500 tuition grant from the state to help defray the cost of the first two years of a college education.

8. In 2003–04 proficiency was defined in relation to MEAP performance levels. The levels were 1, 2, 3, and 4, with 1 the highest; *proficient* was defined as "met/exceeded expectations" (levels 1 and 2); students scoring at levels 3 and 4 were defined as "did not meet expectations." At the time of this writing, these four levels had been renamed advanced, proficient, partially proficient, and not proficient, respectively.
9. We would remind the reader that the term *catch-22* connotes a situation in which a desired outcome or solution is impossible to attain because of a set of inherently illogical rules.
10. Members included C. Philip Kearney, professor emeritus, University of Michigan, Ann Arbor, MI; Sharon Johnson Lewis, director of research, Council of Great City Schools, Washington, DC; Lawrence Lezotte, president, Effective Schools, Ltd., Okemos, MI; Mark Reckase, professor of measurement and quantitative methods, College of Education, Michigan State University; and Edward Roeber, vice president, Measured Progress, Dover, NH.
11. For the reader interested in more detail, we suggest requesting a copy of the committee's report from the office of the SBE.
12. See Note 6.
13. At the time, high school scores were not yet available. However, following the same procedure, shortly thereafter a second panel was created to examine and recommend cut scores and grades for the high school achievement status measures.
14. See, for example, Harris (2009).
15. At the current time, the MDE has proposed removing the performance indicators from the scoring scheme and including them simply as one of eight compliance items to be answered with a simple yes/no to the question of whether the school submitted its performance indicators as a part of its annual reporting to the MDE.
16. See Note 8.
17. This requirement has a purpose analogous to the accreditation advisory committee's recommendation of placing more weight on the scores of low achievers in calculating the achievement status score. See p. 66.
18. Secretary of Education Arne Duncan recently announced that he would entertain a state's request for waivers of the AYP requirement if a state had in place an acceptable long-term plan to improve student achievement and proficiency. The waiver provision responds to the problem that, despite a district meeting the AYP requirement for its total student group, it could still fail because it did not meet the requirement by one or more of its four student subgroupings singled out in the legislation—1) major racial/ethnic groups, 2) students with disabilities, 3) limited English proficient students, and 4) economically disadvantaged students—the so-called trip wire (see Higgins [2011c]).
19. For a succinct recounting of some of the many problems faced by the states, see Ritter and Lucas (2006). For a detailed recounting of the creation of NCLB, see Vinovskis (2009).
20. See Note 14.
21. The titles of the categories may be a bit confusing. A school would be considered state accredited if it fell into either of the first two categories: accredited or interim

status. If it did not meet state accreditation standards, it would fall into the third category: unaccredited.

22. Recent legislation now requires a local school district to determine and report whether its teachers and administrators are highly effective, effective, or ineffective. The evaluations are to be tied to local decisions regarding promotion and retention of teachers and administrators, including tenure and certification decisions (see Revised School Code, Act 451 of 1976).
23. See, for example, Lewin (2010).
24. As of the present writing, it seems that Michigan legislators are having second thoughts about high school graduation requirements. One house of the Michigan legislature has introduced and passed a bill to rescind the recently adopted requirement that all high school students must take and pass algebra II in order to graduate.

4
Assessing the Academic Outcomes of Schooling

FROM OPPOSITION TO ACCEPTANCE

Today in Michigan there is an abundance of comparative information available on the academic outcomes of schooling, on how public school students are performing in critical academic subjects such as reading, writing, mathematics, science, and social studies. This information is broken out by individual schools and school districts, and is collected and publicly reported annually by the MDE. The information is not only available by school, but also by grades within a school. A parent in East Lansing can easily review the results and see how the 4th grade pupils as a group in the Donley elementary school are doing in reading, writing, and mathematics. A parent in Ann Arbor can look at reading scores for 7th graders in the Tappan middle school, or the mathematics scores for the same 7th graders. A parent in Muskegon can find out how 11th graders in the Muskegon high school scored on the Michigan Merit Exam, including how those 11th graders scored as a group on the ACT. This information on student academic performance also is aggregated at the state level and publicly released, so the interested Michigan citizen is able to get a clear sense of the degree to which the state's public school pupils are achieving proficiency in critical school subjects, whether it be reading, writing, mathematics, science, or social studies. And interested parents or citizens can go one step further by looking to see how Michigan pupils, and schools, are doing in comparison to pupils and schools in other states and in the nation as a whole. They can ask, "How are Michigan schools doing compared to Ohio schools? How is Michigan doing compared to the nation as a whole?" And they can easily find the answers, because now there is comparative information from the NAEP readily available on the Internet and in the print media that allows one to view the levels of reading proficiency and math proficiency in each of the 50 states as measured by the NAEP.

But it was not always so. Prior to 1969, it was not possible to find out how the state's public schools were doing in reading and math. It was not possible for a parent to find out how his or her child's school or school district was doing in these two critical academic areas. There was no statewide academic performance information available whatsoever. While most schools and school districts did administer one or more of the many available standardized testing programs, there was no common testing program across the entire state. Nor for that matter were the results of the district and school testing programs made public. Comparing schools and school districts on the basis of pupils' academic achievement was considered anathema. In many cases, results were not even to be shared with a parent. Test results most often were "embargoed," to be shared only with teachers, counselors, and administrators, and perhaps, from time to time, with members of the local school board. There existed a deep and ingrained opposition to sharing test results with anyone other than a professional educator. And there was even stronger opposition to building a state system that would produce student achievement information and allow comparisons among schools and school districts within a given region or state. To build a national system that would allow comparisons between and among states was considered an equal if not greater offense.

But in spite of opposition from the professional education community, these systems were built and today they produce a rich array of information on the academic achievement of pupils in our public schools. The breakthrough in Michigan came in 1969 with the launch of the MEAP. The breakthrough at the national level came in 1970 with the initial public report of the NAEP. But before they became a reality, each of these programs had to undergo a gauntlet of strong opposition from the entrenched forces of the profession—the teacher unions, the professional curriculum and subject matter associations, the administrator associations, and in many cases even recalcitrant legislators.

Some sense of the nature of this ingrained opposition in Michigan to the MEAP can be gleaned from the comments back in 1970 of the curriculum director of an affluent, suburban school district: "The [program] is really politics masquerading as research. Promise after promise has been broken. Plans have been dictated and changed by the legislature . . . It is not an operational purpose of the assessment project to improve instruction by identifying promising practices . . . The conclusions were written before the project was undertaken . . . Educators at the district level have not been included in designing the tests and are not included in plans for the development of future tests" (Grosse Pointe Public Schools 1970).

Nor was the press silent. Apparently expressing the views held by their local school district superintendent, a city newspaper had this to say: "The damage already has been done this time, but we hope that someone does a little more checking the next time before the State Department of Education is allowed to pull another stunt like the one foisted on thousands of public school pupils this week" (*Ypsilanti Press* 1970, p. 4).

In the same issue, a local legislator gave his view of the effort: " . . . rotten, just out and out Communist propaganda—rotten all the way through" (*Ypsilanti Press* 1970, p. 4). Still others saw the effort as an invasion of privacy (*Mt. Clemens-Macomb Daily* 1970, p. 1). On the first public release of the 1969–70 MEAP results, the furor increased. A local superintendent wrote to the state superintendent expressing his utter dismay, seeing the public release as " . . . a complete breaking of trust . . . [and as] extremely unethical" (Kearney and Huyser 1973, p. 56). Similar brickbats were hurled by representatives of the teacher unions, the professional administrator associations, and several of the professional subject matter associations—all reflecting again and again an ingrained opposition to the public release of test results if not to testing itself. And it was a good number of months, if not years, before the opposition to the MEAP began to wane.

In like fashion, the early developers of the NAEP faced a similar gauntlet of opposition from the professional education associations. John Gardner, the then president of the Carnegie Corporation and one of the initial funders of the NAEP effort, speaking in a more recent interview commented on the nature of the opposition the early developers faced back in 1963. He noted that the American Association of School Administrators (AASA) didn't want anyone to measure them, that the National Education Association (NEA) backed the AASA, and that the Council of Chief State School Officers (CCSSO) did as well (Jones and Olkin 2004, pp. 116–117). The AASA was and is the national professional association of school superintendents; the NEA was and is the more powerful of the two national teacher unions; and the CCSSO was and is the professional association of chief state school officers—state commissioners, state superintendents, and secretaries of education. Lloyd Morrisett, a vice president of the Carnegie Corporation at the time, also speaking in a recent interview, remarked that they [the early developers] had to overcome very substantial political resistance in the educational community, adding that the assessments and the sampling had to be designed in a form that "would not seem to be dangerous to the people that resisted the idea of comparative testing" (Jones and Olkin 2004, p. 124). A third recent interviewee, David Goslin, had served as a recorder for the two initial conferences organized by the Carnegie Corporation in 1963–64 to explore the feasibility and desirability of establishing a national assessment program. Goslin corroborated the views of Gardner and Morrisett: "I think that as a political position, nobody could acknowledge then that you might one day have comparisons of states, localities, and schools on the NAEP test. The idea that this would be the basis for a national curriculum would have been an anathema; it would not have gone anywhere" (Jones and Olkin 2004, p. 137).

To get a sense of the roots of this ingrained and strong opposition to the gathering and reporting of comparative information on schools and school districts that prevailed in the 1960s and prior years, one need only review any number of publications of that era addressing the proper roles of state government and the federal government when it came to public education. For most who wrote on the subject, the concept of local control reigned supreme. As an example, in a small booklet published in 1963, one of the authors addressing the question of local control begins by noting that "many Americans would hold that the local management of public schools is best. The intrusion of other levels of government on local operation is often looked upon with disfavor. Action by the Federal government is most suspect, but even the states, which legally have plenary power with respect to education, are not always welcome in their endeavors to control education" (Campbell and Bunnell 1963, p. 1).

None other than President John F. Kennedy expressed in the prior year a similar sentiment, at least as far as the federal government was concerned: "The control and operation of education in America must remain the responsibility of state and local governments and private institutions. This tradition ensures our educational system of the freedom, the diversity and the vitality in support of public elementary and secondary education" (U.S. 1962, p. 1544).

Yet it is somewhat ironic, or perhaps simply a portent of what was to come, that President Kennedy's first U.S. Commissioner of Education was Frank Keppel. It was Keppel who first suggested and advanced the idea of a national assessment of public education. And it is Keppel who is most often touted as the father of national assessment (Jones and Olkin 2004, p. 11).

Despite the long-standing hostility of the professional educational community, the efforts to mount state assessment programs as well as a national assessment program proceeded apace. In large part, these efforts were aided and abetted by a public that had become disenchanted with its schools. As we noted in Chapter 3, beginning in the 1960s there arose across the nation and in the individual states a growing dissatisfaction with American public education. This dissatisfaction was being voiced in the media, in educational and secular journals, in public reports, and in any number of published books and monographs. As a consequence, the long-standing wall of opposition by the professional education community to state and federal intrusion into the governance and management of schools was beginning to crumble. Arguments for educational reform abounded, and central to many of the arguments was the lack of meaningful and readily available information on the academic performance of students. So the nation was soon to see a significant change of attitude about testing and about the public release of test results begin to take place among the professional educational community. It didn't happen rapidly, but it did happen. To look back now, in 2011, to the 1960s and prior years, is to see an almost complete reversal of the mindset of education professionals and their associations in the several states when it comes to their own state assessment programs, and increasingly the same reversal across the country when it comes to the NAEP.

Against this backdrop, we turn now to a brief telling of the story of the development and implementation of these two assessment programs, the MEAP and the NAEP, and also take a look at what the two programs tell us today about the academic achievement of pupils—across the entire nation, and particularly in the public schools of Michigan. We begin by recounting briefly the history and development of the NAEP.

THE NATIONAL ASSESSMENT OF EDUCATIONAL PROGRESS: THE NATION'S REPORT CARD

The Genesis and Development of the NAEP

As noted above, it was Frank Keppel who in early 1963 first advanced the idea of a national assessment of public education.[1] Keppel at the time was the U.S. Commissioner of Education, having been appointed to the post by President John F. Kennedy. Keppel broached the idea to Ralph Tyler and asked him to prepare a memorandum suggesting a way to evaluate education in the United States. Tyler at the time was the director of the Center for Advanced Study in the Behavioral Sciences at Stanford University, and a noted scholar and researcher in education and the social sciences. On the receipt of Tyler's memorandum, Keppel turned to John Gardner, the president of the Carnegie Corporation, for financial support to hold two conferences to discuss Tyler's memorandum. The conferences were held in December 1963 and January 1964.

Out of these two conferences was born the unprecedented effort to design and develop a national assessment of educational progress. It was an effort that extended over the next 40-plus years, marked by a number of ups and downs, first funded by the Carnegie Corporation and later the Ford Foundation, and subsequently entirely by the federal government; experienced a number of changes over the years in responsibilities for governance and administration; worked assiduously to break down the intense opposition emanating from the professional education community; saw expansion of the initial assessment to seven subject areas and additional age groups and grades; and—most radical of all—witnessed its responsibilities being extended to producing results not just for the nation as a whole but also for individual states, and soon thereafter for large urban school districts.

Following the two Carnegie-sponsored conferences in late 1963 and early 1964, a decision was made to create the Exploratory Committee for the Assessment of Progress in Education (ECAPE), with Ralph Tyler as chair. Carnegie again came to the fore and provided a grant of $100,000 to support the work of ECAPE. In late 1965, the Ford Foundation awarded a grant to ECAPE to supplement the continuing financial support already being provided by Carnegie, and in early 1966 the U.S. Office of Education for the first time lent its financial support to the effort. The U.S. Office of Education, and later the U.S. Department of Education, eventually assumed full financial responsibility for the NAEP.

While financial support for the NAEP moved from Carnegie and Ford and eventually became fully lodged in the federal government, the administration, management, and governance of the program over the years followed a more checkered path. How checkered can be seen by briefly tracing this path. In July of 1968, the "E" was dropped from ECAPE and it became CAPE, the Committee for the Assessment of Progress in Education. Shortly thereafter, responsibilities for the administration and management of the NAEP, as well as the governance, were transferred to the Education Commission of the States (ECS) in Denver. Further changes in the administration and management of the NAEP took place in 1983, when the ECS was dropped from the picture and a new NAEP contract was awarded to the Educational Testing Service in Princeton, New Jersey. By contracting for the NAEP, the federal government chose to take a more active role in determining NAEP policy, which was not a popular position among educators, who feared the role of the government dictating what would be tested, and hence what would be taught. In 1988, further changes in the governance of the NAEP came about when the Congress enacted Public Law 100-297, establishing the National Assessment Governing Board (NAGB) as an independent body responsible for setting policy for the NAEP tests. Over this same general time period, federal administrative oversight of the NAEP was transferred to the National Center for Educational Statistics, then to the National Institute of Education, and eventually back again to the National Center for Educational Statistics, where it is lodged today. The National Center for Educational Statistics currently remains responsible for the administration and management of the program, enlisting from time to time outside contractors to assist in carrying out the myriad tasks of implementation, evaluation, and further development of the program. The NAGB continues to provide policy oversight for the program.[2]

Breaking down the deep and ingrained opposition to building a national system that would allow comparisons of student academic achievement between and among states was a major challenge that faced the initial designers and developers of the NAEP. As we remarked earlier, several of the major professional organizations voiced rather strident opposition to the notion, with the executive committee of the American Association of School Administrators (AASA) adopting a formal resolution recommending "that its members refuse to participate in NAEP tryouts or in any subsequent operational NAEP" (Jones and Olkin 2004, p. 12). The NEA, the largest teacher union in the nation, soon followed suit by endorsing the AASA resolution, as did the professional association of those men and women who led the nation's 50 state departments of education, the Council of Chief State School Officers (CCSSO). And as Vinovskis (1998) has observed, the subject matter associations were not far behind, with the president of the National Council of Teachers of English admonishing teachers "to fight tooth and nail to prevent a proposed plan to measure the quality of American education" (p. 6).

As we stated earlier, a major reason for opposing the NAEP arose primarily from professional educators' ingrained opposition to comparing test scores between and among local school districts and, more to the point, between and among states. Comparison of states led to ranking of states, and ranking led to losers and winners—there would be those states at the top of the heap, those at the bottom, and those in the middle. And the same could be said for districts and for schools within a district. A second reason was opposition to a national curriculum. The opponents claimed that national tests would lead to national standards, which in turn would lead to a national curriculum and the loss of local control, a much-cherished principle of American public education. It would be bad enough to have state standards and a state curriculum, but as David Goslin remarked in the interview cited earlier (Jones and Olkin 2004, p. 137), the idea that the NAEP would serve as the foundation for a national curriculum would not have gone anywhere. There also was the concern that a national assessment would become, in essence, a nationwide individual testing program, again seriously violating the principle of local control as well as being an unprecedented invasion of students' (and families') individual privacy by the federal government.

This last concern was quickly addressed and put to rest with the emergence of the NAEP's sampling design. No single student would take an entire test, thus no individual results would be available. In addition, district and state comparisons would not be possible. The student population would be sampled; results would be valid and reliable only for groups of students. The design of the sampling frame would limit those groups to representing the nation as a whole, and four large regions, namely, the four quadrants of the United States—the northeast, southeast, southwest, and northwest. The sampling frame would make it impossible to deliver state results, much less district results.[3] While this safeguard initially assuaged the opposition, it was only a few short years until the pressure for state-level results would force a change in the sampling frames and the NAEP would begin producing results state by state, thereby allowing for much-feared comparisons between and among states.

The full story of how Ralph Tyler and his colleagues in the early days of the NAEP were able to work around if not overcome the opposition to the program is well told by others, as is the account of external pressures that arose in subsequent years and led to a significant change in if not reversal of the mindset of those who opposed NAEP (and MEAP) in the 1970s and 1980s.[4] Today this resistance is a thing of the past. Indeed, not only is there a growing acceptance of the NAEP in the professional education community, but also growing support for the NAEP's public release of its results on a state-by-state basis. A recent statement from Gerald N. Tirozzi, the executive director of the National Association of Secondary School Principals, stands in stark contrast to the 1970s resolution of opposition adopted by the AASA:

> The significant disparities among states leap from the page when state proficiency test scores are compared with National Assessment of Educational Progress (NAEP) scores—currently the only national barometer available . . . Sadly some states have set their bars exceedingly low and have given their "proficient" students a false sense of achievement . . . If Congress truly wants to drive an education agenda for higher standards . . . [it] should shift the law at its foundation to institute national standards and a national test in reading and math. (Tirozzi 2009)

David Goslin, whom we quoted earlier, must now chuckle a bit to himself as he surveys the current education scene and the increasing calls for national standards. He might be one of the first to agree that the times indeed have changed. The NAEP now enjoys growing support from not only the professional education community, but also the Congress and the nation's governors, and it appears that that support is here to stay. And on that note, we turn now to the NAEP as it exists and operates today, and take a look at some of its more recent test results for Michigan students.

The NAEP Today and Michigan's Public Schools

Over the past 40 years, from its first offerings in April of 1969 of three assessments in citizenship, science, and writing for in-school 17-year-olds, to its current schedule of offerings in nine different subject areas at three different grade levels, the NAEP indeed has come a long way. Reading and math assessments now are offered every other year at grades 4, 8, and 12. Science and writing assessments are offered every four years at grades 4 and 8. And the remaining subjects—the arts, civics, economics, geography, and U.S. history—are cycled in periodically at one or more grade levels. All of these subjects are reported at the national level, and beginning in 1990, four of these subjects—reading, math, science, and writing—began to be reported at the state level, for public schools only. The full range of NAEP offerings scheduled up through the year 2017 is depicted in Table 4.1.[5]

Table 4.1 The Schedule of Upcoming NAEP Assessments

Subjects	Grade levels	Year	Reported at state level
Reading	4, 8, 12	2009, 2011, 2013, 2015, 2017	4, 8, 12[a]
Writing	4, 8	2011, 2015	4, 8
Mathematics	4, 8, 12	2009, 2011, 2013, 2015, 2017	4, 8, 12[a]
Science	4, 8	2009, 2013, 2017	4, 8
The Arts	8	2008, 2016	No
Civics	4, 8, 12	2010	No
Economics	12	2012	No
Geography	4, 8, 12	2010	No
U.S. History	4, 8, 12	2010	No

[a]For 2009, there is a pilot study of state-level results, for which 11 states volunteered.

SOURCE: National Center for Education Statistics, the Nation's Report Card: http://www.nces.ed.gov/nationsreportcard/about/assessmentsched.asp.

A Quick Look at Recent Results

In Table 4.2, we present Michigan's NAEP scores over the past several years in the four academic subject areas that NAEP reports on a state-by-state basis—reading, mathematics, science, and writing. Only about one-third of Michigan students, irrespective of grade level, scored at or above the "proficient level," which by NAEP standards represents ". . . solid academic performance at each grade level—4, 8 . . . It will reflect a consensus that students reaching this level have demonstrated competency over challenging subject matter and are well prepared for the next level of schooling" (Vinovskis 1998, p. 45).

As depicted in Table 4.2, the NAEP results over the immediate past years paint a fairly dismal picture of academic achievement in Michigan's public schools. Two things are most striking in the results. First, among the 37 separate scores presented, in only eight cases—grade 4 math in 2003, 2005, 2007, and 2009; grade 4 science in 2009; and grade 8 science in 2000, 2005, and 2009—does the percentage of students attaining proficiency exceed 33 percent. And the eight exceptions fall in the 34–38 percent range. To put it more bluntly, most often more than two-thirds of Michigan's grade 4 and grade 8 students fail to achieve academic proficiency in reading, science, math, and writing as measured by NAEP standards.

Second, over the period of years included (1990–2007) the scores were essentially flat with the exception of grade 4 math and, to a lesser extent, grade 8 math. In grade 4 math, the percentage of students attaining proficiency doubled from 1992 to 2007; the percentage figure in 1992 was 18 percent and by 2007 it had more than doubled to 37 percent. In the most recent administration, 2009, we see a small drop-off to 35 percent. In grade 8 math the increase was comparable, from 16 percent in 1990 to 31 percent in 2009. However, while the increase was quite sharp in the first three administrations—12 percent from 1990 to 1996—the scores then leveled off for the next five administrations, with the small increase to 31 percent noted above in the most recent year, 2009. The grade 4 and grade 8 reading scores were essentially flat over a similar period. In grade 4 and grade 8 science, while fewer years were involved, the scores also remained essentially flat, albeit there were only three years involved at grade 4—2000, 2005, and 2009—and four

Table 4.2 NAEP Results for Michigan, Percent Proficient, Available Years 1990–2009, Grades 4 and 8

	Grade 4 reading	Grade 8 reading
1992	26	—
1998	28	—
2002	30	32
2003	32	32
2005	32	28
2007	32	28
2009	30	31
	Grade 4 math	Grade 8 math
1990	—	16
1992	18	19
1996	23	28
2000	28	28
2003	34	28
2005	38	29
2007	37	29
2009	35	31
	Grade 4 science	Grade 8 science
1996	—	32
2000	32	35
2005	30	35
2009	34	35
	Grade 4 writing	Grade 8 writing
2002	19	24
2007	—	27

NOTE: For the NAEP, percent proficient includes the number of students who score at or above the "proficient" level. The NAEP uses three levels: 1) basic, 2) proficient, and 3) advanced. Basic denotes partial mastery of knowledge and skills that are fundamental for proficient work at each grade level; proficient represents solid academic performance at each grade level; advanced signifies superior performance beyond grade level mastery. There are, of course, students who score "below basic" on the NAEP tests, i.e., a fourth level; however, for some reason, it is not a standard or level set or used by the NAGB.

SOURCE: National Center for Education Statistics, the Nation's Report Card: http://nces.ed.gov/nationsreportcard/states/profile.asp.

years at grade 5—1996, 2000, 2005, and 2009. The overall flatness of these scores tells us that academic achievement of Michigan students is not improving, at least based on NAEP results. In short, Michigan students are not on an increasing trajectory to reach 100 percent proficiency by school year 2013–14 as called for by NCLB and as measured by the NAEP.

And perhaps more telling and of greater cause for concern is Michigan students' decline over time in performance on NAEP when compared with other states. For example, Michigan's rank among participating states in 4th grade reading fell from 22nd among 42 states in 1992 to 30th of 51 states in 2007, while Michigan's rank in 8th grade mathematics fell from 21st among 42 states to 36th of 51 states over the same period. The measured performance of African American students is particularly alarming, with Michigan's 8th grade math scores ranking next to last in 2007 among 41 reporting states.

An even greater cause for concern is the dreadfully low NAEP reading and math scores for 4th and 8th grade students in the Detroit Public Schools that were announced in early December 2009, as well as the science scores for Detroit 4th and 8th graders announced in February 2011, following the release of the NAEP's first Trial Assessment of Urban Districts. By NAEP standards, only 5 percent of Detroit 4th graders and 7 percent of Detroit 8th graders were proficient in reading. In math the scores were even worse—3 percent at grade 4 and 4 percent at grade 8.[6] Table 4.3 depicts Detroit's scores as compared to all other U.S. cities involved in the Trial Assessment of Urban Districts.

We turn next to the overall 2009 MEAP results and ask how these results compare with the quite dismal picture painted by the NAEP results. Do they paint the same picture or a different picture, and if so, why? However, before we turn to an exploration of recent MEAP scores and attention to these two questions, let us first look briefly at the history and development of the MEAP.

Table 4.3 Academic Achievement in Selected Subjects, NAEP Trial Urban District Assessment, Percent Proficient, 2009

	Detroit	U.S. large cities
Reading		
Grade 4	5	23
Grade 8	7	21
Math		
Grade 4	3	31
Grade 8	4	24
Science		
Grade 4	40	19
Grade 8	30	16

NOTE: Proficient is defined as a score of proficient or above.
SOURCE: National Center for Education Statistics, the Nation's Report Card: http://nces.ed.gov/nationsreportcard/states/profile.asp.

THE MICHIGAN EDUCATIONAL ASSESSMENT PROGRAM (MEAP)

The Genesis and Development of the MEAP

We noted in the previous chapter that back in the fall of 1968, Ira Polley, Michigan's State Superintendent of Public Instruction (SPI) and staff members in the MDE's newly formed Bureau of Research began to lose faith in input-oriented school accreditation.[7] They focused instead on creating a system that annually would gather and report information on the academic performance of students in Michigan's public schools. These efforts eventually led to the drafting of a proposal for creation of a statewide educational assessment program, starting with reading and math at grades 4 and 7. In the spring of 1969, the SBE responded favorably to the proposal and directed Polley "to prepare and submit appropriate legislation for the periodic assessment of educational progress in the public elementary and secondary schools of Michigan" (Kearney, Crowson, and Wilbur 1970, p. 16).

While the SBE did indeed have the power to mandate such a program, the program also would require a relatively high level of funding, and the only realistic source for such funding was the legislature. Two possibilities existed: either seek the introduction of a new piece of legislation, which would not only mandate the program statutorily but also provide the necessary funds, or establish the program and acquire the funds through the simple expedient of adding a line item to the MDE's annual budget request. Both alternatives, of course, would require legislative approval, but the latter had the advantage of not treating the assessment program as an entirely new and separate issue. Polley made the decision to go the route of asking for a line-item addition to the annual budget request, along with the necessary language. The first overture, to the Senate Appropriations Committee, met with no success. A second approach made to the House Appropriations Committee, after lengthy discussion and persistent lobbying by Polley, did meet with the approval of the committee. Following passage by the full House and subsequent passage by the Senate, with the assessment funding and language included, the bill went to the governor's desk for signature in late July of 1969.

At the time, there was some thought that the governor, while basically favoring the idea, might choose to veto the assessment item and seek additional political mileage by introducing state assessment as a fresh, new program arising from the work of his ongoing Commission on Educational Reform. These fears were unfounded, and on August 12, 1969, the governor did sign the MDE's budget bill with the assessment provision intact. Thus was born the Michigan Educational Assessment Program.

The MEAP's first year—1969–70

Time quickly became the major problem facing MDE staff charged with mounting the initial offering of the MEAP. The language accompanying the appropriation called for putting in place a statewide assessment of all 4th and 7th graders no later than January 1970—a mere six months after the governor's signing. With little time to spare, and no time to build new measures, the MDE turned to the Educational Testing Service in Princeton, New Jersey, contracting with it to develop and administer the new tests.

The major portion of the assessment battery developed by the Educational Testing Service consisted of shortened achievement tests in four basic skills areas: 1) reading comprehension, 2) vocabulary, 3) English expression, and 4) mathematics. The tests purposely were put together as shortened versions of regular size achievement tests, thus making the scores valid and reliable only for groups of students, but not for individual students. As planned, no individual pupil reporting could or would take place in the first year. The assessment battery also included a Section 1, entitled "General Information," which contained 26 questions designed to provide indirect group measures of socioeconomic status and pupil attitudes and aspirations. All of the measures, the achievement tests as well as the items in Section 1, were norm-referenced.

In launching the 1969–70 MEAP, the MDE faced the same obstacles faced by the early developers of the NAEP, namely, the school community's deep and ingrained opposition to sharing test results with anyone other than professional educators. The decision not to produce individual pupil results allayed some of the opposition, but certainly did not address the major concern of the school community, namely, public release of comparative results. To speak to that concern, the MDE made the promise that test results would be made available only to school superintendents, principals, and classroom teachers. There would be no public release of school or school district results. But even this did little to further assuage the opposition. As Roeber (1986, p. 2) put it, ". . . if the [1969–70] state assessment program was strong on anything, it was strong on generating controversy! Teachers disliked the achievement measures. Low scoring districts disliked the percentile ranks. Parents and students were offended by the questions in the SES measure and turned off by the attitude scales. Administrators were defensive about potentially unfair comparisons, while teachers were worried about evaluation based on these test results."

Despite the initial opposition and the accompanying controversies, the first-year program did go forward, the assessments were administered, answer sheets were collected and scored, and reports of the results were prepared.[8] The reports were of two types. The first type was a public report, which contained only general information on the levels and distribution of student performance for the state as a whole (Michigan Department of Education 1970). No individual school or school district information was included. The second type was the confidential local district reports sent individually to each local district in August of 1970.

These reports included the actual assessment scores for each local district—each district receiving data only on its schools.

When it was made known that local districts had received their individual results, there immediately arose pressure from several sources calling on the MDE to provide, in one document, comparative data on all the schools in the state. The requests came from the news media, the governor, legislators, and state government officials: "The Chair of the Senate Appropriations Committee wanted the data, the House Appropriations Committee, the House Education Committee, the House Special Committee on the Quality of Elementary and Secondary Schools, the Legislative Fiscal Agency, and several individual legislators all wanted the data" (Kearney and Huyser, 1973, p. 52).

The MDE was caught squarely between the interests of two competing groups—1) the governor, legislators, and other state officials who demanded the data; and 2) local school personnel who felt that they had been assured that no such disclosures would be made.[9] Needless to say, disclosure won out. The MDE somewhat reluctantly made the decision that not only would it publicly release local district results for future MEAP administrations beginning with the 1970–71 MEAP, it also would go back and prepare for public release a district-by-district summary of the 1969–70 results.

We also should note that a second turn of events reinforced the MDE's decision to publicly release the results of the 1969–70 MEAP. During the 1968 session of the Michigan legislature, a categorical aid program was added to the State School Aid Act, called Section 3, aimed at assisting those schools marked by "a high degree of concentration of economic and cultural deprivation." In the three school years from 1968–69 through 1970–71, under this provision certain schools became eligible for categorical aid based on criteria developed by the MDE. In the 1970–71 School Aid Act, the legislature raised the level of funding, but also changed the criteria. The new criteria required use of the 1969–70 MEAP results to determine a school's relative standing on two measures: 1) the percentage of students with socioeconomic deprivation, and 2) the percentage of students with low achievement levels. The legislation, in effect, required the MDE to prepare a ranking of all schools in the state and, on the basis of that ranking, publicly release the point scores of all the schools falling in the bottom quartile. The MDE was then required to allocate the categorical aid on the basis of that ranking. Thus, for practical purposes, the Section 3 legislation removed from the jurisdiction of the MDE the question of whether or not MEAP results would be publicly released.[10]

New challenges, new directions, new accomplishments

The MEAP endured the trials and tribulations of its first year of operation, receiving not only continuing funding for 1970–71 but also its own statutory authority in the legislature's adoption of Act 38 of the Public Acts of 1970. Still, the protests of local educators continued, including a threatened boycott of the program by several local school district administrators. And the protests in the early years of MEAP were not limited to school administrators. The Michigan Education Association, the state's largest teacher union, mounted its own protests, including enlisting its parent organization, the NEA, in a campaign to discredit the MEAP and the MDE (see House, Rivers, and Stufflebeam [1974]). Nor were strong critiques of the program limited to members of the school community; university professors, both within the state and on the national level, also got in their licks (see, for example, House, Rivers, and Stufflebeam [1974] and Murphy and Cohen [1974]). It would be some years before Michigan witnessed any lasting change in the school community's opposition to assessment testing, and particularly the sharing of assessment results with anyone other than professional educators. But that change did eventually come.

Despite the initial obstacles and difficulties, the MEAP held on, and significant changes in the architecture of the program began to take place in the immediate years following 1969–70. The first was the introduction of every-pupil testing in 1970–71. As noted above, the 1969–70 MEAP had been designed so that the basic—or smallest—unit of analysis was a school building. There was to be no reporting of individual pupil results, nor was any such reporting possible. Many parents, along with educators at the local school level, even while having serious reservations about the new testing program, were nevertheless displeased that the MEAP did not deliver individually reliable pupil scores. In response, the MDE directed a redesign of the 1970–71 MEAP so that the assessments would begin to provide individually reliable pupil results. In addition, the MDE began to turn away from exclusive reliance on the Educational Testing Service, and started to recruit and train Michigan classroom teachers as item writers. The teacher-developed items soon became perceived as better measures of achievement for Michigan students and, not surprisingly, became better accepted by Michigan teachers. At about the same time, a decision was made to jettison the MEAP's norm-referenced approach and move to objective-referenced testing. The MDE, working with a new contractor, the California Test Bureau, and again enlisting Michigan educators in the effort, undertook the development of the performance objectives that would form the basis for building the new objective-referenced tests. The 1973–74 school year witnessed the MEAP's first use of these new objective-referenced tests. Additional changes were to follow. In 1979, grade 10 assessments in math and reading were added to the MEAP offerings. In 1985, science was added.

Over the next several years, the MEAP underwent additional improvements, as well as a host of continuing trials and tribulations. And the MEAP endured, even though at times its continued existence seemed in doubt. A failed attempt to establish a grade 1 assessment led in 1975 to legislative threats of a moratorium on further expansion, if not also discontinuation of the MEAP, a threat that was headed off by the SBE itself adopting a moratorium on immediate expansion. MDE and MEAP staff had to deal continually with the competing pressures of meeting immediate program demands versus finding time for thoughtful and considered deliberation as ever newer demands were being placed upon the MEAP. Less than positive reviews by external scholars, as well as continuing brickbats from local educators and their state and national associations, added to the tension and strain (House, Rivers, and Stufflebeam 1974).[11] But the program persisted and, one might say, took on a life of its own. Work was undertaken to develop additional performance objectives in other academic areas, including social studies, art, music, health, and physical education. MEAP tests in these areas were constructed, piloted, and initiated on a sampling basis in order to provide state and regional level information on how Michigan students were doing in these areas. Annual every-pupil testing in reading and math at grades 4, 7, and 10, as well as every-pupil testing in science at grades 5, 8, and 11, continued to be a mainstay of the program through the 1990s.

During this same time period, the MEAP introduced a new reporting scheme that was to become a harbinger of the "percent proficient" reporting scheme later adopted under the pressures of EducationYes! and NCLB (see Chapter 3 in this volume). Called the *Proportions Report*, the new reporting scheme presented test scores, averaged over a three-year period, in a format that indicated the percentage of students (in the school and in the district) who had scored within each of four bands or levels. Band 4 included those students who achieved 75–100 percent of the objectives tested; band 3 contained those students who achieved 50–74 percent of the objectives tested; band 2 held those students who achieved 25–49 percent of the objectives; and band 1 held those who achieved 0–24 percent of the objectives.

For example, a school might find in grade 4 reading that only 10 percent of its pupils scored within the top band, 15 percent of its students scored within the next band, 20 percent of its students within band 2, and 55 percent of its students within band 1, the bottom band. The MDE would designate this as a "high-needs" school, for it did not have at least 50 percent of its students scoring in the top band. A moderate-needs school did not have at least 65 percent of its students scoring in the top band, and a school with at least 75 percent of its students scoring in the top band was a low-needs school. Based on the up or down movement of the school's scores in subsequent years, it would be designated as improving or declining. The *Propositions Report* indeed was a harbinger, a forerunner, of what was to come under NCLB and EducationYes!

In Chapter 3, we refer to the fact that in the 1990s the SBE was having its own problems with Governor John Engler, who at the time was challenging the authority of the SBE on several fronts by issuing a number of executive orders transferring major functions of the SBE and the MDE to other departments of state government.[12] Included in these executive orders was the transfer of the MEAP to the Treasury Department. As we noted, aside from the governor's growing dissatisfaction with the SBE, the ostensible rationale behind the transfer was that the Treasury Department administered the Michigan Merit Scholarship Program, which awarded financial scholarships to secondary school students who passed the MEAP before completing high school.[13]

Thus the MEAP, first established in 1969 by the SBE and operated for over 20 years as an integral unit of the MDE, now became lodged in a different department of state government—one that, in truth, had little to do with public education. To further compound the problem, by executive order, the governor also created the Center for Educational Performance and Information, and made it responsible for handling the MEAP data and related performance information on the schools. The SBE and the MDE, one might say, were left out in the cold. It was not until late 2004, two years into the administration of Governor Jennifer Granholm, that the MEAP was transferred back into the MDE and recovered its appropriate place in the state administrative framework. During the years of its exile, the kindest thing one can say is that the MEAP endured, although some might argue that it simply languished, if it did not come close to "melting down." Today, the MEAP and its sister programs are the centerpiece of the Bureau of Assessment and Accountability, a new MDE unit initially established in 2004 as the Office of Educational Assessment and Accountability.[14]

Before we leave our brief and somewhat selective account of the history and development of the MEAP, there is one other significant structural change in the program that needs to be mentioned, namely, the introduction in 2007 of the ACT as the central piece of a new grade 11 Michigan Merit Exam to take the place of the existing grade 11 MEAP exam. The decision to add the ACT, one of the nation's two most widely required and used college admissions tests—the other being the SAT—has an interesting lineage. As we noted earlier, throughout the 1970s and 1980s the nation witnessed a growing concern and dissatisfaction with American public education and particularly with the American high school. As one response to this, sometime in the late 1980s the legislature placed an "unasked for" $783,000 in the MDE's annual appropriation, along with language that called for the MDE to develop and administer to high school seniors an Employability Skills Test.

Enquiring of the legislature what it meant by *employability skills*, the consensus seemed to be that the legislature expected the MDE to develop a high school graduation test, assuming that the term employability skills was just educational jargon. In the years immediately following the appropriation, the MDE did develop an innovative employability skills project that would require each exiting high school student to leave with a portfolio that would document her or his readiness for subsequent education and work. Unfortunately, this portfolio requirement never took off. With the advent of the Engler administration in early 1991, the program was more or less scrapped.

Subsequently, during the summer of 1991, the Michigan legislature adopted a requirement that the high school MEAP become a graduation test. After substantial lobbying on the part of the MDE and local educators, the legislature repealed the graduation requirement, but put in its place a requirement that all high school transcripts carry scores on the grade 11 MEAP, along with an entry indicating that the particular student's score represented performance at one of three levels: proficient, novice, or below novice. These performance-level designations were quite different from any of those used previously in the MEAP or, for that matter, in other testing programs such as the ACT.

While students still faced the requirement of the grade 11 MEAP and the entry of their scores and performance on transcripts, there remained a waning interest in sitting for the test, much less exerting the effort to score well. A growing movement among some parents and others in opposition to outcomes-based education, to state assessment, and particularly the grade 11 MEAP, buttressed this attitude. To counter the negativity, state government enacted an "incentive" by way of instituting the Michigan Merit Scholarship Program. Under this program, a student's scores on the grade 11 MEAP, if high enough, made the student eligible to receive a $2,500 tuition grant from the state to help defray the cost of the first two years of a college education.

However, a serious problem eventually arose from the use of the proficient, novice, or below novice designations on a student's transcript, since in a good many cases the designations apparently were way out of line with a student's ACT scores. Some students who were admitted to top-tier universities and colleges were labeled novice—or worse, below novice—on the grade 11 MEAP. Cases were reported, for example, of students with ACT scores in the mid- and high 20s being marked on their transcripts as novice on the basis of the grade 11 MEAP scores. (The ACT has a range of 1 to 36, with a presumed mean of 18; a score in the mid- or high 20s is quite good, and certainly not the score of a novice learner.) This fomented a rebellion among the parents of many of these students and particularly suburban parents, as well as serious unrest among the state's high school principals. It also later opened the door for the executive director of the Michigan Association of Secondary School Principals to mount a successful legislative lobbying effort to add the ACT to a modified grade 11 MEAP, all packaged as the Michigan Merit Exam (MME), a comprehensive battery that includes the ACT plus writing college entrance exam, portions of ACT's WorkKeys work skills assessment, measures in reading, writing, total English language arts, math, science, and social studies (see Ballard 2005). Today, each Michigan student in grade 11 is required to take the MME in the spring of the school year. The student then has available an ACT score, free of charge, to send to a college or university of his or her choice; he or she also becomes eligible for a $4,000 Michigan Promise Scholarship (which replaced the Michigan Merit Scholarship program), provided he or she take the entire MME and receive valid scores in math, reading, writing, and science.[15]

At best, we only have skimmed the surface of the history of the MEAP over the past 40-plus years, attempting to hit some of the high points to give the reader a sense of the factors that affected and shaped the program over that period of time. A full account of the history and development of the MEAP demands and deserves much more than we have presented here. We only hope that some future scholar might see fit to embark upon a definitive study of a program that, warts and all, has had a significant impact on Michigan education—an impact that promises to become even greater in the immediate years ahead. It is worth noting the comment of a MEAP staffer responsible for the program in its early days who left the MDE in 1991 only to return in 2003 to again head up the program. When asked how the MEAP program in 2003 differed from the MEAP program he left in 1991, his response was that there was no longer any argument from locals as to why the state was assessing student performance.[16] MEAP had become an accepted part of the educational landscape in Michigan.

The MEAP Today and Michigan's Public Schools

Over the past four decades, from its first offerings in January of 1970 of assessments at grade 4 and grade 7 in reading comprehension, vocabulary, English expression, and math, plus a general section of 26 questions designed to produce indirect group measures of socioeconomic status and pupil attitudes and aspirations, to its current schedule of offerings in six different subject areas at eight different grade levels, the MEAP has come a long way. Reading, writing, and math assessments now are offered every year at grades 3–8, science at grades 5 and 8, social studies at grades 6 and 9, and the comprehensive MME at grade 11. Student performances in all these subject areas are reported at the student and classroom levels confidentially, and at school, district, and state levels publicly. Table 4.4 shows the current range of MEAP and MME offerings.[17]

A Look at Recent MEAP and MME Results

In Table 4.5, we present a statewide summary of MEAP scores at grades 3–9 for fall 2010, and MME scores at grade 11 for spring 2010, the most recent years for which results are available.

In reading, from grades 3–8 we find that 79–87 percent of Michigan students have attained proficiency, with the scores being slightly higher at the lower grades (3–6). In MEAP writing, the scores are of some concern. However, we should note that the 2010 offering was a redesigned writing assessment administered for the first time in fall 2010. Additionally, the MEAP no longer calculates a total ELA score. Students in grades 3 and 4 appear to do particularly well in math, with between 91

Table 4.4 Annual MEAP and MME Assessments, Subjects and Grade Levels

Subjects	Grade levels
Reading	3–8
Writing	3–8[a]
Total English language arts	3–8
Mathematics	3–8
Science	5 and 8
Social studies	6 and 9
MME	11
ACT composite	
ACT WorkKeys	
English[a]	
English + writing	
Mathematics	
Science	
Writing	

[a]Grades 4 and 7 only beginning in 2010–11.
NOTE: As of the 2008–2009 school year.
SOURCE: MDE.

Table 4.5 Statewide MEAP and MME Results: Fall 2010—Grades 3–9, Spring 2010—Grade 11, Percent Proficient

Grade	Reading	Writing[a]	Total ELA[b]	Math	Science[c]	Social studies[d]
3	87	—	—	95	—	—
4	84	48	—	91	—	—
5	85	—	—	80	81	—
6	84	—	—	84	—	73
7	79	48	—	85	—	—
8	82	—	—	78	76	—
9	—	—	—	—	—	71
11	69	47	—	54	62	82

[a]In fall 2010, the revised MEAP writing test was offered only at grades 4 and 7.
[b]In fall 2010, no MEAP total ELA score was calculated. In addition, no MME total ELA score is calculated at grade 11.
[c]Science is offered only at grades 5, 8, and 11.
[d]Social studies is offered only at grades 6, 9, and 11.
NOTE: For the MEAP, percent proficient includes the number of students who score at or above the proficient level. The MEAP uses four score levels: 1) not proficient, 2) partially proficient, 3) proficient, and 4) advanced. Not proficient means the student needs intensive intervention and support to improve achievement. Partially proficient means the student needs assistance to improve achievement. Proficient means the student's performance indicates an understanding and application of key grade level expectations defined for Michigan students. Advanced means the student's performance exceeds grade level expectations and indicates substantial understanding and application of key concepts defined for Michigan students.
SOURCE: MDE.

and 95 percent scoring at or above the proficient level. In the next four grades, 5–8, the percentages increase from grade 5 to grade 6, level off at grade 7, and experience a drop at grade 8. In science and social studies, students at only two grade levels were tested: grades 5 and 8 in science, and grades 6 and 9 in social studies.

While the MEAP scores for grades 3–8 at face value appear pretty good, we still find upward of 15–30 percent of these students who have yet to attain proficiency in these basic subject areas. Still, pretty good is not good enough, particularly judged by NCLB's goal of having 100 percent of Michigan students reaching proficiency by school year 2013–14. Additionally, the writing scores continue to be quite troublesome.

The MME scores for grade 11 students are cause for even more concern: 31–53 percent of 11th graders have yet to reach proficiency in reading, writing, math, and science; in social studies, only 18 percent fail to meet the mark.

The summary results presented in Table 4.5 provide only a snapshot of student performance, a single cross-sectional look at one moment in time, school year 2010–11. What do the scores look like in prior years? Are the scores improving, declining, or staying the same? In Table 4.6 we have arrayed the same scores for the same grades over the most recent five-year period in which the MEAP and MME were administered and scores were available, that is, from school year 2006–07 through school year 2009–10. We use the scores in Table 4.6 to explore a bit further and see what trends may exist in each of the six subject areas, from grade to grade and over time.

COMMENTS ON THE MEAP SCORES

In reading, with the exception of grades 6 and 7, the scores across the rows have been essentially flat from year to year, varying no more than 3–4 percentage points and hovering in the 80 percent range. At grade 6, this pattern is broken by an uptick of 8 percentage points in 2009–10, but drops back 4 percentage points in the most recent year, 2010–11. At grade 7, the percent proficient first dips down from 80 percent to 72 percent over 2006 and 2007, but then jumps back up to 79 percent in 2008 and tops out at 82 percent in 2009–10, followed by a drop back to 79 percent in 2010–11. The flatness across years rings the same alarm bell we mentioned above: upward of 20 percent of students consistently are falling short of reaching the goal of 100 percent proficiency. But even more worrisome is the pattern we see when looking down the columns. With two exceptions, in each of the years, there is a drop of approximately 10 percentage points from grade 3 to grade 8, with the biggest single drop—10 percentage points—coming between grades 6 and 7 in 2007–08. At grade 8, with the exception of the two most recent years, roughly 25 percent of the students have yet to reach proficiency. In 2009–10 and 2010–11, the percentages drop to 17 and 18 percent, respectively, but are still troublesome.

Table 4.6 Statewide MEAP and MME Results, Grades 3–9 and 11, 2006–07, 2007–08, 2008–09, 2009–10, Percent Proficient

Reading					
Grade	2006–07	2007–08	2008–09	2009–10	2010–11
3	87	86	87	90	87
4	85	84	83	84	84
5	84	82	81	85	85
6	83	82	80	88	84
7	80	72	79	82	79
8	76	77	76	83	82
11	63	66	64	69	67
Writing					
Grade	2006–07	2007–08	2008–09	2009–10[a]	2010–11[b]
3	52	67	61		—
4	45	44	44		47
5	57	59	63		—
6	74	73	76		—
7	65	77	78		48
8	67	70	74		—
11	43	45	47	47	51
Total ELA					
Grade	2006–07	2007–08	2008–09	2009–10[c]	2010–11[c]
3	79	81	83		
4	78	76	77		
5	78	78	78		
6	78	80	89		
7	76	74	80		
8	71	75	77		
11	—	—	—		
Mathematics					
Grade	2006–07	2007–08	2008–09	2009–10	2010–11
3	88	90	91	95	95
4	85	86	88	92	91
5	76	74	77	79	80
6	69	73	80	82	84
7	64	73	83	82	85
8	68	71	75	70	78
11	50	50	53	54	56

(continued)

Table 4.6 (continued)

			Science		
Grade	2006–07	2007–08	2008–09	2009–10	2010–11
5	83	82	83	81	78
8	75	79	77	76	78
11	60	61	60	62	65
			Social studies		
Grade	2006–07	2007–08	2008–09	2009–10	2010–11
6	73	74	74	73	75
9	74	71	72	71	73
11	87	84	84	87	81

[a]In fall 2010, the MEAP writing test at grades 3–8 was undergoing revision.
[b]In fall 2010, the revised MEAP writing test was offered only at grades 4 and 7.
[c]In fall 2009, no MEAP total ELA score was calculated. In addition, no MME total ELA score is calculated at grade 11.
NOTE: For the MEAP, percent proficient includes the number of students who score at or above the proficient level. The MEAP uses four score levels: 1) not proficient, 2) partially proficient, 3) proficient, and 4) advanced. Not proficient means the student needs intensive intervention and support to improve achievement. Partially proficient means the student needs assistance to improve achievement. Proficient means the student's performance indicates an understanding and application of key grade level expectations defined for Michigan students. Advanced means the student's performance exceeds grade level expectations and indicates substantial understanding and application of key concepts defined for Michigan students.
SOURCE: MDE.

The available writing scores vary considerably and certainly are not what one would call sterling. The grade 4 scores across the first three years—2006–07 through 2008–09—are particularly low and flat. The good news is that at grade 7 the scores have risen by 13 percentage points over the three years, and at grades 5 and 8 they have risen by 6 and 7 percentage points, respectively. Grade 3 appears somewhat puzzling, going from 52 percent to 67 percent between 2006 and 2007, but then dropping to 61 percent in 2008. As we noted above, the MDE is not satisfied with the writing assessment and currently is developing a new and expanded writing assessment that was not offered in 2009–10 and administered only at grades 4 and 7 in fall 2010. This, of course, raises questions about the validity of the new writing assessment at both grade levels.

The available total ELA scores present a set of patterns not unlike those we see in the reading scores. At three levels—grades 3, 4, and 5—the scores across the rows are essentially flat. At the other three levels—grades 6, 7, and 8—they increase over the three-year span. At grades 6, 7, and 8, the percentage point increase is 11, 4, and 6, respectively. Looking down the columns, we see almost the same general pattern of declining scores that we saw in reading, although not quite as large—6–8 percentage points versus 10 percentage points. However, in 2008 there is a bit of an anomaly at grade 6. The score at grade 6 jumps up 11 percentage points over grade 5, but then drops down again by 9 percentage points at grade 7. Again, as we noted above, no total ELA score was calculated for 2009–10 since the writing test was being redesigned. And the decision was made not to calculate a total ELA beginning in 2011.

The mathematics scores are interesting on a couple of accounts. First, the scores across the time span at grades 6–8 are increasing appreciably: at grade 6 there is an increase of 15 percentage points; at grade 7 the increase is 21 percentage points; at grade 8 the increase is much smaller, but still an increase. The trajectory is upward and therefore hopeful, even though there is still a good ways to go to reach 100 percent proficiency in math. Second, even more interesting is grade 7, where the percent proficient has increased from 64 percent in 2006, to 73 percent in 2007, to 83 percent in 2008, to 82 percent in 2009, and to 85 percent in 2010–11—increases of about 10 percentage points from year to year with the exception of the final two years. Something certainly seems to be happening here, and it is happening in the central year of middle school, the proverbial bugbear of mathematics teaching.

In science and social studies, MEAP assessments are given only at two grade levels, thus we are limited in examining patterns. Acknowledging this limitation, we do see that in science the patterns across the two rows, grades 5 and 8, are essentially flat, except for a slight drop-off at grade 5 in the most recent year, 2010–11. Looking down the columns, we see percentage point decreases ranging from 3 to 8. But given that there are only two entries in each column for the MEAP, we should be cautious in drawing any conclusions. The same can be said for grade 6 and grade 9 social studies. Indeed, both the rows across and the columns down are essentially flat.

COMMENTS ON THE MME SCORES

The final rows in Table 4.6, labeled grade 11, display results from the five most recent administrations of the MME. In the spring of 2007, the MME replaced the grade 11 MEAP assessment and is now administered each year during the month of March. The MME includes several parts: the ACT plus writing college entrance exam, portions of the WorkKeys work skills assessment, and several Michigan components developed to assess Michigan high school content standards. The MME delivers scores in reading, writing, mathematics, science, and social studies, as well as the ACT scores. The specific score categories delivered by the MME are listed in Table 4.4. The MME also is an integral part of the Michigan Promise Scholarship. To qualify for the $4,000 scholarship, students must take the entire MME and receive valid scores in reading, math, science, and writing.[18]

In Table 4.7, at the risk of being redundant, we have summarized the MME results that first appeared as the grade 11 rows in Table 4.6. Once again, the scores are reported in terms of the percentage of students who scored at the proficient or higher levels as approved by the SBE.

Percentage-wise these scores overall tend to be lower than the grades 3–9 scores, with the single exception of the social studies scores, which are more in line with the grades 3–9 scores in the several subject

Table 4.7 Statewide Grade 11 MME Results, Percent Proficient

	Reading	Writing	Total ELA[a]	Math	Science	Social studies
2006–07	63	43	54	50	60	87
2007–08	66	45	56	50	61	84
2008–09	64	47	56	53	60	84
2009–10	69	47	—	54	62	82
2010–11	67	51	—	56	65	81

[a]No total ELA for the MME results at grade 11 was calculated in the school years 2009–10 through 2010–11.

NOTE: In addition to reporting on subject matter achievement, the NAEP also reports on instructional experiences and school environment for populations of students (e.g., all 4th graders) and groups within those populations (e.g., female students, Hispanic students). For those interested in more information, see the IES Center for Educational Statistics Web site: http://www.nces.ed.gov/nationsreportcard/about/.

SOURCE: MDE.

areas. In terms of the NCLB goal of 100 percent proficiency by 2013–14, the grade 11 scores also are cause for serious concern.

THE ACT EXAM

The ACT is a college entrance exam, not unlike the SAT. Many colleges and universities do require the exam as part of their admission processes, and most likely, a student's scores on the ACT (or the SAT) enter into admissions decisions to one extent or another depending on the college or university in which a student seeks to enroll. The minimum possible score on the ACT is 1, and the maximum possible score is 36. ACT lists its presumed mean or average score as 18. The writing score, however, has a different range; the minimum possible score is 2 and the maximum possible score is 12; the presumed mean is 6.

In Table 4.8, we present the statewide ACT results for 2007–2011. For all five years, 13 of the scores are slightly above the presumed mean of 18.0—composite, math, reading, and science. For four of the years, the scores in English plus writing are slightly below the presumed mean. The scores in English over the four-year period increase

Table 4.8 Statewide ACT Results, Grade 11

	Composite	English	English + writing	Math	Reading	Science	Writing
2007	18.8	17.6	17.3	18.8	18.9	19.3	6.4
2008	18.8	17.6	17.5	19.0	18.8	19.5	6.6
2009	19.0	18.0	17.9	19.2	19.0	19.4	6.7
2010	19.3	18.3	17.9	19.3	19.4	19.7	6.5
2011	19.3	18.7	n/a	19.8	19.2	19.9	n/a

SOURCE: MDE.

from 17.6 to 18.3. Finally, the four writing scores are slightly above the presumed mean of 6.0. Overall, these are respectable if not outstanding scores, particularly remembering that the ACT in Michigan is not a self-selected test but rather one that all grade 11 students are required to take as one part of the MME. But we leave it to the reader to make her or his personal judgments about what the scores in Table 4.8 tell us about the academic performance of Michigan's high school youth.

Having now completed our presentation of recent MEAP and MME assessment scores, let us return to the critical question we raised earlier, namely, how do these MEAP results compare with the disheartening picture presented earlier in the NAEP scores?

A COMPARISON OF MEAP AND NAEP SCORES

As we see in Table 4.2, the NAEP state-level score results for Michigan are dismaying, but Michigan is not alone. Many other states do not fare well on the NAEP, and when comparing their NAEP scores to the corresponding scores reported in their own state assessment programs, the differences often are also stark, as can be seen in Table 4.9. For example, judging Michigan on the basis of its MEAP scores paints a much rosier picture than judging Michigan on the basis of its NAEP scores. By Michigan standards, fully 84 percent of its combined 4th and 8th graders are proficient in reading in 2009; by NAEP standards that figure falls to 31 percent. Almost identical differences are seen in Michigan's combined 4th and 8th grade mathematics scores. A simi-

Table 4.9 Academic Achievement in Reading and Mathematics, Percent Proficient, Grades 4 and 8 Averaged

	State assessments 2009[a]		NAEP 2009	
	Reading	Math	Reading	Math
Michigan	83.5	81.0	30.5	33.0
United States	67.4	70.5	32.5	36.5
Nebraska	90.5	89.7	35.0	36.5

[a]The state assessment scores for Michigan are 2009 scores; the state assessment scores for the United States and Nebraska are 2007 scores.
SOURCE: *Education Week* (2009).

lar picture results when examining Michigan's state assessment scores compared to the U.S. average state assessment scores, and then also comparing those scores to NAEP scores. The NAEP scores come in 48–53 percentage points *lower* than Michigan scores and 34–35 percentage points lower than the U.S. average scores. The difference between a state's assessment scores and its NAEP scores is most stark in the case of Nebraska, where the NAEP reading score is almost 56 percentage points lower than its own state assessment reading score; its NAEP math score is 53 percentage points lower.[19]

In Table 4.10, we present 2010 NAEP scores for two critical subject areas and two critical transition points in a student's journey through the grades. Reading is absolutely essential to success in school, and particularly for students as they leave the primary or elementary phase and enter the middle years of schooling. Unfortunately, the NAEP scores in 4th grade reading are, to say the least, underwhelming. By NAEP standards, only 30 percent of Michigan 4th graders are proficient in reading, and while that score is just 3 percentage points shy of the U.S. average,

Table 4.10 Academic Achievement in Reading and Mathematics, Percent Proficient, NAEP 2009, Grade 4 Elementary and Grade 8 Middle School

	NAEP grade 4 reading	NAEP grade 8 math
Michigan	30	31
United States	33	34
Massachusetts	47	52

SOURCE: *Education Week* (2009).

it is still 17 percentage points below Massachusetts, the highest scoring state in the nation. Mathematics also is a critical school subject, and mathematics achievement in middle school, or the lack thereof, is of serious and growing concern. The student who exits middle school without a solid base in mathematics will face serious challenges in high school. Yet only 31 percent of Michigan 8th graders are deemed proficient in 2010 by NAEP standards—3 percentage points under the national average and trailing Massachusetts again, this time by 21 percentage points.

Table 4.11 lists comparative figures for the percent proficient on selected MEAP scores and NAEP scores for the year 2010 for reading and math. The comparative figures for science are for MEAP 2006 and NAEP 2005, the most recent somewhat comparable scores. The comparisons indeed are startling. As measured by MEAP scores, Michigan 4th and 8th graders are doing quite well in reading, math, and science. But these same students are not doing nearly so well, indeed quite poorly, as measured by NAEP scores. In reading, the difference at grade 4 is 54 percentage points, and at grade 8 it is 52 percentage points. Math and science scores also paint an equally dismal picture with differences ranging from 36 to 53 percentage points. The fall 2009 MEAP scores indicate that from 70 percent to better than 92 percent of the

Table 4.11 Academic Achievement in Selected Subjects, Percent Proficient, MEAP Fall 2009 versus NAEP Spring 2010

	MEAP	NAEP
Reading		
Grade 4	84	30
Grade 8	83	31
Math		
Grade 4	92	39
Grade 8	70	34
Science		
Grade 5	83[a]	30[b]
Grade 8	75[a]	35[b]

[a]From year 2006.
[b]From year 2005.
SOURCE: MDE and National Center for Educational Statistics, the Nation's Report Card: http://nces.ed.gov/nationsreportcard/states.

Michigan students in question have attained the state's proficient level in their respective subject matter areas. The spring 2010 NAEP scores, on the other hand, paint a far different picture—no more than one-third of Michigan 4th and 8th graders attained the NAEP's proficient level in their respective subject matter areas—reading, mathematics, and science (the sole exceptions being grades 4 and 8 math scores and grade 8 science scores, which, at 34 percent, 39 percent, and 35 percent slightly exceed the one-third mark).

MEAP versus NAEP—Further Considerations

From our examination of the data in Tables 4.9, 4.10, and 4.11, it is patently clear that judging Michigan only on the basis of its MEAP scores paints a much rosier picture than judging it on the basis of its NAEP scores. As we see in Table 4.9, by Michigan standards nearly 84 percent of the state's combined 4th and 8th graders are proficient in reading in 2009, but when using NAEP standards that figure falls to 31 percent—a drop of more than 50 percentage points. Almost identical differences are seen in combined 4th and 8th grade math scores. In Table 4.10, we are witness to the sorry state of Michigan's grade 4 NAEP reading scores and grade 8 NAEP math scores. The differences become even more obvious in Table 4.11. (And looking back to Table 4.3, we witnessed the absolutely abysmal NAEP reading and math scores for the Detroit Public Schools.)

Why do we see such differences? What are the reasons? Some will argue that Michigan has set the bar too low; others will argue that the NAEP has set the bar too high. Some will argue that Michigan's assessment tests are not rigorous enough; others will argue that the NAEP's assessments are too rigorous. And some argue that such comparisons are inappropriate if not invalid. Let's look at some of the possible explanations for these sizable differences.

The problem of content standards

Assessment tests, whether national or state, are based on content standards. Thus, a problem arises from the fact that the content standards employed by the MEAP and the NAEP are different. Content standards should set forth a near complete description of what it is that a student should know and master in a particular subject at a particular grade or level. They are the bedrock of any given achievement test. For example, an NAEP assessment test will be based on specific descriptions of a body of knowledge and skills that the NAEP governing board believes a student should know and master, say, in 4th grade math. Correspondingly, a MEAP assessment—or any state's assessment—in the same subject matter field and at the same grade level will be based on specific descriptions of a body of knowledge and skills that the SBE—or any state's governing board—believes a student should know and master in 4th grade math. Problems quickly arise because the NAEP standards and the MEAP standards—or any individual state's content standards—are not the same; indeed it is fair to say that that they differ considerably, and furthermore were developed for different purposes. The NAGB board members are on record as stating that the NAEP content standards should be "aspirational," that they should address what "ought" to be taught (Vinovskis 1998, p. 44). In effect, they are intended to establish a very high set of expectations, nothing but the best, so to speak, or, as is often claimed, they constitute "the gold standard." The MEAP content standards, on the other hand, lie more on the pragmatic side, designed to link closely with classroom instruction. In any event, there is no question that the MEAP content standards differ appreciably from the NAEP content standards and, by and large, so do the separate content standards established by each of the other 49 states.

Earlier, we referred to a published statement by the executive director of the National Secondary School Principals Association calling for resolving this problem by moving to establish national standards and a national test: "Sadly some states have set their bars exceedingly low and have given their 'proficient' students a false sense of achievement . . . If Congress truly wants to drive an education agenda for higher standards . . . [it] should shift the law at its foundation to institute national standards and a national test in reading and math" (Tirozzi 2009).

Thus, it would seem that the answer to the problem of so many different separate sets of content standards among the 50 states—and content standards that differ appreciably from the NAEP content standards—is for the states to forgo their own separate content standards and buy into the establishment of a common set of national standards.

But the question of forgoing separate state standards and establishing national standards, and a national test, quickly presents another set of problems. After all, as we note in Chapter 3, under the 10th Amendment to the U.S. Constitution education is a matter left to the states. Still, the national government properly gets into the mix on the basis of Article I, Section 8, of the U.S. Constitution—Congress's authority and responsibility to provide for the general welfare and common defense of the nation. So immediately we become involved in questions of federalism—to what extent will citizens in the separate states accept, or even tolerate, further federal inroads into deciding what subjects and what content ought to be taught in our public schools?[20] Is this properly a decision that should be reserved to the separate states, respecting the principle of subsidiarity? Or is it more properly a matter of the nation's general welfare and common defense? If not the federal government, could the task be assigned to a nonfederal or nongovernmental body created for the purpose? If the nation were to move in the direction of national standards, what of the costs of jettisoning 50 separate states' sets of content standards and replacing them with a new or revised set of national assessment standards? Who should, and who would, assume responsibility for the costs? The Congress? The individual states? Or would it necessitate establishing some sort of shared responsibility?

In mid-2009, the nation's governors and state education chiefs set out to answer these questions. Under the auspices of their two professional organizations, the National Governors Association and the Council of Chief State School Officers, the governors and the chiefs launched a first attempt to establish common core standards for the nation's public schools. On July 21, 2010, the two organizations jointly announced that not only had they completed work on common core standards in English language arts and math, but that 27 states had adopted the standards and about a dozen more were expected to do so in the following weeks (see Lewin [2010, p. A:1]). The three states mentioned earlier apparently were holdouts—Texas, Alaska, and Virginia. So, it appears that 40 or more states were now ready to jettison their separate sets of core content standards and begin moving toward the adoption of a set of common core standards—common content standards for what it is that children should know and be able to do as a consequence of their public schooling. Yet much remains to be done, not the least being to successfully mount similar efforts in other subject matter areas such as science, social studies, and the arts and humanities (see Dillon [2011b]). And even if these efforts are wholly successful, there remain a second and third problem. The second problem is the question of setting performance standards. The third problem is the question of constructing a common test to measure the performance of students against the common core standards.

The problem of performance standards

The second problem, in fact one that is inextricably linked to the problem of content standards, is what score levels should be established to determine whether a student has attained proficiency in any given subject at any given grade level. In addressing the problem of performance standards, the NAEP has set four performance levels: 1) basic, 2) proficient, 3) advanced, and 4) below basic.[21] For the NAEP, proficiency is defined as scoring at or above its proficient level. The MEAP has set four performance levels: 1) advanced 2) proficient, 3) partially proficient, and 4) not proficient. For the MEAP, proficiency is defined as scoring at or above the proficient level. The MEAP's not proficient level is analogous to the NAEP's below basic designation. It goes without saying that the performance standards used by the NAEP are different from those used by the MEAP, even though the names or descriptive titles for the levels look similar. Each set of performance standards—the MEAP's and the NAEP's—is separately established, based on different tests, and each of the tests, in turn, is based on different content standards. In addition, NAEP scores are based on sampling frames; not every pupil is tested. MEAP scores are based on every-pupil testing.[22] So, at the risk of appearing somewhat facetious, comparing performance results on the MEAP and the NAEP is, as the saying goes, like comparing apples and oranges.

The problem of a common test

Assuming that current efforts to develop and adopt nationwide common core standards prove successful, and that agreement can be reached on what the student performance levels ought to be, the third problem to be addressed is the development and adoption of a common national test to measure the performance of students against the standards. We do, of course, already have the NAEP, but it is unlikely that it could or would be used for the purposes we have in mind. It was designed and developed to sample the learning and knowledge of groups of students, to provide a periodic check on the educational progress of individual states and the nation, not to measure the academic achievement of individual students. To modify it to do the latter would be a huge if not prohibitive task. The NAEP is not given annually but rather periodically. It does not cover the entire 3–8 grade span, but rather only select grade levels. For example, the NAEP reading and math tests cover only grades 4 and 8 and are given only every other year (see Table 4.1). The NAEP is a national—not nationwide—test, funded by the federal government and governed by a federally appointed board of directors. As such, it again would lead one to become quickly enmeshed in questions of federalism. To have each state develop its own assessments (and performance standards), even when based on nationwide common core standards, would seem to run awry from the goal of common academic measurement across the nation. Thus, it seems that the effort, without question, would necessitate the development of a new nationwide test, built on core standards and common across the 50 states. It would be a substantial but doable task, one that would require considerable time, effort, and cost.

Indeed, work already is under way on addressing the problem. In September 2010, two consortia were awarded federal grants to begin the task of constructing common assessments. The first set of common assessments, aligned with the common core standards, will be developed in English language arts and math. As of February 2011, 45 states and the District of Columbia had signed on to participate in the work of the consortia. The MDE is a member of one of these two consortia and has assumed a leadership role in the consortium's work. The target date for the first administration of the common assessments is the 2014–15 school year. If all goes well, by school year 2015–16, Michigan's state assessment scores, as well as the assessment scores of some 40-plus other states, should be well in line with the NAEP scores. However, saying that the results of the two tests should be well in line begs the question, of course, of whether the score levels—the percent proficient on either or both tests—will satisfy the parents, legislators, educators, and other citizens of Michigan.

Shorter-term solutions

But short of moving to common core content and performance standards and a common test, there are some steps that might be taken in the short run to better align the results of the states' and the NAEP's testing programs. First, for Michigan, perhaps the easiest if not the most desirable or defensible step would be to raise the cut scores that are used to set the performance levels on the MEAP. Other states could do the same. The current MEAP cut scores are judgments made through a formal standard-setting process. In setting cut scores the MDE convenes standard-setting panels broadly representative of teachers, administrators, parents, and members of the business community. The panels meet, are trained, and then examine actual score profiles. Based on that examination and its judgments, the panel offers its recommendations on cut scores to the MDE, which in turn recommends acceptance, acceptance with revisions, or nonacceptance to the SBE. The SBE then takes action to adopt, revise and adopt, or reject the recommendations. The NAEP follows a similar judgmental process in setting its cut scores and performance standards.

A second way the MDE could set new cut scores would be by statistically recalibrating them against an enhanced set of content standards or expectations. In February 2011, the SBE took action to do just that. The board directed the MDE to recalibrate the current MEAP cut scores "to make them consistent with the skills students need to be prepared for college and careers" (Higgins 2011a). Spring of 2011 is the target for approving the new cut scores which then will be applied to the 2011–12 MEAP assessments. The good news is that the SBE's action is a first step in bringing the MEAP scores into closer alignment with the NAEP scores. The bad news is that, at least initially, this will result in a precipitous drop in the MEAP scores, resulting in a far lesser percentage of Michigan students attaining proficiency. For example, it is estimated that the percent proficient in grade 3 math will drop from 95 percent in 2009 to 34 percent in 2011, bringing the MEAP scores much more in line with the NAEP scores. This action also is bound to have a significant impact—probably a substantial drop—on the number of Michigan schools that meet the federal requirement for AYP.[23] To say the least, many schools—and their communities—will be in for a rude awakening. But one cannot reasonably argue against raising expectations and inducing more rigor into the system, provided of course that the increased expectations and demands are accompanied by ample resources and renewed efforts to improve the quality of teaching and instruction.

A third but more difficult step, at least politically, to move toward closer alignment with the MEAP and NAEP scores would be to convince the NAGB to include in its definition of proficiency those students who score at its basic or higher level, in effect lowering the current NAGB cut scores. There are fairly strong arguments for doing this. Martineau (2007, p. 15) makes a somewhat compelling case that "the available evidence indicates that NAEP cut scores are inaccurate representations of proficiency." His comments follow on a long history of controversy and contention over the advisability and validity of the NAEP's performance standards (Vinovskis 1998; Beaton and Johnson 2004; Bourge 2004; Linn 2004).

At first, the two descriptions—the NAEP's basic and the MEAP's proficient—do not seem that far apart. For the NAEP, basic "denotes partial mastery of knowledge and skills that are fundamental for proficient work at each grade level." For the MEAP, proficient "means the student's performance indicates an understanding and application of key grade level expectations defined for Michigan students."

Without attempting to resolve the dispute it would seem useful, at the least, to examine what some of the comparisons might look like if the NAGB governing board chose to include in its definition of proficiency those students who score at its basic level or higher. In Table 4.12, which is a revision of Table 4.11, we have done just that. In the NAEP column, we changed the original scores to now reflect the percentage of those Michigan students who scored at the basic level or higher on the spring 2010 NAEP.

While one might question the validity of the comparisons, they do present quite a different and, at least from Michigan's point of view, more positive picture. There still remain some substantial differences—for example, in grade 4 reading, grade 4 math, and grade 5 science. But the new comparisons do better align the MEAP scores and the NAEP scores. At the least, it should make one pause and ask whether the problem is not so much in the MEAP performance standards as it is in the NAEP performance standards—or, for that matter, in the MEAP or NAEP content standards.

One also might ask whether a part of the problem is in the media's reporting of the scores. While Detroit's MEAP and NAEP scores are not a very good example, it is interesting to note again that the two Detroit newspapers reported Detroit's Trial Urban District Assessment (TUDA)

Table 4.12 Academic Achievement in Selected Subjects, Percent Proficient, MEAP 2009 versus NAEP 2009

	MEAP	NAEP
Reading		
Grade 4	84	64
Grade 8	83	72
Math		
Grade 4	92	78
Grade 8	70	68
Science		
Grade 5	81[a]	69[b]
Grade 8	76[a]	66[b]

[a]From year 2006.
[b]From year 2005.
NOTE: For the NAEP, in this table proficient is defined as a score of basic or above. In addition to reporting on subject matter achievement as measured by MEAP, the MDE in its school report card also reports on the extent to which local districts are meeting a number of other legislative requirements. For information on these requirements, see the MDE Web site: http://www.michigan.gov/mde.
SOURCE: MDE and National Center for Educational Statistics, the Nation's Report Card: http://nces.ed.gov/nationsreportcard/states.

scores using basic and above rather than NAEP's criterion of proficient and above. This gave Detroit's absolutely abysmal NAEP scores a slight boost, as depicted in Table 4.13. Indeed, while it improves the picture for Detroit, even very large, huge differences still remain, making Detroit's MEAP scores appear even more suspect.

But we will have to leave a definitive answer to the questions raised to the measurement experts and, more appropriately, to the policymakers. For it is the policymakers—whether the SBE or the NAGB—who have made and will make the ultimate decisions on what the performance standards will be, as attested to by the most recent SBE action in Michigan mentioned earlier.

A cautionary note

It is with some trepidation that we offer the foregoing, for a good many experts in the measurement community would argue that it is with considerable risk that one undertakes comparisons of state assessment

Table 4.13 Detroit Public Schools, Academic Achievement in Selected Subjects, Percent Proficient, MEAP 2009 versus NAEP 2009

	MEAP	NAEP[a]	NAEP[b]
Reading			
Grade 4	64	5	27
Grade 8	69	7	40
Math			
Grade 4	76	3	31
Grade 8	40	4	23

[a]Proficiency is defined as a score of proficient or above on the NAEP scale.
[b]Proficiency is defined as a score of basic or above on the NAEP scale.
SOURCE: MDE and National Center for Educational Statistics, the Nation's Report Card: http://nces.ed.gov/nationsreportcard/districts.

results with NAEP results, and that such comparisons at best should be used with extreme caution (NCES 2007). Ho and Haertel (2007), for example, writing on the underlying assumptions of state-NAEP comparisons, point out that while there is a large body of literature on linking state tests to the NAEP, much of it is indeed cautionary. Still, such comparisons, driven largely by NCLB, have become widespread, and public school personnel, as well as state and national policymakers, are forced to answer to them. In doing so, educators and policymakers would do well to heed the advice offered by Ho and Haertel: "As awareness of the fundamental differences between state tests and NAEP grows more widespread, we hope and anticipate that State-NAEP discrepancies will be used, not to confirm suspicions of invalid state results, but to begin deeper explorations into the differences between tests and testing practices" (p. 5).

A FINAL OBSERVATION

Irrespective of whether one favors moving to nationwide standards and a nationwide test, or raising cut scores on the state assessment, or defining students who score at the basic level on the NAEP as proficient, or simply giving up on trying to link state results with NAEP results, we can certainly celebrate the transparency that has come about in public education as a consequence of the NAEP and of state assessment programs such as the MEAP. No longer is information on the academic attainments of students in our public schools the sole province of the professional educator. The doors and the windows have been thrown open, and any one of us—parent, advocate, citizen, businessperson, legislator, state executive—has access to a wealth of comparative information on the performance of our local schools and school districts, our state public school systems, and our nation.[24] Such information alone, of course, will not automatically alleviate the educational problems facing the state or the nation; it will, however, further empower those concerned with improving the quality of our public schools. Used creatively and thoughtfully, that information can result in improved education for the children and youth of Michigan and the nation.

Notes

1. For this section, we draw on Jones and Olkin (2004), who provide a lengthy and detailed account of the history and development of the NAEP.
2. For the reader interested in further detail, we recommend consulting either of the following two publications: Jones and Olkin (2004) or Vinovskis (1998).
3. The NAEP also drew samples by community type (e.g., urban core, suburban, town, and rural), socioeconomic status, racial-ethnic group, and sex.
4. See Note 2 above, and Chapter 3 in this volume.
5. In addition to reporting on subject matter achievement, the NAEP also reports on instructional experiences and school environment for populations of students (e.g., all 4th graders) and groups within those populations (e.g., female students, Hispanic students). For those interested in more information, see the IES Center for Educational Statistics Web site: http://www.nces.ed.gov/nationsreportcard/about/.
6. Both Detroit newspapers reported these results as 69 percent and 77 percent of Detroit 4th and 8th graders, respectively, scoring below basic on the NAEP assessments, which is bad enough. However, by NAEP standards the situation is even worse. The NAEP does not include the basic category in its definition of proficiency. Only the two top NAEP score categories, proficient and advanced, are included in the NAEP definition of proficiency. Thus, discounting scores of students who scored at the basic and below basic levels, and including only scores of students who scored at the proficient and advanced levels, we arrive at the 3 percent and 4 percent proficiency scores reported here. That is, by the NAEP's scoring protocol, more than 90 percent of all DPS 4th and 8th graders were not proficient in either math or reading.

7. For this section I draw extensively on Kearney (1970, 1971), Kearney and Huyser (1973), and Brictson and Roeber (n.d.).
8. A fuller account of the controversies that surrounded the program in its initial year is provided in Kearney (1970).
9. For a fuller account of the demands for public release of the assessment results and the MDE's acquiescence to these demands, see Kearney and Huyser (1973).
10. The program still exists today but in substantially amended form. No longer are MEAP results used. Rather, allocations are now made to school districts that have a high incidence of children coming from poverty circumstances, as measured by the number of children eligible for free and reduced price lunches. The allocations are effected by adding 0.115 weighting per eligible pupil (counting each of those pupils as 1.115) to the foundation allowance of those districts eligible for the aid.
11. See Kearney and Huyser (1973); House, Rivers, and Stufflebeam (1973); and Murphy and Cohen (1974).
12. During his tenure, Governor Engler issued over 100 executive orders transferring existing units of state government from one agency to another, as well as orders that created new departments including the Center for Educational Performance and Information.
13. Under this program, a student's scores on the 11th grade MEAP, if high enough, made the student eligible to receive a $2,500 tuition grant from the state to help defray the cost of the first two years of a college education.
14. In addition to the MEAP, the bureau also offers a continuum of alternate assessments to serve special needs students, including MEAP (with accommodations), MEAP-Access, MI-Access Functional Independence, MI-Access Supported Independence, and MI-Access Participation. For information on these assessments, see the MDE Web site: http://michigan.gov/mde.
15. Unfortunately, funding for the Michigan Promise scholarship was eliminated by legislative action in July 2010 as the state moved to eliminate a pending $2.8 million shortfall in the FY 2011 budget.
16. Telephone interview with Edward D. Roeber, April 29, 2009.
17. In addition to reporting on subject matter achievement as measured by MEAP, the MDE in its school report card also reports on the extent to which local districts are meeting a number of other legislative requirements. For information on these requirements, see the MDE Web site: http://michigan.gov/mde.
18. See Note 15 above.
19. For the reader interested in how other states fared, see *Education Week* (2009).
20. As we shall see later in this chapter, three states—Texas, Alaska, and Virginia—already are on record in opposition to the development of common standards.
21. While there are, of course, students who score below basic on the NAEP tests, for some reason the NAEP claims it is not a standard set or used by the NAGB—that is, the NAGB claims only three levels.
22. This is not to say the sampling isn't capable of producing valid and reliable results. For the doubters, there is a time-tested rejoinder: "If you don't believe in sampling, the next time you have a blood test, tell them to take it all."

23. It remains to be seen if the AYP requirement will be significantly altered, if not eliminated, under the scheduled Congressional reauthorization of NCLB.
24. A contention further corroborated by the announcement in the *Detroit Free Press* on August 13, 2011, that the state is launching a Web site that "will eventually provide parents—and everyone else—a way to gauge how well individual high schools prepare their graduates for college . . . the site will give parents and everyone else access to more data about Michigan schools in one spot than ever before" (Higgins 2011b).

5
Charter Schools

Following the 1983 publication of *A Nation at Risk*, opinion leaders, policymakers, and the public became more vocal in their dissatisfaction with U.S. public schools. Indeed, this discontent triggered an astonishing wave of reforms covering teacher licensure requirements, improved teacher pay, longer school days and years, more stringent high school graduation requirements, early childhood education, and more standardized testing. Further, because these reforms cost money, the 1980s saw large increases in funding levels for public schools, with aggregate support more than doubling during the decade, from $106 billion in 1980 to $223 billion in 1990 (U.S. Department of Education 2006).

The passage of so much school reform legislation in the 1980s was a remarkable political achievement and was not without some apparent academic successes. In particular, from the mid-1970s to the mid-1980s, results of the NAEP showed black-white test score differences cut in half, as schools focused on "facts and drill" education. Nevertheless, despite the spate of reforms and some evidence of improved academic outcomes, popular support for school reform remained high as the 1990s began. Critics pointed to the poor showing of U.S. students on international comparisons of reading, mathematics, and science achievement. And with most of the traditional reforms already enacted across the states (e.g., more time in school, higher standards, and better teacher pay), reformist energies turned to the organization and governance of public schools.

Specifically, reformers pointed to school bureaucracies as a principal reason for underperforming schools and called for more school autonomy and greater parental choice in U.S. public education. Indeed, the emergence of school choice as an idea in good standing was perhaps the most important development in K–12 education policy in the late 1980s and early 1990s. It also marked a change in public attitudes or perceptions, given the popular rejection of vouchers and tuition tax credit proposals during the preceding decade. This new interest in public school choice was fueled, in part, by an influential study published by the highly regarded and politically moderate Brookings Institution in 1990. *Politics, Markets, and America's Schools*, by John Chubb and Terry Moe, called for nothing less than fundamental reform of the institutions through which public K–12 education is controlled in the United States.

Analyzing data from random samples of roughly 400 schools and 9,000 students from the Administrator and Teacher Survey of the High School and Beyond data set, Chubb and Moe (1990) estimate that a student in an effectively organized school gains at least a half year in achievement over a student in an ineffectively organized school over the last two years of high school. Extrapolating that finding to the normal four-year high school experience, the authors argue that an effectively organized high school may increase the achievement of its students by more than one full year. Now, what are the observable characteristics of an effective school? Chubb and Moe see such schools as "coherent, strongly led, academically ambitious, professionally grounded, team-like organizations" (p. 141). Schools with these characteristics are high performers. Certainly, the personal qualities of the students in the school and the support and nurturing of their families are important determinants of their academic performance. Nevertheless, the organizational qualities of the school exert a significant and independent influence on student learning. The question then becomes: How are these organizational qualities fostered in schools? For the authors, the answer is the school environment, which is shaped, in turn, by the school's institutional structure. The effective school is unburdened by bureaucratization and centralized control. Essentially, the effective school runs itself, with minimal, if any, direction from a district or state authority.

For Chubb and Moe, excessive school bureaucracy and centralization, the main barriers to school effectiveness, are rooted in America's institutions of democratic control. And their policy prescription to promote school autonomy and professionalism was nothing less than "fundamental reform of the institutions through which education is controlled" (Chubb and Moe 1990, p. 142). Specifically, Chubb and Moe called for a system of public school choice that would encourage the creation of new schools, remove authority over the schools from the traditional players (e.g., school boards, superintendents, central offices, state departments of education), and vest that authority in parents, students, and the schools themselves. In the authors' words,

> Schools would be legally autonomous: free to govern themselves as they want, specify their own goals and programs and methods, design their own organizations, select their own student bodies, and make their own personnel decisions. Parents and students would be legally empowered to choose among alternative schools, aided by institutions designed to promote active involvement, well-informed decisions, and fair treatment. (p. 229)

With their influential publication, Chubb and Moe raised public awareness of the possibility of school choice through the creation of new public schools, referred to as *charter schools*, that were free from the policy control of locally elected boards of education, and free from most, if not all, state school laws and rules. This notion of innovative public schools of choice was not new. The idea had been discussed in the 1980s by Ted Kolderie, Al Shankar, and others, but the Brookings study emphasized the legal autonomy of the new schools and greatly expanded the exposure of the new concept.[1]

Minnesota passed the first charter school law in 1991. Since then, 40 states and the District of Columbia have passed charter school statutes, and by 2009 more than 4,700 charter schools enrolled more than 1.4 million students nationwide (Center for Research on Education Outcomes [CREDO] 2009). Of course, education policy is determined in the political arena, and the unique politics of each of the 50 states will determine whether some form of charter schools will be established and will forge different sets of compromises when drafting charter school legislation. However, while state charter school statutes vary considerably across the states, Buckley and Schneider (2007) identify several defining characteristics of charter schools:

> Broadly defined, charter schools are publicly funded schools that are granted significant autonomy in curriculum and governance in return for greater accountability. In addition, the charter establishing a school is, ideally, a performance contract that details the school's mission, its program and goals, the population served, and ways to assess success (or failure). Charters are granted for fixed lengths of time (usually three to five years), at which time the body that authorized the charter reviews the performance of the school and decides whether or not to renew it. (p. 2)

States writing charter school statutes then must decide such core provisions as the length of the charter, which public bodies may grant them, the extent of charter school autonomy from existing public school laws and rules, and the like.

MICHIGAN NEGOTIATES A CHARTER SCHOOL STATUTE

John Engler was sworn in as Michigan's 46th governor on January 1, 1991. In his campaign, Engler promised greater parental choice in K–12 education. During his first year in office, Michigan was visited by Chubb and Moe, Shankar, and several times by Kolderie. In public speeches and private meetings with government, business, and school leaders, these scholars and educators outlined their conceptions of a new system of charter schools. Rep. Bill Bryant (R. MI) became an early and staunch supporter of this innovation and sponsored legislation, drafted in concert with the governor's office, to enact such a system of autonomous public schools in Michigan.

Michigan's first charter school statute passed the legislature in December 1993 and was signed by Governor Engler in January 1994. Public Act 362 of 1993, which termed the new schools *public school academies* (PSAs), remains one of the most expansive charter school statutes in the country. That is, charters may be granted by local boards of education, boards of intermediate school districts, and the governing boards of community colleges and public universities. In all, more than 600 boards are empowered to issue charters (although the vast majority has thus far declined to do so). This widely distributed chartering authority has produced one of the largest charter school programs in the United States, with only Washington, DC, Arizona, Colorado, and Delaware enrolling a higher percentage of public school students in charter schools in 2006–07 (MDE 2007). However, while Michigan's charter school program is one of the nation's largest, it is also one of the least autonomous, with the statute requiring PSAs to "comply with all applicable law . . . "[2] In essence, Michigan's PSAs are subject to all the laws and rules applicable to traditional public schools. The one notable exception is that teachers and other employees of PSAs are not unionized, save for the few PSAs chartered by local school district boards.

Financing Public School Academies

Under the statute, PSAs were considered school districts, but unlike traditional districts, they had no geographic boundaries beyond their walls, no service area other than the state as a whole, no local property tax base, and no taxing authority of any kind. Except for federal aid available to all Michigan public schools (about 7 percent of operating revenue, on average), public funding for PSA operations would consist entirely of state aid. The question for the legislature at the time was the level of per pupil funding, or foundation allowance, for the new public schools.

Although the 1994 Proposal A reform package had significantly narrowed differences across local districts in per pupil funding, substantial disparities remained. The prevailing sentiment among legislators was that the foundation allowance for a PSA should be set at the level of the traditional district ("host") in which the PSA is located. In this way, PSAs and traditional districts would be on roughly the same financial footing as they compete for students.[3] However, in light of the vast differences in local district foundation allowances, ranging in 1994–95 from $4,200 in many rural districts to more than $10,000 in the most affluent suburban districts, the legislature concluded that PSA allowances should match those of the host district only up to a specified limit. This limit was set at $5,500 for 1994–95, or $500 above the state basic foundation allowance. As such, this cap would be adjusted annually with this basic allowance and would be high enough to guarantee that PSAs established in Michigan's urban districts, where the need for new school choices was perceived to be greatest, would have per pupil funding equal to their hosts. In this way, prospective PSA organizers might be attracted to districts like Detroit, Flint, Saginaw, Pontiac, and Grand Rapids, but would not be tempted to locate in an affluent suburb nearby and reap a financial windfall while luring children away from the inner city.

The Proposal A reforms, and particularly the state's new foundation funding formula, greatly simplified the funding of school operations, including PSAs. But the funding of PSA construction and other capital projects eluded such easy resolution. Proposal A did nothing to change capital funding for Michigan's public schools. All such funding continued to be raised entirely from local property taxes. No state aid was available to local districts for capital projects. This means, of course, that property-rich districts like Bloomfield Hills, Birmingham, Southfield, Ann Arbor, and Jefferson can build new schools or upgrade old ones with relatively low millage rates, while property-poor districts, including most of Michigan's urban districts, have to levy high tax rates to finance capital projects or allow their capital infrastructure to deteriorate.

The legislature decided not to address capital funding for PSAs. The new schools would have to lease or acquire and renovate buildings with a portion of their operating revenue.[4] This financial restriction substantially hindered efforts by independent groups seeking to establish charter schools to acquire sites and undoubtedly contributed to the extraordinary prominence of for-profit educational management organizations (EMOs) in Michigan.[5] These organizations have access to private equity to cover school start-up costs, including school construction or acquisition. Indeed, most of the state universities that have authorized PSAs in Michigan have required that the schools have an EMO contract, largely because of the financial support they provide to the school (Horn and Miron 2000).

EARLY CONTROVERSIES

Ironically, despite the relative lack of autonomy accorded Michigan PSAs by the new law, the statute was challenged in 1994 by a coalition of education groups on the grounds that it violated constitutional requirements for oversight by the SBE (*Council of Organizations and Others for Education about Parochiaid, Inc., et al. v. Engler* 1997). Following the plaintiffs' victory in district court, the Michigan legislature repealed Public Act 362 and passed Public Act 416 of 1994, which explicitly cited the SBE's oversight powers and marginally strengthened state control over PSAs. In passing the new bill, however, the Republican-controlled legislature hedged its bet on the final disposition of the case by inserting a section that would repeal the new law if Public Act 362 were to be subsequently upheld on appeal. Indeed, in 1997 the Michigan Supreme Court reversed the district and appellate courts, holding that the original statute was constitutional and that the repealer inserted into Public Act 416 was valid and enforceable (*Council of Organizations and Others for Education about Parochiaid, Inc. v. Governor* 1997). In the high court's opinion, the original statute in no way compromised SBE "leadership and supervision" of public school academies.

Noah Webster Academy

The new charter statute, however, also eliminated the authority of non-K–12 school district boards to grant charters, and this provision remained in effect throughout the appeals process. This issue arose soon after passage of the original statute when the local board of a small K–6 district in Ionia County, seeing an opportunity to eliminate a district budget deficit with authorizer fees, chartered the Noah Webster Academy, a virtual school linking homeschool families to a small headquarters in Ionia. Backed by Governor Engler, this network quickly preenrolled about 1,300 students on the promise of state revenue for home computers and college trust funds for participating families. However, in the face of strong opposition from the legislature and the State Department of Education, the charter was revoked, the law amended, and academy representatives were unable to obtain a charter from any remaining authorizing body.[6]

The Cap

Initially, the Michigan legislature did not impose any limit on the number of schools that could be chartered by any authorizer. However, concerns over the large number of charters granted by the trustees of Central Michigan University in the early years of the program led the legislature to amend the statute in 1996 to limit the total charters issued by the governing boards of Michigan's 15 public universities to 150. This limit, which was reached in 1998, has constrained university chartering ever since.

The "Bay Mills Loophole"

Bay Mills Community College (BMCC), located in the Upper Peninsula's Baraga County, is Michigan's only tribally controlled community college. Unlike the 28 community colleges organized under state law, each with a designated service district, the BMCC district is statewide. Michigan's PSA statute empowers community college governing boards to authorize charter schools anywhere within their respective districts. In 2001, the BMCC Board of Regents chartered PSAs in Bay City and Pontiac. A coalition of traditional public school organizations and supporters challenged these charters by requesting a formal opinion of the Michigan attorney general regarding the scope of BMCC chartering authority. In an opinion issued in September 2001, then Attorney General Jennifer Granholm upheld the authority of the BMCC regents to issue charters statewide.

In essence, BMCC enjoys chartering authority commensurate with that of a public university but without the restriction of the cap. With virtually no room remaining under the university limit, petitioners now had a new source of school charters. Following the 2001 ruling, the

Figure 5.1 Number of PSAs in Michigan

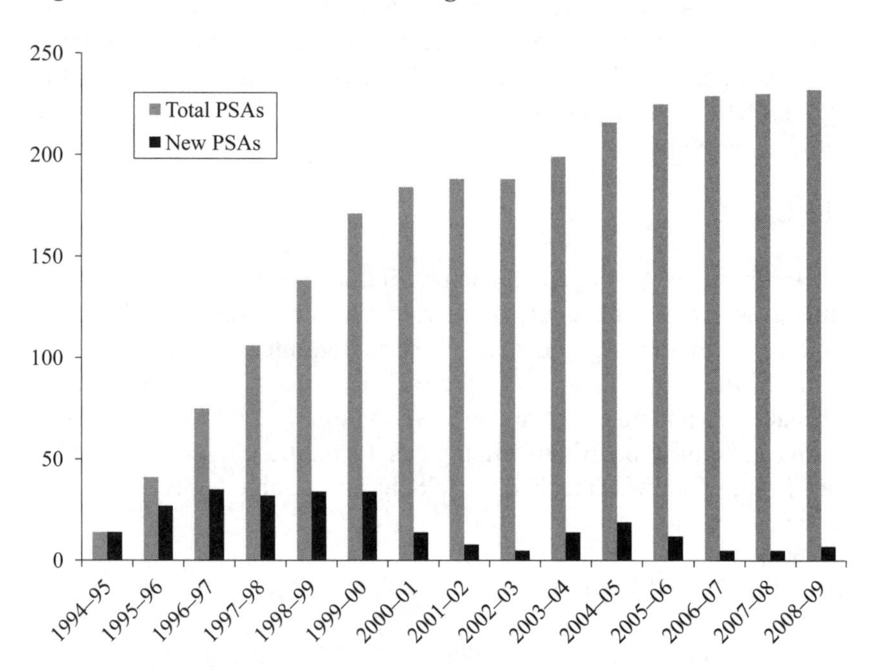

SOURCE: MDE (2008b).

Figure 5.2 Enrollments in Michigan PSAs

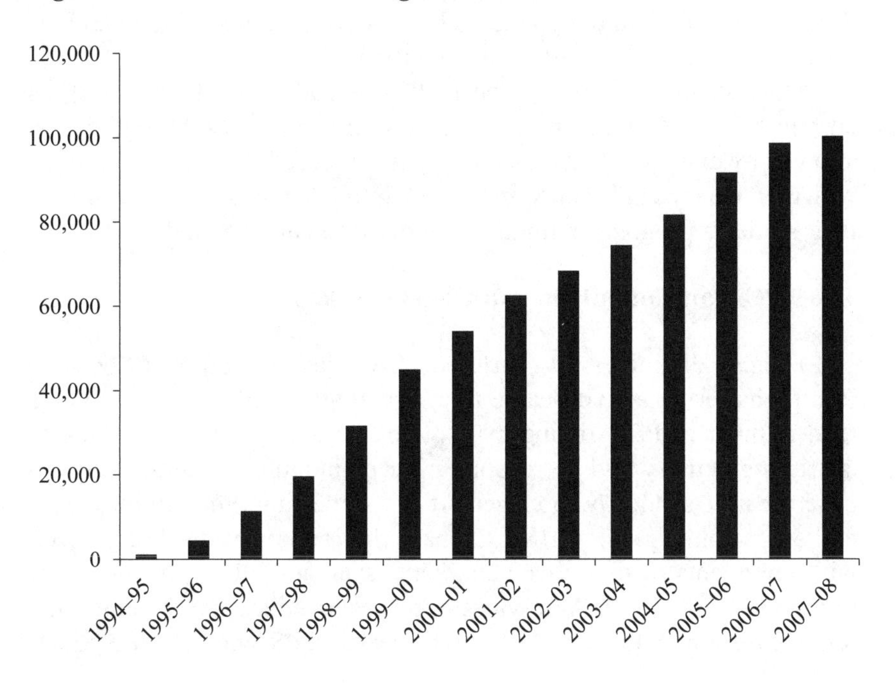

SOURCE: MDE (2008b).

number of BMCC-chartered PSAs grew dramatically, from two in 2001–02 to 35 in 2006–07. Only Central Michigan University, with 57 PSAs, has more. During this six-year period, the BMCC regents accounted for 33 of 68 new PSAs authorized in the state. The growth of Michigan's charter school program is depicted in Figures 5.1 and 5.2.

As Figure 5.1 shows, growth in the number of Michigan PSAs has slowed dramatically in recent years, with net increases of just 7 schools over the last three years examined. Of the 10 new schools opened in 2006 and 2007, 5 were authorized by BMCC. This pattern of slowing growth may be temporary, or it may be an indication that Michigan's charter school movement is reaching maturation. If the latter, then perhaps the pool of potential school organizers is nearing depletion. More likely, however, the state's willing authorizers not subject to the cap (a very small group led by BMCC) are now more concerned with monitoring and supporting their current schools rather than authorizing new ones. Currently, statewide growth in the number of charter schools is difficult to predict, although more charters can be expected in Detroit as state-led reform efforts unfold in the city.

More steady growth is seen in PSA enrollments (Figure 5.2), as current schools expand enrollments and, in some cases, add grades as allowed by existing or amended charters. Often, PSAs begin operations with elementary grades only and "grow into" their charters over time as their students progress to middle school grades and beyond.

The Michigan Commission on Charter Schools

The cap on university-chartered PSAs was reached by 1999. As a result, chartering activity came to a virtual standstill, with Michigan's total number of PSAs rising by a mere two in 2001–02. This lack of chartering activity and corresponding accumulation of unmet demand upset charter school proponents. At the same time, the attorney general's opinion regarding BMCC chartering authority did not sit well with opponents of the movement. This issue and others, including an apparent dearth of PSA services for special education students, the relative responsibilities of PSA authorizers and PSA boards, and poten-

Reprinted with permission.

tial conflicts of interest involving PSA managers and board members, prompted the Michigan legislature in October 2001 to create a special commission on charter schools "to conduct a complete and objective review of all aspects of public school academies in Michigan."

The eight-member commission, chaired by Michigan State University President Peter McPherson, gathered data and commentary through hearings, Web site postings, research, and mail and e-mail communications during late 2001 and early 2002 and issued its report, *Charter Schools in Michigan*, in April 2002.[7] Key recommendations included a stronger role for the superintendent of public instruction in overseeing PSA authorizing bodies, greater protections against possible conflicts of interest involving PSA board members, administrators, and school management companies, and greater emphasis on PSA responsibilities in special education. Most notably, the commission recommended that the cap on conventional charters issued by public universities be raised from 150 to 205 over six years and that BMCC, as a statewide authorizing body, be subject to this restriction. The report also called for the creation of up to 175 "special purpose" charters over 15 years for children with academic or socioeconomic deficits. A bill incorporating most of the commission recommendations, including BMCC, the higher cap on university-authorized PSAs, and enhanced state oversight, was quickly introduced in the legislature but fell one vote short of passage in the House. A second House vote garnered even less support, and the highly touted commission report was quietly left for dead. At that point, the Michigan legislature turned its attention to the state's dwindling employment level and mounting budget deficits, an issue that has occupied much of their attention ever since.

STUDENT ACHIEVEMENT IN CHARTER SCHOOLS: THE NATIONAL PERSPECTIVE

Although our national experience with charter school programs is now entering its 17th year, the impact of charter schools on student achievement remains a most contentious question among researchers and educators nationwide. The central question, of course, is whether charter schools are more effective than traditional, district-based public schools in improving student achievement. The greatest challenge in making this comparison arises from the selectivity of charter schools. That is, students are not randomly assigned to charter schools; rather, they choose to attend. Consequently, comparisons of the achievement levels or growth in charter schools and traditional schools must be conditioned on differences between the two student populations. Ideally, this research question requires longitudinal student-level data on students who are randomly assigned to charter and traditional public schools. Two such experimental research projects have been launched by the U.S. Department of Education's Institute for Education Sciences, but definitive findings are probably three to five years away (Buckley and Schneider 2007).

While we await the results of this experimental research, we have conflicting findings from several statistical studies. A 2004 study by the National Center for Education Statistics reports that, for students from the same racial and ethnic backgrounds, achievement levels in reading and mathematics in charter schools do not differ from those in other public schools (U.S. Department of Education 2004). However, analyzing the same NAEP data in 2004, researchers with the American Federation of Teachers (AFT) report that charter school students had lower achievement in reading and mathematics than students in traditional public schools. The differences were significant for all students as well as low-income students and students from the inner city. No significant difference in achievement was found for minority students (Nelson, Rosenberg, and Van Meter 2004).

This AFT study, reported favorably on the front page of the *New York Times*, drew a critical response. Harvard economist Caroline Hoxby argued that the study was flawed because it relied on an inadequate sample and failed to properly consider differences in educability between charter and traditional school children. Hoxby's own study (2004) examined a matched sample of charter and traditional schools. Specifically, Hoxby matched each charter school with its nearest traditional public school, both geographically and in terms of racial composition and then computed the difference in the percentage of students proficient in reading and mathematics in the 4th grade on the state assessment. Hoxby concluded that: " . . . although it is too early to draw sweeping conclusions, the initial indications are that the average student attending a charter school has higher achievement than he or she otherwise would . . . " (p. 3).

Hoxby's study was praised by critics of the AFT study, but sharply criticized by researchers at the Economic Policy Institute, a liberal Washington, DC, think tank, who argued that her methodology did not adequately control for differences in student characteristics. By their reanalysis of Hoxby's data set, supplemented with additional data to control for these differences, the achievement advantage for charter schools disappears for both reading and mathematics (Roy and Mishel 2004).

The question of charter schools' impact on student achievement is inextricably tied to the question of whether charter school students are harder to educate than their traditional public school counterparts. Buckley and Schneider (2007) analyze data from the 2002–03 school year in Washington, DC, to answer this question: Do charter schools enroll students who are harder to educate, do they attract more motivated or more socioeconomically advantaged students in their communities, or do they do both to some extent?

Using a sophisticated Bayesian statistical model and Markov Chain Monte Carlo estimation method, Buckley and Schneider (2007) find mixed evidence for a difference in educability as proxied by free/reduced price lunch, special education, and English language learner student categories. While they find greater concentrations of low-income children in DC charter schools on the average, the charter schools had proportionately fewer English language learners and about the same fraction of special education students. The authors also examine student-level survey data on additional characteristics related to educability, including student mobility, attitudes toward school, home environment, and peers. They conclude: "In general, we find scant evidence that charter-school students in DC are harder to educate than students in the traditional schools" (p. 94).

The most comprehensive and sophisticated charter school evaluation reported to date has been undertaken by researchers at Stanford University's CREDO. The researchers assembled longitudinal student-level achievement data from 14 states and the District of Columbia to assess the impact of charter schooling on student learning gains.[8] This landmark study compares the educational achievement levels and academic growth of charter school students to equivalent students in traditional public schools that the charter students themselves attended before enrolling in charter schools. This national "head-to-head" assessment of the performance of charter schools reveals that 17 percent of the charter schools outperformed their traditional district school counterparts, nearly half of the charter schools showed results that were statistically indistinguishable from local public schools, and 37 percent of the charter schools significantly underperformed their traditional counterparts.

This study, which is rich in detail and only briefly summarized here, also finds that charter students in elementary and middle school grades make greater progress than their traditional public school peers, but students in charter high schools and charter multilevel schools have significantly worse results. At the same time, however, the study also reveals significant variation in charter school performance across the states (CREDO 2009).

CHARTER SCHOOL PERFORMANCE: EVIDENCE FROM MICHIGAN

As we've pointed out, any valid assessment of Michigan's charter schools must recognize that their students are not randomly selected from the local school-age population; rather, they are self-selected.[9] Even in instances where charter school slots are oversubscribed and enrollees are selected by lottery, the self-selection bias remains because the families electing to enter the lottery may differ in important ways (e.g., level of interest or involvement in the child's school and education) from families who do not. Accordingly, this section will examine the characteristics of Michigan's PSA students as compared with those of traditional public schools in both host districts and statewide. Also, in view of the rapidly growing research literature affirming the importance of teacher quality for student learning (e.g., Rockoff 2004; Murnane and Steele 2007), we will consider some important differences between PSA teachers and teachers in traditional public schools.

PSA Students

PSA students in Michigan are disproportionately urban, minority, and poor. Over half are eligible for free or reduced price lunch, compared with 34 percent of traditional public school students statewide. However, as indicated in Figure 5.3, the ethnicities of PSA students closely resemble those of the 17 urban school districts that house three-fourths of them.[10] African American students comprise 56 percent of PSA enrollments and 59 percent of host district enrollments, but only 18 percent of traditional school enrollments statewide. Caucasian students comprise 34 percent of PSA enrollments and 29 percent of host district enrollments, but fully 74 percent of traditional school enrollments. Hispanic, Asian, and other races comprise the balance of enrollments in the schools.

Figure 5.3 Student Enrollment by Ethnicity, 2006–07 (%)

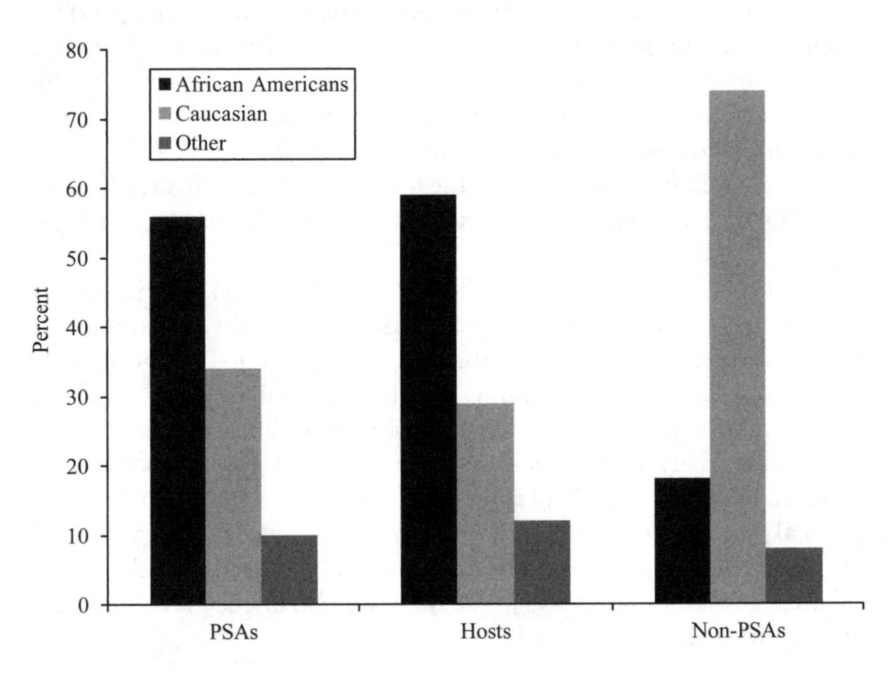

SOURCE: MDE (2007).

PSA Teachers

The quality of a charter school, or any school, is determined by the teachers in the school. A growing "teacher effects" literature confirms the importance of good teaching for student learning (Rockoff 2004; Rivkin, Hanushek, and Kain 2005; Murnane and Steele 2007). These findings based on measures of student achievement gains confirm our intuition, but researchers have been challenged to identify observable teacher characteristics or credentials that may be associated with effectiveness in the classroom. The question is important. Principals, department heads, and parents need to identify good teachers without benefit of *ex post* analyses of student achievement gains. Instead, they must rely on a review of standard teacher credentials such as license or certification held, undergraduate school, major and minor areas of study, and teaching experience. Selecting those who will excel in the classroom can be daunting.

Two characteristics that have been indicative of teaching effectiveness and are often used as proxy measures of teacher quality are certification or license held and teaching experience. Teachers with the highest level of professional certification have been found to demonstrate effectiveness in the classroom (Darling-Hammond 2000). And recent research has confirmed that teachers improve dramatically over the first three or four years on the job (Rivkin, Hanushek, and Kain 2005).

A recent analysis of 2005–06 data on Michigan public school teachers has revealed some sharp contrasts in the quality proxies noted above between PSA teachers and teachers in traditional public schools (Gawlik, Addonizio, and Kearney 2010). These findings, along with data on relative salary levels, are summarized in Table 5.1.

As the analysis reveals, Michigan PSAs employ proportionally fewer fully certified teachers and more substitute teachers than their traditional counterparts. Further, PSA teachers are much less experienced than teachers in traditional public schools and earn substantially lower salaries, as one would expect given the lower experience levels and the absence of teacher unions in PSAs.[11]

Table 5.1 Teacher Characteristics and Salary Levels in PSAs and Traditional Public Schools, 2005–06

Dependent variable	PSAs	Traditional districts
Percent certified	57.77	74.51
	(16.39)	(8.89)
Percent substitute	42.23	25.49
	(25.04)	(10.40)
Average years teaching	4.15	12.00
	(1.35)	(2.17)
Average salary ($)	37,337	54,739

NOTE: Standard deviations are in parentheses.
SOURCE: Gawlik, Addonizio, and Kearney (2010).

ACADEMIC OUTCOMES

As noted earlier, the best comparison of charter school performance with that of traditional public schools would be drawn from a randomized experiment. Unfortunately, no such experiment has been conducted here in Michigan, so we draw our comparisons from published, nonexperimental research studies that attempt in various ways to deal with the issue of student comparability between PSAs and traditional schools. As we will see, these studies also vary in the statistical rigor used to control for important differences between these two student populations.

Horn and Miron (2000) analyze MEAP data for five years—from 1995–96 to 1999–2000. They compare charter schools as a group with the aggregate performance of their host districts (i.e., the school district in which the PSA is geographically located) and then compare change scores in the percentage of students demonstrating proficiency for individual PSAs over two, three, and four years with change scores for traditional schools in host districts. In general, they find that host district students outperform charter school students in percentage of students achieving proficiency. This finding was consistent in all subjects and grade levels tested through grade 7.[12] The authors add, however, that many individual charter schools showed greater yearly improvement in test scores than the traditional host schools. Finally, the authors compare the performance of students in EMO-run charter schools with their counterparts in non-EMO charters and find roughly equal four-year proficiency rates across all subject areas for the two school groups.

Eberts and Hollenbeck (2001), using a more rigorous statistical methodology to control for differences in PSA and traditional school student populations, analyze student MEAP scores for 4th and 5th graders for three school years, 1996–97 through 1998–99. They use a set of models to estimate differences in achievement between charter students and traditional public school students in the host districts. Each charter school was paired with its host public school district, and statistical controls were used for differences across students, schools, and districts. The authors find that students attending a charter school scored about 2–4 percent lower on 4th grade reading and math assessments than their traditional public school counterparts. They also find PSA students lagging traditional school students in host districts by about 4 percent on the 5th grade science test and about 6–9 percent on the 5th grade writing test. And the authors note that their results may understate the achievement gaps between PSA students and students in traditional schools because, despite their sophisticated methodology, they were unable to fully control for the bias resulting from the self-selection of PSA students. Finally, the authors find evidence that Michigan's PSAs appear to improve their relative performance over time.[13]

Michigan Department of Education

The most up-to-date analysis is provided by the MDE. As with the earlier studies, the measure of academic achievement is taken from the MEAP, the sole assessment available for all PSAs and traditional schools in the state.[14] The following results are taken from the fall 2006 elementary and middle school testing and spring 2007 high school testing. As we have emphasized, the effect of charter schools on student achievement can be reasonably accurately gauged only by comparing the performance of charter school students with the performance of traditional, district-based students of equivalent social and economic backgrounds. Accordingly, the MDE compares aggregate PSA scores on MEAP and the MME with the aggregate scores of traditional schools in the host districts as well as with aggregate scores of all traditional schools statewide. While the latter comparison is of interest, the former is a more valid indicator of the relative effectiveness of PSAs.

Elementary and Middle Schools

For aggregate performance in grades 3–8, as measured by the percentage of students who met or exceeded state standards, PSA students outperformed their traditional public school counterparts in the 17 host districts in both English Language Arts (ELA) and mathematics, although the advantage is not substantial. These comparisons are depicted in Table 5.2.

The MDE analysis shows also that both the PSAs as a group and the host districts badly lag the state's traditional public schools in both ELA and mathematics at the elementary and middle school levels.

Some evidence indicates that charter schools improve modestly the longer they are open, at least over the short term. The MDE compared aggregate ELA and mathematics proficiency for grades 3–8 for fall 2006 for three PSA groups: 1) schools open one to three years at the time of testing, 2) those open four to six years, and 3) those operating seven years or more. Aggregate proficiency was slightly higher in both ELA and mathematics for the schools in the four- to six-year category as compared with the new schools, although the advantage is so small as to be inconsequential. The difference in aggregate proficiency is more substantial between the PSAs that have operated seven years or more and both groups of newer schools. These comparisons are depicted in Figure 5.4.

This finding is intuitive. As noted above, the rapidly growing research literature on teacher quality reveals that teachers are the most important school-based influence on student achievement and that their effectiveness improves dramatically over the first three or four

Table 5.2 Fall 2005 and Fall 2006, Grades 3–8, MEAP Percent Proficient

	ELA		Math	
	2005	2006	2005	2006
PSAs	62.9	65.7	57.3	61.3
Hosts	59.3	61.2	51.7	56.1
Non-PSAs	75.2	77.4	72.2	75.7

SOURCE: MDE (2007).

Figure 5.4 Grades 3–8 MEAP Proficiency by Age of PSA, Fall 2006 Percent Proficient

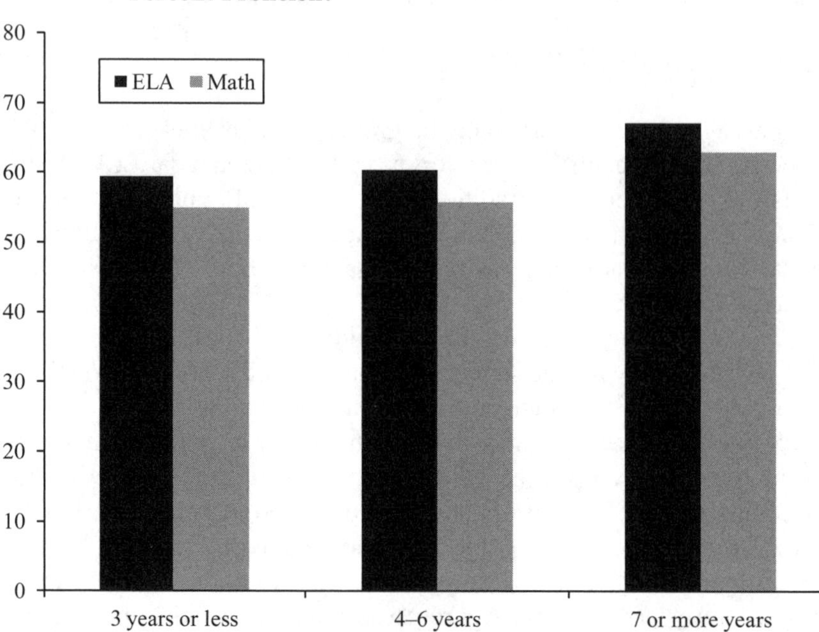

SOURCE: MDE (2007).

years of teaching (Rockoff 2004; Rivkin, Hanushek, and Kain 2005; Goldhaber 2007). The evidence on improvement in teaching effectiveness after four years is mixed, with some studies finding improvement over many years (Clotfelter, Ladd, and Vigdor 2006) and others not (Rivkin, Hanushek, and Kain 2005). It is entirely possible that the age of the PSA in the MDE analysis is a proxy for staff experience and competence. A study of teachers and administrators working in Michigan's PSAs would shed light on this important question of PSA quality and maturation.

Student Subgroups

The MDE analysis also disaggregated 2005 and 2006 MEAP data to examine achievement for four major student subgroups: 1) economically disadvantaged, 2) African Americans, 3) Hispanics, and 4) students with disabilities. These comparisons are presented in Table 5.3.

The panels of Table 5.3 reveal that PSAs consistently outperformed the host district schools, with an advantage in both subjects and both years across all four student groups. The advantage is most pronounced with special education students, the group for which the issue of self-selection, or nonrandom student sorting, may be the most serious. That is, students with more serious learning deficits may remain in traditional public schools where specially trained staff are more readily available. Nevertheless, the apparent advantage of the PSAs over the host district schools is notable and calls for closer statistical analysis to disentangle school effects from effects of family and peers.

Also noteworthy is the advantage of Michigan PSAs over all traditional schools with respect to African American students in mathematics for 2005 and 2006 and for ELA in 2006. The differences are small and

Table 5.3 Aggregate Achievement of Student Subgroups, 2005 and 2006, Grades 3–8, Percent Proficient

	2005		2006	
Student subgroup	Math	ELA	Math	ELA
Economically disadvantaged				
PSA	51.1	55.3	54.8	59.2
Host	44.7	52.0	49.9	55.2
Traditional	57.1	60.0	62.0	64.0
African American				
PSA	46.4	54.6	51.9	59.3
Host	42.0	52.4	47.3	55.2
Traditional	45.2	55.0	50.9	57.9
Hispanic				
PSA	60.1	60.7	59.8	61.4
Host	50.5	52.6	55.3	56.2
Traditional	59.2	61.0	63.8	64.4
Students with disabilities				
PSA	35.1	31.2	37.6	35.4
Host	23.4	22.4	28.2	24.5
Traditional	41.1	37.0	45.1	39.3

SOURCE: MDE (2007).

may be statistically insignificant and so too for the traditional schools' relative advantage over PSAs in 2005 ELA results. Nonetheless, these results should dispel any impressions that PSA performance systematically lags that of traditional schools in all student categories. On the contrary, these descriptive analyses suggest that Michigan's PSAs are relatively effective with our hard-to-educate student subgroups.

Of course, aggregate analyses like this one mask substantial differences among individual schools. In an analysis of 2005–06 MEAP scores for elementary and middle schools in the Detroit metropolitan region (i.e., Wayne, Oakland, and Macomb counties), Gawlik, Addonizio, and Kearney (2010) find substantial variation across PSAs in the percentage of students achieving proficiency. These findings are summarized in Table 5.4.

High School Achievement

Administered for the first time in spring 2007 to 11th graders, the MME consists of three parts: 1) the ACT college entrance examination;

Table 5.4 MEAP Performance for PSAs in Wayne, Oakland, and Macomb Counties, 2005–06

Percent proficient	*N*	Minimum	Maximum	Mean	Standard deviation
ELA					
Grade 3	85	18.80	97.00	61.0941	17.12612
Grade 4	84	8.30	96.40	53.9226	17.28403
Grade 5	82	15.80	94.70	54.0256	18.03876
Grade 6	80	21.80	94.70	60.4313	16.31519
Grade 7	68	10.20	90.40	55.2559	18.42338
Grade 8	66	0.00	86.50	51.8697	18.96947
Math					
Grade 3	85	28.60	100.00	73.7541	15.46249
Grade 4	85	22.20	100.00	59.1329	16.49170
Grade 5	82	7.90	94.70	47.7012	19.96498
Grade 6	80	7.10	96.40	37.8600	21.03768
Grade 7	68	2.60	89.30	32.9176	18.44046
Grade 8	66	0.00	90.90	37.9985	20.54055

SOURCE: Gawlik, Addonizio, and Kearney (2010).

2) the WorkKeys job skills assessments in reading and mathematics; and 3) Michigan assessments in mathematics, science, social studies, and persuasive writing. The aggregate percent proficient for PSAs, host-district high schools, and traditional high schools are depicted in Figure 5.5.

As Figure 5.5 makes clear, Michigan's high school PSAs substantially underperformed their host district counterparts on the 2007 MME in both ELA and mathematics. Further, both of these school groups lagged far behind all traditional Michigan high schools in both subjects. Aggregate student proficiency was particularly dismal (9.5 percent and 4.2 percent in ELA and mathematics, respectively) in PSA high schools that had been open three years or less. Proficiency was substantially higher in older PSA high schools, but still lagged the levels of traditional high schools by a wide margin. This pattern of lagging PSA achievement is also found for economically disadvantaged students and African American students.[15] These comparisons are presented in Table 5.5.

Figure 5.5 High School MME, Spring 2007, Percent Proficient

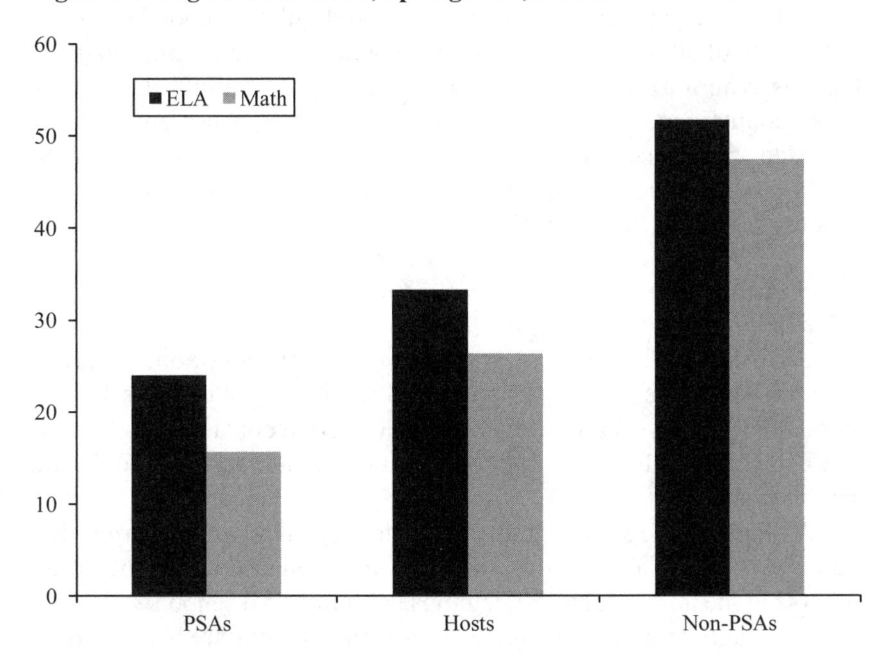

SOURCE: MDE (2007).

Table 5.5 Aggregate Achievement of Student Subgroups Spring 2007 MME, Grade 11, Percent Proficient

	ELA	Math
Economically disadvantaged		
PSA	14.6	7.7
Host	19.9	12.8
Traditional	30.1	25.2
African American		
PSA	14.8	5.9
Host	22.6	12.9
Traditional	23.5	14.6

SOURCE: MDE (2007).

Attendance Rates

Both the federal NCLB statute and Michigan state law require that public school attendance and graduation rates be monitored. Further, the Michigan School Code requires a minimum attendance rate of 70 percent for the payment of state aid for an individual school day. Obviously, school attendance is viewed as essential for academic progress. On this criterion, Michigan's PSAs appear to lag behind their traditional counterparts. For the 2005–06 school year, 17.8 percent of PSAs recorded attendance rates below 90 percent, compared with 5.9 percent for traditional schools in host districts and 6.2 percent for traditional schools statewide (MDE 2007).[16]

Graduation Rates

Statistics on high school graduation rates are notoriously unreliable. Different methodologies can yield wildly disparate rates for the same school or district. However, application of a consistent methodology can yield a valid comparison of graduation rates across schools and school systems.

As Figure 5.6 reveals, graduation rates for Michigan's charter high schools compare favorably with rates reported for traditional high schools in the host districts but lag those of traditional schools statewide by a substantial margin. Of course, these comparisons are hampered by the small size of the PSA high school population, with just over 17,000

Figure 5.6 High School Graduation Rates, 2005–06 (percent of schools in each category)

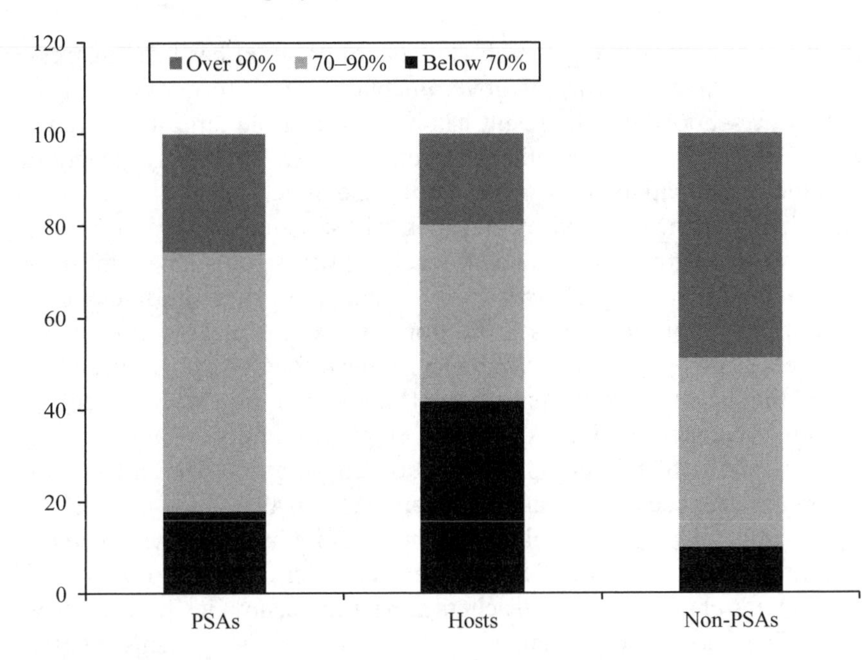

NOTE: Based on unweighted school counts.
SOURCE: MDE (2007).

students, and the lack of PSA data disaggregated by student subgroups.[17] And, again, these mean values mask variation across individual PSAs.

Nevertheless, the data on PSA graduation rates are roughly consistent with the general pattern of outcomes described earlier for elementary and middle schools. Public school academies tend to be located in districts with low-achieving schools and equal or exceed the academic performance of these schools on average. At the same time, Michigan's charter schools fall well below the average academic performance of Michigan's traditional public schools, hardly an unexpected outcome given the disproportionately high poverty rate among PSA children.[18]

SUMMING UP

In one sense, Michigan's charter school program has been aggressive in that a wide array of governmental bodies are empowered to authorize schools and the result has been one of the largest programs in the United States. In another respect, however, Michigan's program is quite conservative. That is, unlike the theoretical ideal of new public schools unencumbered by state school laws and rules and offering innovative programs fashioned by teachers, Michigan's PSAs are subject to the full panoply of laws and rules that apply to traditional public schools, save for those laws (e.g., property taxation and election laws) that reflect differences in governance. Indeed, one could persuasively argue that Michigan's PSAs represent innovation only with respect to school governance and the absence of employee unions.[19]

The result of this compromise between program size and school autonomy has been the creation of many schools that "play it safe," as opposed to progressive, teacher-led centers of innovation envisioned by the intellectual founders of the charter movement. In fact, in many of Michigan's charter schools, teachers appear to occupy positions clearly subordinate to school managers. As noted earlier, Michigan's charter school program is unique among the states in the prevalence of EMO-run schools, with their prepackaged curricula, policies, and procedures. Teachers are often untenured, at-will contractors with little autonomy and professional discretion. At the same time, however, the resulting tendency toward uniformity as opposed to experimentation and innovation has its appeal. Charter school observers have noted that the freedom inherent in some state programs is no guarantee of success. As several education scholars have observed, "Freed from bureaucratic regulations and union rules, many of the best educators can design excellent charter schools. But freed from these rules, many of the worst educators can design terrible schools" (Carnoy et al. 2005, p. 118).

Perhaps it is not surprising, then, that Michigan's PSA program has been neither a disaster nor an unqualified success. Some schools are excellent, many have waiting lists, some struggle with poor management and poor outcomes for students, and some have been closed. And the system has slowly evolved, despite the Michigan legislature's quick relegation of the charter school commission report to the circular file. The cap on university-authorized charters, the main issue prompting the commission's creation, remains in place for now but has been attenuated to a degree by the rise of BMCC as a statewide authorizer. However, BMCC may be nearing their capacity for acceptable PSA oversight as reflected in the slowing growth of their program. In any event, they remain Michigan's sole statewide authorizer not subject to the cap and it is difficult to know whether the dearth of new charters in recent years reflects limited demand on the part of school organizers or limited capacity of authorizers.

Another notable addition to Michigan's PSA law was a provision empowering public university governing boards to authorize up to 15 "urban high school academies" in Detroit.[20] Urban high school academies may employ as a classroom teacher any full-time tenured or tenure-track faculty member from the authorizing university. Each academy must operate grades 9–12 within three years of opening and may include any other grades, including kindergarten and early childhood education. At the time of this writing, two urban high school academies were operating in Detroit and a third was being prepared for a fall 2009 opening. All three academies were authorized by Grand Valley State University.

LOOKING AHEAD: SOME OUTSTANDING ISSUES

Aside from the cap, the commission addressed two additional policy issues that continue to engage policymakers. Both are discussed at length in the *MDE 2007 Report to the Legislature*. The first concerns the lack of authority of the superintendent of public instruction over authorizing bodies to ensure they fulfill their responsibilities for PSA oversight, while the second arises from the apparent inability of many PSA boards to effectively oversee the activities of the EMOs they hire to run their schools. In effect, the EMOs control the boards in many instances. Both issues arise from the rather elaborate but loosely structured regulatory system created by the legislature to govern their large charter school system. Let's consider each in turn.

The Role of the Superintendent

The Michigan Constitution assigns general leadership and supervision of public schools to the SBE and empowers it to hire a superintendent of public instruction to execute SBE policy. The superintendent and the State Department of Education are mandated by statute to enforce laws relating to public schools, including PSAs. However, while the Michigan School Code empowers the superintendent to enforce school laws for PSAs, including rulemaking regarding pupil and financial accounting and school safety, the commission found substantial gaps in the superintendent's statutory authority over PSAs, particularly PSA authorizers. Specifically, although the commission stated that PSA authorizers should exercise primary oversight of charter schools, the commission called for amendments in the charter school law to require the superintendent to periodically certify the authorizers' performance in four areas: 1) holding PSA boards accountable for meeting academic standards, 2) enforcing contracts they sign with PSA boards and EMOs, 3) ensuring compliance with state law, and 4) the financial management of the schools.

The Role of the Authorizer

The authorizing body lies at the heart of charter school governance. It is the charter school's source of legitimacy as a public school. Initially described by Kolderie as "a publicly elected body with an education mission," these entities substitute for the elected local board of education as the charter school's source of legitimacy as a public institution.[21] They are designated and empowered by statute to authorize charter schools and hold them accountable to the public by issuing and enforcing contracts that specify the educational and financial responsibilities of the school. The authorizer's regulatory role consists of monitoring the actions of charter school boards and ensuring their compliance with the charter contract and all applicable law. The authorizer also acts as the fiscal agent for its charter schools. All state aid to which the school is entitled flows through the authorizer. Michigan's charter school statute allows authorizers to charge oversight fees of up to 3 percent of total state aid. In return, authorizers are responsible for ensuring that their PSAs uphold the public trust.

The Role of the PSA Board

The commission report stated that "the frontline responsibility to run the school" rests with the PSA board and expressed concern over testimony about the apparent lack of independence of PSA boards from the EMOs they hired to run their schools. The commission called upon the legislature to amend the charter school statute to require authorizers to include in their contracts with PSA boards a set of requirements that would strengthen both authorizer and board control over EMOs. These requirements were intended as safeguards against conflicts of interests whereby PSA boards would hire close relatives to run the schools, pay individual PSA employees for more than one full-time position (e.g., assistant principal and teacher), and generally place the interests of EMO principals and shareholders before those of the students and the public. The recommended amendments also required authorizers to approve all contracts between PSA boards and EMOs.

These policy issues continue to be debated in Michigan and are addressed in the *MDE 2007 Report to the Legislature*. However, while the commission report recommended specific amendments to Michigan's charter school statute, the MDE report calls on the legislature to grant the superintendent of public instruction rulemaking authority over authorizers and raises specific concerns about PSA board relationships with EMOs. First, EMO administrators are often involved in recruiting board members and recommending their appointment to authorizers. Second, many EMO contracts are turnkey agreements by which the EMO controls all revenue available to the PSA board and manages all aspects of school operations. Moreover, in many instances the EMO owns the school building and much of the school's furniture and equipment (Horn and Miron 2000). Such an arrangement can easily compromise the board's ability to effectively represent the school's and students' interests when negotiating service agreements and fees with the EMO. The MDE report also expresses concerns over the lack of statutory requirements for authorizers' oversight of these PSA-EMO contracts and concludes with a call for legislation giving the superintendent rule-making authority to set specific standards for such authorizer oversight.

POLICY EQUILIBRIUM OR POLICY STALEMATE?

These concerns, raised in several studies of Michigan's charter school program, including both the 2002 commission and 2007 MDE reports, and the legislature's unwillingness to address them reflect Michigan's ambivalence toward its charter schools. That is, these schools should stand apart from the traditional public schools and provide families with alternative educational options. But they should not constitute a separate public school system. They should be autonomous from local district boards but not from state laws and rules. They should be judged on the basis of student achievement, but their administrative practices should be closely scrutinized by the state. The program should be large in scale, but should not approach the degree of independence envisioned by Chubb, Moe, Kolderie, and other intellectual founders of the charter school movement. Indeed, observing the abundance of Michigan's franchise-like, EMO-run PSAs, with 100 schools run by eight companies and 34 by NHA alone, one is left to wonder what happened to the program creators' vision of autonomous, teacher-led centers of educational innovation, free from the bureaucratic burdens of traditional schools.

On the other hand, it is entirely possible that the evolution of Michigan's charter school program, including the ascendency of EMOs, reflects an equilibrium or consensus that has emerged from the state's political and economic environment. Certainly charter school laws in Michigan and across the states have been motivated by a desire to improve children's academic achievement. But they serve other ends as well. Charter schools provide families in urban areas with an opportunity to send their children to smaller and, at least in their view, safer schools. Charter schools also introduce competition to the public school system, and they respond to the public's demand for educational choice while stopping short of, and perhaps guarding against, more radical and controversial voucher proposals. Viewed this way, Michigan's charter school program is not an unfinished educational innovation derailed by political stalemate and economic distress, but rather a workable compromise emerging from the state's evolving political economy and one of Michigan's most important school reforms of the past 30 years.

Notes

1. The term *charter school* was coined by Ray Budde (1974), a retired education professor, in a 1974 conference paper. American Federation of Teachers President Al Shankar (1988a,b) further developed the concept in a 1988 address to the National Press Club and in a *New York Times* column. Both Budde and Shankar envisioned these new public schools as teacher-run laboratories for instructional innovations, created with permission from the local school district board (Vergari 2007).
2. As one might expect, this point was the subject of vigorous debate in the legislature. An early draft of the bill limited PSAs' mandates to only a relatively short list of statutory citations, but proponents of greater state control (generally Democrats) held sway on this issue and inserted the broader language.
3. Such "equality" would be rough, indeed, as the overall financial condition of a school district depends on enrollment trends, operating costs, cash management, and other factors.
4. Some PSA boards have taken innovative approaches to capital funding. For example, the boards of Chandler Park Academy and Detroit Community High School issued tax-exempt, fixed-rate revenue bonds backed by future school operating revenue (*Gongwer News Service* 2005).
5. The MDE reports that for the 2006–07 school year, 61 percent of Michigan's PSA boards (serving two-thirds of the state's charter school students) elected to hire an EMO to run some or all of their school operations. These contracts range from facility management to personnel management, accounting and payroll, curriculum development, and professional development for teachers and administrators. Michigan's percentage of EMO-run schools far exceeds the national average of 10 percent. Indeed, the next highest states are Ohio and New York, at merely 33 percent and 26 percent, respectively.
6. A much smaller school, with students in attendance at the Ionia County facility, was subsequently chartered, but the notion of a virtual school was abandoned.
7. Coauthor Addonizio served on the commission. In addition to Chairman McPherson, the commission included Superintendent of Public Instruction Tom Watkins, Michigan Education Association President Lu Battaglieri, local school board member Sheri Thompson, educator Carmen A. N'Namdi, Professor Louann Bierlein Palmer, and attorney Richard McLellan.
8. The states participating in this study are Arizona, Arkansas, California, Colorado (Denver only), Florida, Georgia, Illinois (Chicago only), Louisiana, Minnesota, Missouri, New Mexico, North Carolina, Ohio, and Texas.
9. This section draws primarily on Horn and Miron (2000), Eberts and Hollenbeck (2001), and MDE (2006b, 2007).
10. In 2006–07, these host districts were Ann Arbor, Benton Harbor, Dearborn, Detroit, Flint, Grand Rapids, Hamtramck, Highland Park, Inkster, Jackson, Lansing, Muskegon, Pontiac, Port Huron, Saginaw, Southfield, and Wayne-Westland.
11. The sole exception with respect to unions applies to those few PSAs that are authorized by the boards of local school districts.

12. The authors did not compare charter high school student scores with host high school student scores because the specialized nature of some charters (i.e., serving at-risk students) threatened the validity of such comparisons.
13. Interestingly, Eberts and Hollenbeck (2001) find that PSAs managed by EMOs had lower test scores relative to traditional schools than self-managed PSAs. This finding is particularly notable because of the extraordinary presence of EMO-run charter schools in Michigan, as noted earlier.
14. In addition to MEAP, several authorizers use additional standardized assessments (e.g., Gates-McGinnite, Iowa Test of Basic Skills, Scantron Performance Series) to monitor the academic progress of students in their respective schools as a part of their oversight activities.
15. No analysis of Hispanic students or students with learning disabilities was possible due to insufficient sample size.
16. Figures are based on unweighted school counts.
17. While Michigan's PSAs continued to enroll proportionately more K–5 students (57.4 percent) than either host districts (42.9 percent) or traditional districts (40.7 percent) in 2006–07, the number of PSA high school students more than doubled over the 2001–02 through 2006–07 period, generally through the addition of high school grades by existing PSAs.
18. In 2006–07, over half of Michigan's PSA students were eligible for free or reduced price lunch, as compared with about one-third of traditional school students (MDE 2007, p. 5).
19. Again, the exception would be those PSAs chartered by local district school boards, a very small fraction of the whole PSA program.
20. Public Act 179 of 2003. Chartered under a separate part (6C) of the PSA statute, UHSAs are not subject to the 150-school cap imposed on university-chartered schools.
21. Personal communication with the authors.

6
Schools of Choice

Following passage of Public Act 362 of 1993 and subsequent legislation that created Michigan's charter school program, the Michigan legislature expanded the state's educational choice initiatives by creating a schools of choice program in 1997.[1] This legislation, Section 105 of the School Aid Act, required all local school boards to decide whether or not they would accept nonresident students in their schools. Those districts opting into the program were required to publish the schools, grades, and programs open to nonresidents and then accept applications. If the number of applicants exceeded available slots, enrollees would be selected by random lottery.[2]

Prior to this legislation, students could enroll in other districts as nonresidents in one of two ways. First, they could enroll as tuition students, with tuition calculated according to a (nearly incomprehensible) section of the School Aid Act.[3] Alternatively, the student's district of residence could release the revenue associated with the student to the enrolling district, enabling the student to receive free tuition. As one would expect, such permission was rarely granted. The new "schools of choice" law allowed students to leave any district of residence to enter a choice school within the same intermediate school district (ISD), and the associated revenue (i.e., foundation allowance) followed automatically. Specifically, the enrolling district receives the lesser of the foundation allowance of the resident district and the enrolling district. Further, the enrolling district is prohibited from charging tuition in any form to make up any revenue differences.

Michigan's schools of choice program was expanded in 2000 to include contiguous districts outside the ISD and to include districts in any contiguous ISD the following year.[4] As with the 1997 legislation, local school boards electing to enroll nonresidents were required to select such students by lottery if their district was oversubscribed and, again, the enrolling district receives the lower of its own and the resident district's per pupil foundation allowance. Districts electing to enroll nonresidents are not required to provide transportation to choice schools, although anecdotal evidence reveals that some districts do send school buses into neighboring districts for this purpose.

While adopting both charter schools and schools of choice, Michigan legislators and voters defeated two efforts to institute school voucher programs in the state. In 1999, Senate Bill 31 was introduced to give vouchers to students in cities with a population exceeding 750,000. The proposal, of course, would have impacted only the Detroit school district. Students from families earning less than 150 percent of the federal poverty level would have been eligible for the vouchers. The bill, however, died in committee.

Following the demise of Senate Bill 31, business executive and former Michigan Board of Education member Richard DeVos led a coalition of education, civic, and business leaders in forming Kids First! Yes! which sought to amend the Michigan Constitution to give parents whose children attend school in districts that failed to graduate two-thirds of their students a publicly funded voucher worth one-half of the district's per pupil expenditure to attend a school of their choosing. As a sweetener, Proposal 1 would have guaranteed that public school spending would never fall below the current level and would have required teacher testing in academic subjects.[5] Opponents of the proposal organized under the name All Kids First! On November 7, 2000, Michigan voters defeated Proposal 1 by a margin of more than 2 to 1.

Among the various forms of K–12 school choice, voucher programs, which encompass private as well as public schools, are easily the most controversial. This controversy stems primarily from the use of public revenue to fund religious school education, a practice prohibited by most state constitutions, including Michigan's.[6] In addition to constitutional issues regarding the separation of church and state, critics cite the potential of vouchers to increase social stratification along racial, ethnic, academic, and socioeconomic lines (Goldhaber and Eide 2002). Concern over such stratification has also been raised in connection with charter schools and interdistrict choice, but the objections have been less strident, probably because these reforms involve only public schools, which are tuition-free and, with rare exception, equally accessible to all applicants.[7] Consequently, these public choice initiatives have enjoyed much more public support in Michigan and across the states.

RATIONALE FOR SCHOOLS OF CHOICE

This form of educational choice, often referred to as open enrollment, appears on the surface to be a more modest policy reform than charter schools.[8] These programs do not alter school governance, as do charter schools, and may not hold the same potential for curricular and instructional innovation as the more autonomous charter schools. Rather, open enrollment programs enlarge geographic school attendance boundaries, so students are not limited to their neighborhood schools. The first state open enrollment law was adopted by Minnesota in 1987. Since then, the number of states with open enrollment programs has grown to 42. Of these, 19 states have mandatory laws and 23 have voluntary programs. Mandatory laws require local school boards to promulgate open enrollment policies, while voluntary laws allow such local district policies (Witte, Carlson, and Lavery 2008).

In essence, open enrollment breaks the link between household and school location. In so doing, these programs could reduce the socioeconomic and racial stratification of students, allowing students to cross boundaries of local districts that segregate families along these lines. On the other hand, interdistrict choice could exacerbate such segregation as families further sort themselves without having to change their place of residence.

Advocates of these and other market-based education reforms, including charter schools, vouchers, and tuition tax credits, generally assert that the resulting competitive pressures exerted on schools will improve the productivity of the educational system as a whole (see, e.g., Friedman 1955; Chubb and Moe 1990; Hoxby 2000, 2002). That is, competition among schools will benefit not only those students who actively choose to participate in these programs, but also those who remain in their traditional, neighborhood schools. This argument, which often emphasizes the private rather than public (or civic) benefits of education, rests on the notion that traditional public schools essentially enjoy a monopoly over students living in their attendance areas, and that monopolies, protected as they are from competition, do not use resources efficiently. Choice advocates further assert that if the money follows the student, a market-based choice program will cause good schools to prosper and grow, while bad schools will either improve or disappear (Hoxby 2000).

By this line of reasoning, school choice advocates see the potential for particularly substantial educational gains for minority and low-income children who traditionally attend low-performing schools. Indeed, studies show that support for school choice, whether open enrollment, charter schools, or vouchers, varies by racial/ethnic group and with the quality of available public schools. For example, a 1993 survey of Michigan residents revealed greater support for a proposed public school choice plan among Detroit residents, particularly lower-income minority residents and those less supportive of their neighborhood schools (Lee, Croninger, and Smith 1994).

At the same time, however, these market-based reforms have been criticized on the grounds that they may compromise the public purposes of schools, particularly those regarding civic participation and social cohesion. That is, the idea that schools should contribute to equality of social, economic, and political opportunities for people of different racial and socioeconomic backgrounds suggests that all students be exposed to a common educational experience that ought not be left to the vagaries of individual or family preferences (Levin 1991, 2000; Fiske and Ladd 2000; Gill et al. 2001). For example, school competition could exacerbate the stratification of students across schools by race, class, and ability or deemphasize preparation for citizenship. Such an instance of market failure could arise if schools and parents are interested not only in school quality, but also in the characteristics of the student body. Specifically, if parents select schools at least partly on the basis of the socioeconomic profile of the student body and schools have some ability to influence their applicant pool (e.g., by selective advertising or social networking), then competition could increase stratification (Epple and Romano 2000; Ladd 2002).

Critics say that the school choice initiatives can impair the efficiency of schools that lose students to their competitors. First, more motivated students and parents may be more likely to actively choose their schools, leaving their less motivated counterparts concentrated in the less attractive schools (Levin 1998; Witte 2000). These schools would then become increasingly less capable of competing in the educational marketplace as their positive peer influences leave. Second, as revenues decline in tandem with enrollments but operating costs do not, these schools are forced to cut programs and services, triggering further losses (Fiske and Ladd 2000).

IMPACTS OF OPEN ENROLLMENT PROGRAMS

Although open enrollment is arguably the least innovative of the school choice initiatives, more closely resembling the traditional system of local public schools than either charter school or voucher programs, as a form of school choice, open enrollment can be expected to exert several important effects on students and communities, and these effects may be interrelated. In addition to the straightforward fiscal effects of school choice, other important but less obvious effects are those on school performance and student sorting. In examining these effects, we must consider why families value school choice. To the extent that parents choose schools on the basis of their educational quality, one could expect that school choice would improve school efficiency. That is, schools can be expected to strive for improvements in teaching and learning to attract new students and the resources that accompany them. Conversely, to the extent parents choose schools on the basis of the socioeconomic profile of the student body, choice could compromise school efficiency as school incentives are directed away from academic performance and toward selective advertising and recruitment activities (Ladd 2002; Rothstein 2006).

Despite the widespread adoption of open enrollment programs across the states, researchers have focused primarily on the effects of the alternative school choice mechanisms of vouchers and charter schools. Moreover, although we now have a fairly substantial body of research on the effects of school competition on educational outcomes, much of this work examines the effects of competition from nearby private schools or neighboring public school districts. Reviewing more than 40 studies in the United States, Belfield and Levin (2002) find that competition has modest positive effects on student achievement. The research literature on the effects of open enrollment programs, in contrast, is relatively scant. A study of well-established open enrollment programs in Minnesota and Colorado finds that students tended to leave districts with higher proportions of low-income and low-achieving students and enroll in districts with greater concentrations of middle-class and higher-achieving students (Witte, Carlson, and Lavery 2008). Such effects are not unexpected, but the full array of short- and longer-term impacts of open enrollment programs continue to unfold.

Fiscal Effects

The most immediate effect of children moving from one district to another is the accompanying transfer of revenue and creation of financial winners and losers. The common practice across the states of paying for schooling by the student ignores a number of important realities about the costs of operating schools. First, almost all instruction takes place in classroom groups, so the actual personnel costs of adding a single student to a classroom are essentially zero. And this is certainly so if the open enrollment program is limited to filling empty classroom seats, as is generally true in Michigan. Similarly, overhead costs for such things as buildings, administration, and even transportation are not increased by the addition of even a substantial number of students if seats are available for them. Conversely, the district of residence sees no reduction in operating costs as it loses students to neighboring districts.[9]

As a result, an open enrollment program such as Michigan's, in which a full per pupil foundation allowance follows the child, provides a windfall for the enrolling district and a corresponding loss for the sending district. Further, to the extent students seek transfer to schools in more affluent or more academically successful districts, such a program will likely exacerbate the quality differences between districts and encourage further transfers. At the same time, however, the absence of such financial rewards and penalties would give public school districts little incentive to improve their programs and respond to parents' educational demands.[10]

Educational Effects

Empirical evidence on the academic effects of school choice is mixed. Those studies that do find positive effects also tend to find that minority students living in urban areas benefit the most from school choice (e.g., Goldhaber and Eide 2002). On the other hand, choice reforms could adversely impact such students as enrollments and resources shift from one set of schools to another in these communities (Addonizio 1994). The distinction, of course, depends on who elects to change schools and who does not.

Some evidence of the educational effects of competition among public schools is taken from large-scale intradistrict choice programs in New York City and Chicago. Community District 4 on the upper east side of New York City has been widely acclaimed as an example of a high poverty district serving predominantly minority students that has seen dramatic improvements in student achievement following the introduction of school choice. Starting in 1973, the district formed more than 20 alternative schools from which parents could choose. In creating these alternative schools or programs, District 4 leaders severed the traditional correspondence between buildings and schools. Several programs, usually employing different educational approaches and serving different age groups, were housed in the same building (Elmore 1990).

Most research on District 4 points to the dramatic improvements in student achievement, but researchers disagree as to how much of the gains are attributable to choice and competition. Other possible contributing factors cited by researchers include higher achieving students attracted to the district by the innovations, increased resource levels, and school downsizing (Teske et al. 1999). One could argue, however, that these additional factors are themselves desirable attributes of any well-conceived school choice program that provide educators the resources and latitude to offer new educational alternatives.

One study of Chicago's high school open enrollment program that used distance from a student's home to school of attendance to identify active choosers reveals little impact on academic outcomes district-wide, but it does find a small positive impact on graduation rates for some students attending career academies, a type of vocational school (Cullen, Jacob, and Levitt 2000). A second study comparing academic outcomes between lottery winners and losers in Chicago's high school choice program finds little evidence that attending sought-after programs improves students' academic outcomes, whether standardized test scores, attendance rates, or credits earned.[11] Further, while the study finds some evidence that lottery winners attending sought-after schools were less likely to report that they were disciplined at school or arrested, they were not more likely to expect to graduate college, enjoy school, have positive interactions with peers or teachers, or feel safe at school (Cullen, Jacob, and Levitt 2003).

Peer Effects

In addition to the impact of school choice on student achievement, a second question dominating the school choice debate is whether choice results in greater student sorting or stratification. That is, given a choice of school or district, will families sort themselves by race, socioeconomic class, or some other characteristic in a way that would weaken community bonds and social cohesion? And one could easily imagine such sorting also impairing the educational achievement of particular student groups.

Prior to about 1990, school choice for families in the United States consisted almost exclusively of choosing the school district in which to live or sending children to private school. Accordingly, much of the research on school choice focused on this type of "Tiebout choice," or "voting with one's feet."[12] Clotfelter (1999) finds evidence of student sorting across districts, but Hoxby (2000) and Alesina, Baqir, and Hoxby (2000) conclude that more student sorting occurs within districts across schools. Urquiola (2005), examining the effects of school district concentration and competition in U.S. metropolitan areas, finds that competition among school districts does contribute to student stratification, but adds that this observed sorting may also reflect residential segregation patterns possibly unrelated to schooling and school district boundaries.

The introduction of open enrollment and charter school programs in the 1990s created new avenues for student sorting, as families were no longer restricted by school district boundaries when choosing their public schools. This new sorting could occur in two general ways. First, as noted earlier, households may differ in their interest and ability to exercise this newfound choice. More specifically, choosing households may be of higher socioeconomic status than nonchoosing households, raising the possibility that white students, more academically able students, and students from families with more educational resources will leave their traditional public schools for schools of choice. This hypothesis is supported by a substantial body of research (e.g., Lee, Croninger, and Smith 1996; Armor and Peiser 1998; Witte 2000). Second, active choosers may sort themselves as well, possibly along racial or class lines. Less research is available on this question, but a rigorous study by Weiher and Tedin (2002) of school choice in Texas finds that race is a good predictor of the school choices made by choosing households. Analyzing the choices of 1,006 charter school households, the authors find that whites, African Americans, and Latinos transfer into charter schools where their groups comprise between 11 and 14 percentage points more of the student body than the traditional public schools they are leaving. Further, the vast majority of choosing households transfer their children into charter schools with *lower* performance on the state achievement test than the traditional schools they left. Interestingly, this observed behavior largely contradicted preferences expressed by these households on surveys designed to elicit their criteria for choosing a school.

IMPACTS IN MICHIGAN

Following passage of the schools of choice legislation, many Michigan school districts saw an opportunity to increase their operating revenue. By the program's second year, 45 percent of districts were accepting nonresidents and by the fifth year, fully 80 percent of Michigan's districts had signed on. Statewide pupil counts, however, were quite modest in the program's early years, with schools of choice enrollments rising from 7,836 in 1997 to 33,506 in 2001, about 2 percent of Michigan's K–12 enrollment (Cullen and Loeb 2003). Examining the first two years of the program, Arsen, Plank, and Sykes (2000) find participation highest in rural and central-city school districts.[13] It was much lower in suburban districts and lowest of all in high-income districts and districts with growing resident enrollments. This finding is not surprising. While the fiscal effects are unambiguously positive for a district enrolling nonresident students to fill otherwise empty desks, some districts may decline to participate in the program because of concerns over peer effects, real or perceived. Put simply, local boards of education may fear that without the authority to screen applicants, the district runs some risk of enrolling undesirable students, including low achievers, those with behavioral problems, or racial minorities.[14]

Arsen, Plank, and Sykes (2000) also find that transferring students were moving to districts with higher family incomes, higher MEAP scores, and lower concentrations of minority students than their home districts. For rural districts as a group, student outflows were roughly offset by inflows, while central cities sustained an average 0.7 percent enrollment loss. For some urban districts, however, the net loss of students and revenue was much larger.[15]

RECENT TRENDS

Michigan's schools of choice program has grown in recent years. We obtained data from the MDE on Sec. 105 and Sec. 105C enrollments (full-time equivalent student counts [FTEs]) from the program's inception in 1996–97 through 2008–09.

With the exception of 2001–02, statewide participation in Michigan's schools of choice program has risen each year since its inception. This steady growth in schools of choice enrollments, moreover, has occurred during periods of both growth and decline in Michigan's total public school enrollments. These data are presented in Table 6.1.

As the data show, the rate of participation in Michigan's schools of choice program has grown steadily since its inception and is now approaching 5 percent of Michigan's K–12 enrollment.[16] This growth is undoubtedly fueled by the growing financial pressure on local school districts, a topic discussed in Chapter 3. Because local districts can control the scope of their participation in the program, designating the schools, grades, and number of slots available to nonresidents, they can essentially seek to fill empty desks, thereby gaining revenue while controlling operating costs.

County and Local Impacts

These totals, while showing steady annual growth statewide, conceal the very uneven impact of schools of choice across localities. The majority of local districts in Michigan are largely unaffected by the program, neither losing nor gaining enrollments to any substantial degree. But many districts in major metropolitan areas are significantly

Table 6.1 Statewide Participation in Schools of Choice, 1996–97 through 2008–09

Year	Nonresident enrollment	Total enrollment	Nonresident as % total enrollment
1996–97	7,386	1,680,693	0.44
1997–98	10,576	1,694,320	0.62
1998–99	14,413	1,709,892	0.84
1999–00	19,045	1,714,815	1.11
2000–01	33,506	1,720,335	1.95
2001–02	33,248	1,731,092	1.92
2002–03	39,800	1,750,631	2.27
2003–04	50,247	1,734,019	2.90
2004–05	57,671	1,708,585	3.38
2005–06	63,279	1,697,900	3.73
2006–07	66,673	1,678,480	3.97
2007–08	74,091	1,648,540	4.49
2008–09	76,650	1,615,371	4.75

SOURCE: MDE.

impacted, with some districts enrolling substantial numbers and proportions of nonresident students. Much of this interdistrict student movement has occurred in the tri-county region of southeastern Michigan, consisting of Wayne, Oakland, and Macomb counties. Table 6.2 lists the 28 local districts whose schools of choice enrollments numbered at least 500 and accounted for at least 15 percent of total district enrollment in 2008–09.

While Michigan's total schools of choice enrollment accounted for less than 5 percent of the state's total K–12 enrollment in 2008–09, this 13-year-old state program is the source of a substantial share of student enrollments and operating revenue for some local districts. As noted earlier, participation in the choice program is a local decision, and success in attracting nonresident students depends on local marketing efforts as well as reputation. As a result, local impacts vary, even for neighboring districts. Indeed, competition for students is often most intense among neighboring communities, fostering local rivalries and resentments not seen in the charter school movement. An example of diverse impacts on neighboring districts is provided by Highland Park,

Table 6.2 Districts with High Schools of Choice Enrollments, 2008–09

District	Sec. 105 enrollment	Total enrollment	Percent Sec. 105 enrollment
Highland Park	1,563	2,747	56.9
Inkster	1,526	3,005	50.8
Clintondale	1,758	3,647	48.2
Vandercook	540	1,302	41.5
Carrollton	703	1,792	39.3
Oak Park	1,467	3,771	38.9
Westwood	685	1,923	35.6
Dearborn Heights	1,013	2,847	35.6
Madison (Oakland)	523	1,520	34.4
Riverview	838	2,641	31.7
Corunna	764	2,438	31.4
Lakeview	875	3,132	28.0
Essexville-Hampton	537	1,923	27.9
Pennfield	535	2,029	26.4
Melvindale-N. Allen	654	2,800	23.4
Ypsilanti	898	3,877	23.2
Western	659	2,865	23.0
West Bloomfield	1,567	6,845	22.9
Bangor	553	2,540	21.8
Ferndale	758	4,033	18.8
Southgate	988	5,467	18.1
Lakeview (Calhoun)	685	3,790	18.1
East Lansing	604	3,417	17.7
Berkley	776	4,407	17.6
Allen Park	639	3,730	17.1
Fraser	772	4,802	16.1
Warren Woods	517	3,391	15.3
Saginaw Twp.	805	5,334	15.1

SOURCE: MDE.

which enrolls fully 57 percent of its students from outside the district (with the vast majority of these choice students living in the Detroit Public School District), and neighboring Hamtramck, which enrolls a mere 8 percent from outside the district. A local school board's decision about enrolling nonresidents is multifaceted, involving educational, financial, and political considerations. Moreover, for those local districts choosing to participate, success in enrolling nonresidents depends on the aggressiveness of the district's marketing efforts and the district's image, socioeconomic characteristics, and academic reputation. And, of course, districts must be concerned with loss of resident enrollment whether they pursue nonresident students or not.

Some insight into the dynamics of Michigan's schools of choice program can be gained by examining participation at the county level. Fully 17 of the 28 local districts listed in Table 6.2 are located in the three counties of Michigan's southeastern region, with Wayne, Oakland, and Macomb counties claiming 8, 5, and 4 of these 28 high choice enrollment districts, respectively. At the same time, however, while nonresident enrollments are quite high in these 17 local districts, participation rates are considerably higher in several other counties and zero or near zero in others. Nonresident enrollment rates for selected counties for the past five years are presented in Table 6.3.

The counties (each an ISD) are ordered by their 2008–09 schools of choice enrollment rates, from high to low. The three most active counties in 2008–09, Jackson, Berrien, and Saginaw, were also the most active in each of the last five years, in terms of participation rates. Moreover, nonresident enrollment rates have increased in each of the past four years in each of these counties. Indeed, the numbers and proportions of nonresident enrollments have increased steadily across most of these counties, reflecting the state's steady growth in open enrollment activity. Notable exceptions, however, include Kent and Genesee ISDs, which have eschewed the state's choice program in favor of their own cooperative student transfer programs.

At the same time, nonresident enrollment rates vary considerably across local districts within each county, again reflecting the localized nature of school choice in Michigan. These local district rates are presented for Jackson County in Table 6.4.

As a percentage of total public school enrollment, the level of open enrollment activity in Jackson County has been the highest in the state

Table 6.3 Nonresident Enrollments Selected Counties 2004–05 through 2008–09

	2004–05		2005–06		2006–07		2007–08		2008–09	
County	FTE	%	FTE	%	FTE	%	FTE	%	FTE	%
Jackson	2,918	10.95	2,997	11.26	3,226	12.19	3,379	13.11	3,516	13.94
Berrien	2,429	8.77	2,631	9.69	2,879	10.73	3,009	11.38	3,130	12.01
Saginaw	3,457	9.78	3,526	10.18	3,627	10.75	3,816	11.55	3,855	11.91
Ingham	3,196	6.59	3,364	7.05	3,563	7.56	3,719	8.01	3,847	8.48
Midland	799	5.49	834	5.83	393	2.79	961	6.88	1,011	7.39
Macomb	4,782	3.48	5,703	4.10	6,545	4.69	7,822	5.64	9,244	6.68
Oakland	7,490	3.68	8,056	3.95	8,679	4.24	9,175	4.54	9,452	4.71
Washtenaw	1,229	2.58	1,508	3.15	1,585	3.31	1,695	3.60	1,971	4.19
Wayne	9,307	2.60	9,721	2.76	9,914	2.90	11,893	3.59	11,791	3.70
Kalamazoo	138	0.40	152	0.45	222	0.65	219	0.65	252	0.75
Muskegon	161	0.58	566	1.74	669	2.09	1,100	3.49	165	0.53
Genesee	56	0.07	70	0.08	79	0.10	109	0.14	119	0.15
Kent	0	0	0	0	0	0	0	0	0	0
Group	35,962	3.13	39,128	3.41	41,381	3.65	46,897	4.21	48,353	4.43
State	57,671	3.38	63,279	3.73	66,673	3.97	74,091	4.49	76,650	4.75

SOURCE: MDE.

Table 6.4 Local Districts in Jackson County Nonresident Enrollments 2004–05 through 2008–09

	2004–05		2005–06		2006–07		2007–08		2008–09	
Local district	FTE	%	FTE	%	FTE	%	FTE	%	FTE	%
Western	551	19.5	554	19.2	619	21.0	644	22.2	659	23.0
Vandercook Lake	473	35.5	471	35.0	498	36.8	506	38.3	540	41.5
Columbia	154	8.6	140	7.8	168	9.4	171	9.8	203	12.0
Grass Lake	91	7.8	98	8.3	115	9.5	155	12.5	181	14.2
Concord	118	11.8	110	11.1	136	14.1	150	15.5	160	17.4
East Jackson	315	19.6	312	20.1	310	20.8	329	22.7	297	22.3
Hanover-Horton	218	15.5	247	18.0	255	18.7	275	20.4	306	22.7
Michigan Center	324	22.0	316	21.4	291	20.1	284	20.3	311	22.1
Napoleon	129	7.9	148	8.9	166	10.1	216	13.3	220	13.8
Northwest	143	4.0	143	4.1	158	4.7	183	5.7	174	5.7
Springport	107	10.1	129	12.1	128	12.2	128	12.4	147	14.2
Jackson	296	4.4	329	4.9	381	5.7	338	5.2	318	5.0

SOURCE: MDE.

for each of the past five years. Local districts enrolling the highest proportions of nonresidents have been Vandercook Lake, Western, East Jackson, Hanover-Horton, and Michigan Center. It is no coincidence that each of these districts has recorded high school graduation rates among the highest in the county and well in excess of Jackson Public School District.[17] Jackson City Schools has been the big loser in the county's schools of choice program. The district's enrollment gains and losses in schools of choice are given in Table 6.5. Jackson City was losing enrollment prior to the inception of schools of choice, but the choice program has managed to accelerate this trend in recent years, starting in 2004–05.

Berrien County—a tale of three districts

Two of the three local districts in Berrien County where nonresidents exceed 200 FTEs and 20 percent of enrollment are Coloma and Eau Claire. (The third is Bridgman.) And the district with the smallest nonresident enrollment is Benton Harbor, with a mere 12 nonresidents, or 0.3 percent of enrollment. A five-year history of nonresident enrollments for local districts in Berrien County is presented in Table 6.6. Benton Harbor schools are open to nonresidents but few families in neighboring communities have shown interest in enrolling. Clearly,

Table 6.5 Jackson Public Schools Enrollment Losses Due to Schools of Choice, 2000–10, Fall Pupil Counts (FTE)

Year	Enrollment gain	Enrollment loss	Net loss
2000	102.30	831.01	728.71
2001	92.00	888.67	796.67
2002	162.80	1,052.39	889.59
2003	186.34	1,186.75	1,000.41
2004	251.95	1,345.32	1,093.37
2005	295.52	1,500.68	1,205.16
2006	329.30	1,486.50	1,157.20
2007	381.03	1,527.45	1,146.42
2008	338.00	1,587.00	1,249.00
2009	318.25	1,646.40	1,328.15
2010	284.06	1,756.83	1,472.77

SOURCE: MDE.

Table 6.6 Local Districts in Berrien County Nonresident Enrollments 2004–05 through 2008–09

	2004–05		2005–06		2006–07		2007–08		2008–09	
District	FTE	%	FTE	%	FTE	%	FTE	%	FTE	%
Benton Harbor	4	<0.1	3	<0.1	4	0.1	17	0.4	12	0.3
St. Joseph	5	0.2	75	2.7	140	5.0	215	7.6	234	8.2
Lakeshore	15	0.5	57	2.0	102	3.5	145	4.9	161	5.5
River Valley	96	9.6	91	9.8	91	10.5	87	10.7	81	10.6
Galien Twp.	33	18.9	58	32.6	67	38.3	58	31.0	61	37.0
New Buffalo	182	26.5	192	29.6	195	29.3	185	28.1	164	24.9
Brandywine	194	13.1	202	14.0	228	15.5	212	14.5	235	16.5
Berrien Springs	235	14.5	283	16.6	363	20.5	389	22.2	457	24.3
Eau Claire	205	24.0	221	26.0	248	30.0	252	31.1	207	28.1
Niles	198	4.9	195	4.8	208	5.2	204	5.2	247	6.3
Buchanan	199	11.3	190	11.1	189	11.0	205	12.0	201	12.0
Watervliet	231	16.8	234	17.5	230	17.3	255	19.2	244	19.1
Coloma	512	23.2	510	24.0	482	23.4	425	22.2	424	22.9
Bridgman	233	22.7	231	22.2	238	23.8	267	26.7	292	29.6
Hagar Twp.#6	49	71.0	37	52.2	40	58.0	31	54.4	45	73.8
Sodus Twp.#5	38	61.3	52	80.0	54	84.4	64	85.3	65	91.5

SOURCE: MDE.

the movement of choice students has been away from Benton Harbor and toward Coloma and Eau Claire, among other districts. We can track this migration of students from Benton Harbor with administrative data compiled by the MDE for their state aid payment system. Table 6.7 provides a historical profile of the district's student exodus from 2000 to 2010 under the state's schools of choice program.

Such movement of students across public schools in and around Benton Harbor has been of enormous social, political, and legal consequence for decades. The Benton Harbor, Coloma, and Eau Claire districts were principals in a 35-year federal desegregation case that spanned the period of 1967–2002. The case originated with a lawsuit filed against the Benton Harbor School District by the parent of a student and the NAACP, claiming the district was discriminating against and segregating black students. Specifically, plaintiffs alleged that black teachers were assigned to black schools and white teachers to white schools, and that in the junior high and high schools, which were more integrated than the elementary schools, students were tracked, with most black students placed in the slower sections (Kotlowitz 1998).

The litigation dragged on for 15 years before the plaintiffs eventually prevailed. In 1981, Judge Douglas Hillman of the Western District Court of Michigan found that officials of the predominantly white Coloma and Eau Claire school districts promoted "white flight" from the largely black Benton Harbor School District by taking transfer students, mostly white, from the district on a tuition basis and ordered the desegregation of Benton Harbor, Eau Claire, and Coloma schools. The court order called for voluntary busing between Benton Harbor and the two heavily white neighboring districts "whenever such transfer would result in decreasing segregation in each school system" (*Berry v. School District of City of Benton Harbor* 1981).[18] The court also ordered extraordinary state payments to Benton Harbor for magnet educational programs.

The desegregation order remained in force until April 4, 2002, when Judge Hillman granted the state of Michigan's motion for "unitary status," a declaration that all remaining effects of past segregation in Benton Harbor had been eliminated.[19] The ruling phased out the program of court-ordered state payments, which had totaled more than $116 million, to the district and effectively ended the 35-year-old case.[20]

Table 6.7 The Exodus of Benton Harbor Residents under Schools of Choice, by Enrolling District, 2000–01 through 2010–11

Year	Coloma	Eau Claire	Berrien	Watervliet	Bridgman	St. Joseph	Other	Total
2000	78	70	14	10	5	0	14	191
2001	138	76	10	27	10	0	28	289
2002	167	102	48	41	17	0	54	428
2003	191	102	68	44	35	1	80	521
2004	280	153	100	42	36	0	63	674
2005	378	121	105	53	40	3	86	786
2006	363	166	138	54	29	45	124	919
2007	365	192	207	43	22	100	146	1075
2008	299	194	218	56	28	161	172	1127
2009	270	164	274	63	23	173	175	1142
2010	289	230	315	86	13	177	263	1373

SOURCE: MDE.

Since Judge Hillman's decision terminating the federal desegregation efforts in Benton Harbor, the racial composition of the district has changed little, with the proportion of children who are African American remaining about 94 percent. These students, however, have become even more poor, with the proportion who are economically disadvantaged (i.e., eligible for free or reduced price lunch under the national school lunch act) rising from 79.6 percent in 2002–03 to an astronomical 98 percent in 2008–09. Over this same period, the proportion of African American students has fallen in both Coloma and Eau Claire, and the proportion of economically disadvantaged students has fallen dramatically in Eau Claire. These data on the racial and socioeconomic composition of the students in these districts, along with neighboring Bridgman Public Schools and the public school academies of Berrien County, are presented in Tables 6.8A and 6.8B.

Although these descriptive data do not establish a causal relationship between the advent of schools of choice and the growing socioeconomic stratification across the local districts involved in the court order, the correlation between Michigan's schools of choice program and the increasing socioeconomic isolation of the children in Benton Harbor Public Schools is unmistakable. This phenomenon is depicted in Figure 6.1.

The data draw a stark picture of a school district beset by steadily declining enrollment and rising poverty. Over this period, Benton Harbor Area Schools has lost nearly half its enrollment, while the percentage of its students who are economically disadvantaged has risen to an astonishing 98 percent by 2009, as noted above. Certainly this outcome is not entirely attributable to the state's open enrollment program. Outmigration, charter schools, and generally declining economic activity have all played a role. Nevertheless, it is equally clear that open enrollment activity has contributed substantially to the school district's plight of racial segregation and poverty. A history of the exodus of Benton Harbor residents to neighboring school districts is depicted in Figure 6.2, with the most popular destinations individually identified.

Saginaw County

Saginaw County public school districts are the third most active county group in terms of participation rate in the state's open enrollment program. This is so despite the nonparticipation of two of the

Table 6.8A Percent African American Students Selected Districts in Berrien County

District	2000–01	2001–02	2002–03	2003–04	2004–05	2005–06	2006–07	2007–08
Benton Harbor	92.7	93.9	93.6	94.0	94.8	94.4	94.0	94.3
Coloma	18.9	16.8	14.2	14.6	15.4	14.3	15.0	12.7
Eau Claire	17.4	15.8	14.4	14.2	13.2	15.0	15.8	14.0
Bridgman	0.7	0.7	0.4	0.6	0.7	1.2	0.8	1.4
PSAs					67.1	71.3	72.8	73.4

SOURCE: MDE. PSA figures are enrollment weighted averages.

Table 6.8B Percent of Economically Disadvantaged Selected Districts in Berrien County

District	2000–01	2001–02	2002–03	2003–04	2004–05	2005–06	2006–07	2007–08
Benton Harbor	84.5	80.5	79.6	86.8	89.0	74.3	87.5	92.2
Coloma	40.4	40.7	42.0	50.2	51.0	44.9	52.3	41.6
Eau Claire	51.8	54.4	56.2	58.7	67.0	51.8	27.9	27.0
Bridgman	12.9	11.9	15.2	19.2	19.0	23.6	27.0	23.8
PSAs					76.1	85.5	67.8	59.5

SOURCE: MDE. PSA figures are enrollment-weighted averages.

Figure 6.1 Benton Harbor Area Schools Enrollment History

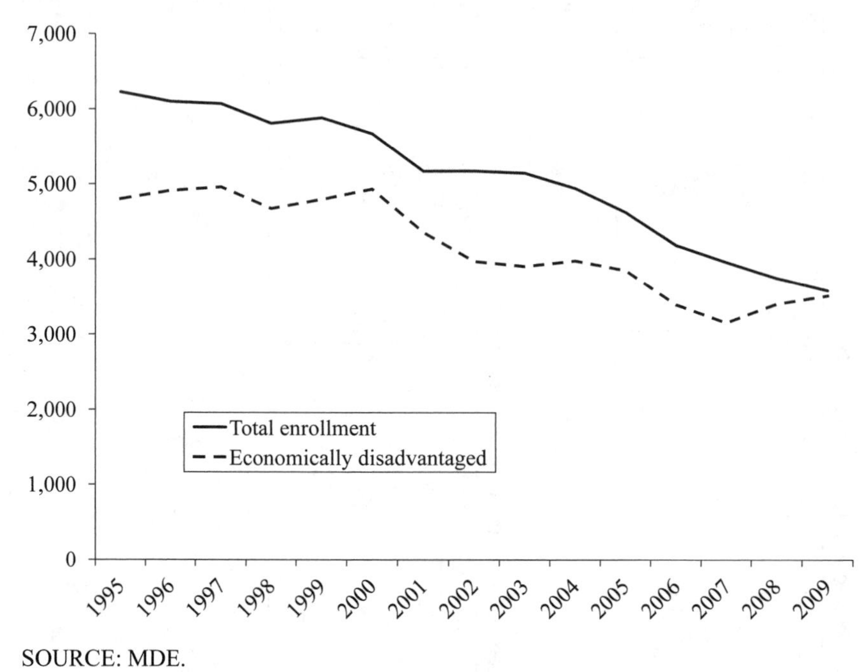

SOURCE: MDE.

Figure 6.2 Benton Harbor Enrollment Losses under Schools of Choice 2000–01 through 2010–11

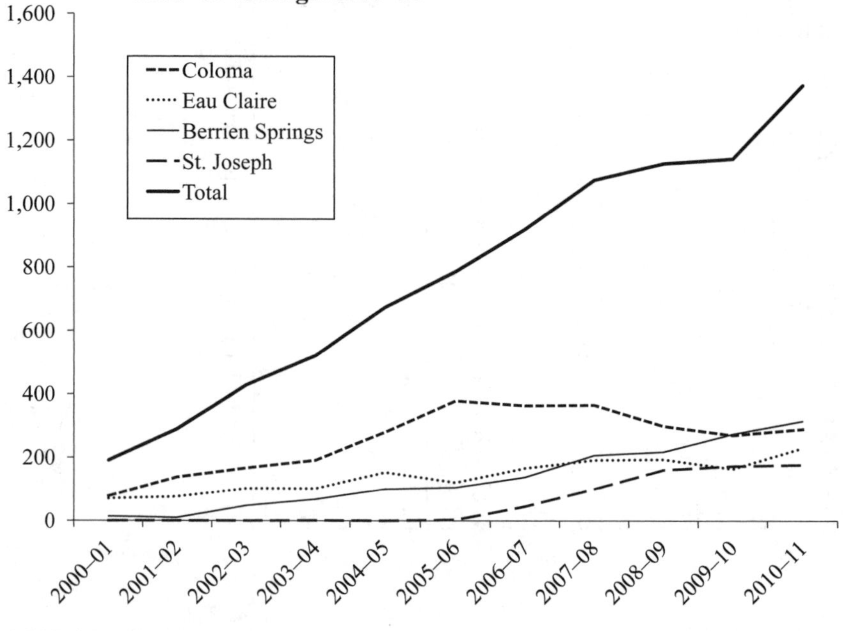

SOURCE: MDE.

county's 13 local districts. One of the nonparticipants, Frankenmuth, is by far the wealthiest district in the county as measured by residential property wealth per pupil, while the other nonparticipant, Freeland, ranks fourth.[21] A history of open enrollment in the county is presented in Table 6.9.

Systematic effects of the county's relatively high rate of participation are not readily apparent from these data. For example, Carrollton, with the greatest proportion of nonresident students, ranks last among the county's local districts in residential property wealth, just ahead of Saginaw City. Further, while Saginaw City School District has steadily lost enrollment since 1991–92 (except for a slight increase in 2002–03), these losses do not appear to have been exacerbated by the state's open enrollment program. Saginaw Public Schools' open enrollment history is presented in Table 6.10 and the district's total enrollment history is depicted in Figure 6.3.

Detroit Public Schools

In absolute numbers, no Michigan school district has lost more students through schools of choice than Detroit Public Schools (DPS). Moreover, this enrollment loss has been just a part of an unprecedented student exodus also fueled by Michigan's charter school program and general demographic trends. These broader trends and their attendant fiscal and political difficulties are discussed at some length in Chapter 7. Here we will focus exclusively on the DPS experience with the state's open enrollment program. A history of DPS enrollment gains and losses stemming from schools of choice is presented in Table 6.11.

The data reveal that DPS is far from a desired educational destination for families in neighboring school districts. The schools of choice traffic has been almost entirely outbound. Where are the students going? Again, state administrative data reveal the enrolling districts for these residents of DPS. A 10-year history of the DPS schools of choice exodus is presented in Table 6.12, with the more popular destinations identified.

While the district's total number of outbound students has grown more or less steadily since the fall of 2000, the distinction of most preferred destination has cycled across several neighboring districts. Throughout most of this 11-year period, Highland Park Public Schools has been the preferred destination, with enrollments from Detroit peak-

Table 6.9 Local Districts in Saginaw County, 2004–05 through 2008–09, Nonresident Enrollments

	2004–05		2005–06		2006–07		2007–08		2008–09	
District	FTE	%	FTE	%	FTE	%	FTE	%	FTE	%
Saginaw City	1,007	8.7	1,006	9.2	989	10.0	1,042	10.9	1,096	11.9
Carrollton	486	29.3	512	31.7	581	33.5	646	37.2	703	39.3
Saginaw Twp.	709	13.7	780	15.1	831	15.7	863	16.0	805	15.1
Buena Vista	245	19.5	196	17.6	202	18.6	142	14.6	173	18.3
Chesaning	107	5.3	76	3.9	73	3.9	91	4.9	89	4.9
Birch Run	62	3.3	66	3.5	119	6.3	143	7.7	157	8.5
Bridgeport-Spaulding	334	15.5	323	15.1	256	12.6	185	10.1	124	7.3
Frankenmuth	0	–	0	–	0	–	0	–	0	–
Freeland	0	–	0	–	0	–	0	–	0	–
Hemlock	90	6.1	106	7.1	103	7.1	128	8.9	115	8.4
Merrill	53	6.2	47	5.7	59	7.1	74	8.8	83	10.5
St. Charles	67	5.6	68	5.7	74	6.2	81	7.0	72	6.4
Swan Valley	298	17.1	346	19.4	341	19.3	423	23.3	438	24.5

SOURCE: MDE.

Table 6.10 Enrollment Losses for Saginaw Public Schools Due to Schools of Choice, 2000–10, Fall Pupil Counts (FTE)

Year	Enrollment loss	Enrollment gain	Net loss
2000	987.13	353.68	633.45
2001	1,004.55	450.16	554.39
2002	1,194.67	653.34	541.33
2003	1,274.31	713.78	560.53
2004	1,459.07	890.16	568.91
2005	1,605.17	1,006.82	598.35
2006	1,694.71	1,005.84	688.87
2007	1,741.05	988.74	752.31
2008	1,778.28	1,041.72	736.56
2009	1,760.66	1,096.38	664.28
2010	1,825.32	1,059.37	765.95

SOURCE: MDE.

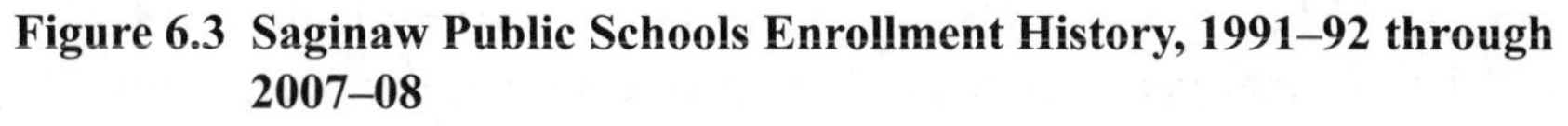

Figure 6.3 Saginaw Public Schools Enrollment History, 1991–92 through 2007–08

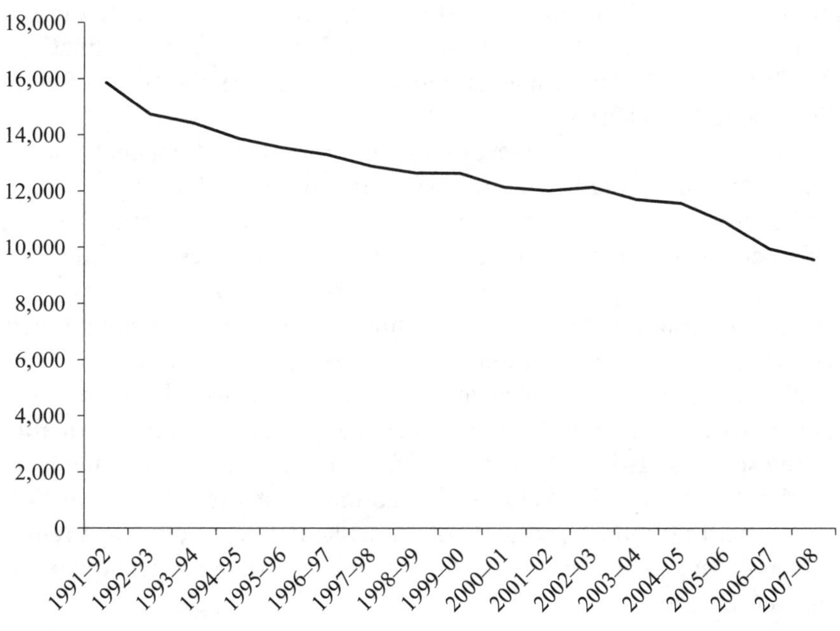

SOURCE: MDE.

Table 6.11 Enrollment Losses for Detroit Public Schools Due to Schools of Choice, 2000–10, Fall Pupil Counts (FTE)

Year	Enrollment loss	Enrollment gain	Net loss
2000	1,466.33	0	1,466.33
2001	3,081.86	0	3,081.86
2002	3,871.04	0	3,871.04
2003	4,005.27	0	4,005.27
2004	6,009.79	210.83	5,798.96
2005	6,587.53	363.56	6,223.97
2006	7,258.60	0	7,258.60
2007	7,605.72	0	7,605.72
2008	9,061.82	6.00	9,055.82
2009	8,606.78	11.00	8,595.78
2010	8,458.46	27.50	8,430.96

SOURCE: MDE.

ing in 2008 at nearly 2,200 and more than doubling Highland Park's enrollment that year. Highland Park's Detroit enrollments plummeted in 2010, however, as educational and financial issues mounted in the district. By that time, Oak Park and Inkster had become the destinations of choice for Detroit residents, while the traffic to Westwood Public Schools reached a new high.

These year-to-year fluctuations in cross-district student movements may be explained by a host of factors, including the adoption of an attractive new program in a district (e.g., full-day kindergarten), enhanced pupil transportation service, favorable press coverage, or more aggressive marketing. District leadership may also choose to suspend or discontinue their open enrollment programs, maintaining their continuing nonresident enrollments but accepting no new enrollees. And while it is unlikely that these annual fluctuations in nonresident enrollment levels are reflective of real changes in the academic quality of the schools involved, a steady outflow of students and revenue from a school or district is likely to damage the reputation of those institutions, spurring more departures of students and resources and eventually inflicting real damage on the academic programs. Undoubtedly, this has been the case in DPS.

Table 6.12 Districts Enrolling DPS Residents, 2000–10, Fall Pupil Counts (FTE)

Year	Ferndale	Oak Park	Dearborn Hts. #7	Highland Park	Redford Union	Westwood	Inkster	Other
2000	2.00	145.00	209.60	965.84	0	0	7.00	136.89
2001	306.11	344.00	225.60	1,327.06	0	15.00	146.00	718.09
2002	328.63	468.66	243.00	1,503.62	225.83	17.00	84.50	999.80
2003	354.50	612.66	483.00	606.32	270.07	44.00	40.50	1,594.22
2004	577.01	720.97	532.00	1,364.78	502.48	222.00	49.00	2,041.55
2005	747.50	670.33	492.50	1,513.38	642.34	278.00	50.00	2,193.48
2006	983.58	593.67	488.83	1,468.13	622.11	341.00	245.00	2,516.28
2007	444.77	1,418.82	467.14	1,551.56	527.00	385.15	120.90	2,691.28
2008	310.00	1,628.40	473.50	2,162.70	410.66	406.00	685.00	2,985.56
2009	330.29	1,285.28	447.50	1,504.03	296.50	337.50	1,122.70	3,282.98
2010	360.00	1,012.49	420.50	791.32	218.50	631.00	1,270.90	3,753.75

SOURCE: MDE.

SCHOOLS OF CHOICE: ADDED VALUE OR ZERO-SUM GAME?

Michigan's schools of choice program is best viewed as part of a broader state movement toward choice and entrepreneurship in K–12 education, one strand in a multifaceted strategy to create incentives to improve public schools. And although it receives less attention than the state's expansive charter school program, Michigan's open enrollment program has had a substantial impact on school enrollments and funding levels in metropolitan areas across the state, including those in Berrien, Jackson, Saginaw, Oakland, Macomb, and Wayne counties.

As a school improvement strategy, however, open enrollment suffers from several shortcomings. First, unlike the charter school program, the open enrollment initiative lacks any supply-side strategy to encourage new school creation. Rather, schools of choice is a zero-sum game in which the gains of the winners in the quest for enrollments and revenue are offset by the losses of the other competitors. Indeed, for those local communities on the losing side in the hunt for student bounties, more than money may be lost. As families remove their children from schools in the communities in which they live, the bonds between school and community are weakened. In particular, this schism jeopardizes public support for local schools, including support for district millage requests for capital projects. Further, such student movement threatens to polarize communities and further segment students by race and socioeconomic status. Evidence of such strains has surfaced in communities in Berrien, Oakland, and Wayne counties, among others.

Finally, the educational effects of Michigan's open enrollment program are not easily discernable and certainly elude the level of public scrutiny given to the performance of charter schools. That is, student achievement data are routinely reported at the school and district level, thereby facilitating the evaluation of charter schools but obscuring the impact of open enrollment on student achievement. As a result, the future of Michigan's schools of choice program will likely depend less on evidence of educational outcomes than on ideology and political preferences. At this time, the long-term effects and policy implications of open enrollment are somewhat ambiguous. The program may result in the further segregation of students by socioeconomic characteristics and academic achievement in metropolitan areas. On the other hand, the program may continue to provide some families with an opportunity to enroll their children in a more desirable school system without the need of relocating their residence. This potential benefit may suffice, at least in the near term, to maintain current levels of political support for the program.

Notes

1. Public Act 300 of 1997.
2. Exceptions were made for siblings of children already enrolled in the district. Also, a district could refuse to enroll an applicant who has been suspended within the preceding two years or who has ever been expelled.
3. Sec. 380.1401 of the School Aid Act states: "Tuition for grades K to 6 shall not exceed 25 percent more than the operation cost per capita for the number of pupils in membership in grades K to 12. Tuition for grades 7 to 12 shall not exceed 12–1/2 percent more than 115 percent of the operation cost per capita for the number of pupils in membership in grades K to 12 . . . The per capita cost used shall not include moneys expended for school sites, school building construction, equipment, payment of bonds, or other purposes not properly included in operation costs as determined by the state board."
4. Public Act 297 of 2000.
5. At the time this proposal was being debated, data on high school graduation rates in Michigan were notoriously unreliable, and the list of districts falling below the two-thirds standard was the subject of much dispute.
6. On July 27, 2002, in a 5 to 4 ruling, the U.S. Supreme Court upheld the constitutionality of a voucher program established by the state of Ohio for families residing in the Cleveland City School District. Many families used the vouchers to send their children to Catholic schools. The court ruled that the Cleveland voucher program did not violate the First Amendment's separation of church and state because the state was not providing the funds directly to the church-run schools. Rather, the state gave the funds to the parents who then paid them to the sectarian schools (*Zelman v. Simmons-Harris* 2002). Although *Zelman* would appear to pave the way for voucher programs that allow parents to choose church-run schools, such programs are prohibited by many state constitutions. Michigan's constitutional prohibition is particularly stringent.
7. Indeed, another reason for the unpopularity of vouchers in the United States is that many proposals have called for relatively small voucher amounts, falling far short of tuition at most good private schools. As such, these plans have been often viewed by the public as more of a "giveaway" to affluent families with children already enrolled in these schools than an opportunity for the less well-heeled to enroll their children. Programs targeted to low-income households, on the other hand, have enjoyed some measure of support in a few states. State-funded voucher

programs currently operate in Maine, Ohio, Vermont, Utah, and Wisconsin, along with a federally funded program in the District of Columbia.

8. The term *open enrollment* has been used to refer to *intradistrict* public school choice programs, a form of choice that predates the *interdistrict* choice created by Michigan's schools of choice program. Here we will use open enrollment to describe the more recent and more expansive interdistrict programs as well as notable intradistrict programs such as those in New York City and Chicago.
9. In microeconomic terms, the marginal cost of educating an additional student is near zero and, conversely, the marginal cost reduction of losing a student is likewise near zero.
10. Intradistrict choice, of course, would generally not create such a powerful economic incentive, since districts can shift funds from school to school or change school attendance boundaries to compensate for enrollment shifts across schools.
11. Because lottery winners are selected at random, winners and losers have the same set of background characteristics on average. Therefore, any observed differences in academic outcomes between lottery winners and losers can be attributed to winning the lottery and not to other influences, either observed or unobserved.
12. Economist Charles Tiebout, in a seminal 1956 article, "A Pure Theory of Local Expenditures," described a mechanism by which individuals choose their community of residence according to that community's combination of local taxes and services. If there are many localities, each with a unique tax/service package, individuals will be able to select their most preferred package in the same manner that they buy goods and services in a private market. This analogy with private markets suggested by Tiebout implies that resources may be allocated efficiently in the public sector as well as in the private sector, a proposition that had been previously dismissed by most economists.
13. In this context, "participation" refers to students attending public schools in districts other than their district of residence. In this way, a student may participate in schools of choice even if his district of residence does not.
14. A 2006 study published by the Harvard Civil Rights Project identified Michigan as one of four states with the highest levels of black segregation in its public schools (Orfield and Lee 2006). This state of affairs is not lost on the residents in many urban areas. As one African American student in author Addonizio's economics of education class at Wayne State University observed, a district may resist the financial incentive for enrolling nonresidents in order to "keep Snoop in the hood."
15. These districts experiencing relatively heavy enrollment losses included Saginaw, Jackson, Pontiac, Niles, Adrian, Inkster, Ecorse, and Hillsdale. Michigan's three largest urban districts, Detroit, Grand Rapids, and Flint, experienced net enrollment losses of less than 1 percent (Arsen, Plank, and Sykes 2000).
16. Section 105/105C is a state program. Alternatively, local districts within the same ISD may develop their own interdistrict plans that operate independently of the state's schools of choice program. While these cooperative programs allow some student movement across local district boundaries, they generally restrict such movement, resulting in fewer interdistrict transfers as compared with the more competitive state program. Notable examples of these more cooperative choice

programs are found in the Kent and Genesee ISDs (Arsen, Plank, and Sykes 2000). Indeed, Kent County public schools report zero participation in the state program (see Table 6.3).

17. The five-year, 2008 graduation rates for these districts, as reported by the Michigan Center for Educational Performance and Information, were Vandercook Lake, 89.0; East Jackson, 86.8; Hanover-Horton, 94.4; Michigan Center, 87.0; and Jackson City, 63.8. Western, with a graduation rate of 72.5 percent in 2008, is somewhat anomalous among this group.
18. In 2007, however, the U.S. Supreme Court ruled that school assignment systems cannot be based on race alone (*Parents Involved in Community Schools Inc. v. Seattle School District* 2007).
19. This ruling was reflective of a general reluctance of the federal courts in the last several decades to insert themselves into the governance of public schools, now viewed as the province of state and local governments. In 1991, the U.S. Supreme Court began to authorize school districts to return to segregated neighborhood schools (*Board of Education of Oklahoma v. Dowell* 1991). The court issued two subsequent rulings that further relaxed desegregation standards. In *Freeman v. Pitts* (1992), the court allowed school districts to terminate desegregation plans even though the schools had not yet become integrated. In *Missouri v. Jenkins* (1995), the court emphasized local control over desegregation as the primary goal of school governance.
20. In his 50-page decision, Judge Hillman wrote, "I accept [the State's evidence] that after adjusting for [socioeconomic] factors and first grade test scores, no statistically significant gap exists between the performance of white and minority students in the Benton Harbor schools. In other words, no 'achievement gap' exists . . . that is attributable to the race of the students . . . " *Berry v. School District of the City of Benton Harbor* (2002).
21. In 2007–08, residential (i.e., homestead) state equalized value per pupil in Frankenmuth was $243,311, far exceeding the corresponding value of $167,152 for Hemlock, the county's second-wealthiest district.

7
The Detroit Public Schools
A Failure of Policy and Politics

As the fall of 2011 and a new school year approached, observers of DPS wondered if this once exemplary district had yet hit bottom. The district's problems had never been more daunting: its budget deficit at the end of school year 2010–11 was $327 million, ballooning $108 million (49 percent) above the 2009–10 deficit level. Moreover, this debt explosion occurred during the two-year stewardship of emergency financial manager Robert Bobb, appointed by Governor Granholm to staunch the flow of red ink in the district.

But the district's problems that year went far beyond financial strains: emergency manager Bobb and the elected school board sued each other over control over DPS, Bobb fired the superintendent whom the board hired, the board president was forced to resign in the wake of sexual misconduct charges, and a debate raged over a mayoral takeover of the schools (Schultz 2010).

Academic performance in the district was just as dire. Both math and reading achievement scores by DPS 4th and 8th graders on the 2009 NAEP were not only the lowest in the nation, but the lowest in the 40-year history of this national testing program.[1]

Bobb, whose term ended in mid-2011, was replaced by Roy Roberts, appointed to the emergency financial manager position by newly elected governor Rick Snyder. Yet, the path forward is far from clear. Roberts, while joining with the governor and the superintendent to launch yet another wide-ranging education reform plan, still faces a serious deficit problem coupled with the added prospect of severe revenue shortages for the 2011–12 school year and beyond (see MDE [2011]).

A LOOK BACK: 1964–81

To fully understand and appreciate the current troubles in which DPS finds itself, it will help to describe briefly the roots of these troubles—roots that stretch back at least 45 years to the early 1960s, if not further. Thus, in this section we set the stage for what will follow in the body of the chapter by first recounting a series of significant events that took place and circumstances that prevailed in the 17-year period from 1964 through 1981.

In our brief review of that 17-year history, we draw heavily on Jeffrey Mirel's (1993) excellent and definitive history of DPS 1907–81, and particularly on Chapter 7, in which Mirel covers the period 1964–81. Mirel introduces what he saw as the impending breakdown that began in the early 1960s with a 1975 quote from political analyst William Serrin (1975): " . . . nowhere in America can the nation's disregard of its cities and the failure of the nation's economic policies be seen so clearly as in Detroit." And, as Mirel notes, Serrin could have said much the same about DPS, which had " . . . slipped to the very edge of financial and educational bankruptcy." In November 1972, staggered by five years of conflict over decentralization, desegregation, and repeated defeats of crucial millage proposals, the school board prepared to shut the system down" (p. 293).

This period of the early 1960s marked the onset of a series of social, economic, financial, legal, and educational forces that over the next several years impinged mightily on DPS and, in so many ways, marked the beginnings of the demise of a once proud and highly respected urban school district. These forces included major shifts in the city and student populations, as well as the racial and economic makeup of both. These same shifts, coupled with growing discontent in the black community, further fed by the devastating 1967 Detroit riots, led to rising demands for community control and decentralization. At the same time, there also arose growing dissension in the citizenry among those arguing for decentralization and community control, and those supporting efforts to integrate the schools and the community—and decentralization won out, for a time. Concurrently, a mounting set of financial woes assailed the school district, which found itself being forced to embark on what Mirel (1993) describes as the "road to financial ruin" (p. 313).

It was during this same time that Detroit's reform school board took steps to initiate a financial equity suit against the state of Michigan, an effort that predated the famous *Serrano I* case in California (*Serrano v. Priest* 1971) but which died in its infancy with the recall of the reform school board as a result of its support for integration. An added set of forces at work in the early 1970s brought on a further array of troubles that saw the school district and the state of Michigan, under *Milliken v. Bradley* (1974) and *Milliken v. Bradley* (1977), deeply engaged with the federal courts in attempts to eliminate de facto segregation in the city schools and surrounding districts. And, as if all of the above wasn't enough, after first having been compelled statutorily in the early 1970s to decentralize its schools, DPS in September of 1981, bowing to an overwhelming vote by the people of Detroit, was forced to cast aside its decentralized system and move to reestablish a centralized structure to govern its schools.

The Exodus Begins

The late 1960s marked the beginnings of a substantial and continuing exodus of citizens from the city of Detroit and students from the city's schools, as well as concomitant changes in the racial and economic makeup of both populations. In the 20-year period between 1960 and 1980, the city of Detroit lost over a quarter of its population, plummeting from 1.67 million to 1.2 million. In the same period, the proportion of black citizens in the population grew from 29 percent in 1960 to 44 percent in 1970 and on to 63 percent in 1980. In the schools, the 1963 enrollment exceeded 293,000 students, and was almost evenly divided between blacks and whites. Shortly after an upswing to 297,000 in student enrollments in 1966, the bottom began to drop out. By 1970, the total number of enrolled students had fallen to just short of 289,000, and the proportion of black students had risen to 64 percent. By 1980, the enrollments in DPS had dipped to 214,736, with the proportion of black students rising to 86 percent. And, as we shall see later in the chapter, the hemorrhaging losses in both the city's population and the DPS student population did not subside, but have continued unabated.

Increasing Demands for Community Control

The loss of citizen and student populations was not the only problem facing the city and the schools in the 1960s and 1970s; Detroit was soon faced with a fast-growing crisis, similar to that which arose in many large urban districts across the nation. It was a crisis given high national visibility in September of 1968, when on the opening day of school New York City was rocked by the strike of over 50,000 public school teachers, marking the first of three walkouts that continued through mid-November and kept over 1 million students out of school for 36 days. The New York City walkouts had their genesis in May of 1968, when the community control board in Brooklyn's black ghetto of Ocean-Hill Brownsville moved to fire several white teachers. The local school community superintendent, Rhody McCoy, had brought no charges against the teachers, but he publicly declared that he wanted an all-black teaching force in the district. Not surprisingly, the teachers union, in the person of its president, Albert Shanker, would have none of it; Shanker reiterated his strong belief that hiring and firing should be color blind. But McCoy had strong support in the local community for his action, a community increasingly becoming disillusioned with the school system and what they saw as the inattention to the overabundance of white teachers when it came to the education of black children.[2] This dissatisfaction of black communities with their public schools was not limited to New York City. The movement soon spread throughout urban school districts across the nation, with growing cries for "power to the people" and "community control" of the schools.

Detroit certainly was not immune to the growing discontent among black urban communities and their resultant calls for community control and decentralization. Well before the New York City walkouts, Detroit found itself in similar circumstances. In the 1965–66 school year, even with the election of a reform school board committed to improving the lot of black students, Detroit witnessed growing discontent, if not anger, with the schools among its black citizens. The signal event of that 1965–66 school year was a massive walkout of students from largely black Northern High School, spurred on by what the students as well as their parents saw as a dramatic deterioration of the educational program that had become reduced to the situation described by Mirel (1993): " . . . most of the majority black high schools in Detroit had essentially become 'general' track institutions dominated by the philosophy that the less teachers demanded of students the more tractable the students would be" (p. 300).

The brouhaha over the Northern walkout and its later settlement, as well as the growing dissatisfaction of the black community, led to the appointment of Norman Drachler as superintendent of schools to replace Samuel Brownell. Despite Drachler's Herculean efforts, the discontent continued apace, and into the middle of this mess came the catastrophic Detroit riots of 1967—six days of utter chaos in which ". . . 43 people died, over 1,000 were injured, in excess of 7,000 arrested, over 2,500 stores damaged, looted, gutted by fire, or destroyed" (Mirel 1993, p. 311). School buildings themselves were not affected, but many observers—surveyed by the *Detroit Free Press* and the Urban League—saw the failure of the schools as a contributing factor.[3]

The Decentralization Experiment

The confluence of these events led to growing and increasingly adamant calls for turning over control of the schools to local neighborhood communities. Giving up on the promises of school reform, responding to the growing influence of the black nationalist movement that was sweeping through the large urban centers of the nation, and urged on by the backlash that followed the assassination of Dr. Martin Luther King, there arose in Detroit an increasingly vociferous movement calling for a thoroughgoing change in the power and governance structure of the DPS system. This movement culminated in April of 1969, with State Senator Coleman Young's introduction of legislation to decentralize DPS.[4]

Senator Young's bill called for two actions: the first was administrative decentralization of the district, the second was increased accountability for teachers and administrators. His bill would create 7–11 regions of 25,000–50,000 students, with each region having a community-elected nine-member school board; each regional board in turn would elect one of its members to an expanded central board, five of whose members would be elected at large from the city. Each regional board would have extensive budgetary, educational, and personnel powers. These would include the right to hire and fire its regional superintendent, as well as employ and discharge its teachers and other employees of the regional district. Young's bill passed both houses of the legislature by overwhelming margins; on August 11, 1970, Governor William Milliken signed it into law. But, as we noted earlier, decentralization did not last long. In a short 10 years, a vote by the citizens of Detroit in September of 1981 forced the recentralization of DPS.

Continuing Financial Woes

In the early 1960s, DPS, while struggling mightily with the mounting array of troubles outlined above, faced at the same time a dire financial future not unlike the financial circumstances that faced many other large urban school districts across the nation. In Detroit's case, the primary causes were threefold. The first was the inadequacy and instability of its revenue stream. The second was the increasing demands the district faced for new programs and services in order to meet the educational needs of mounting numbers of students in the early 1960s, a substantial portion of whom fell into special needs categories. The third was the growing demands of the teachers union for higher salaries and improved working conditions for its members. Detroit Public Schools, in effect, was fast becoming ensnared in the classic financial dilemma of falling revenues and rising demands.

In 1967–68, Detroit educated 14.2 percent of the students in the state but received only 11.4 percent of the total state school aid (Mirel 1993, p. 321). Local financial support for schools fared little better. From 1960 through 1980, Detroit witnessed a fairly sharp decline in its property tax base. Over roughly the same period, 1963–1977, the Detroit Board of Education put some 18 millage proposals before the voters of Detroit. Only 6 of those passed; 12 went down to defeat.

The money supply was fast dwindling, but the demands were fast rising. First, there were increasing numbers of students to educate, at least through the end of the 1960s, and increasing racial, ethnic, and linguistic diversity, as well as spreading poverty. More importantly, the rapidly changing characteristics of the student population presented the schools with new and growing demands for programs and services to meet the needs of special populations of at-risk students—the handicapped, the disadvantaged, the low achievers. More and more students with special needs were showing up on the schools' doorsteps, and more and more special programs and services had to be mounted to meet those needs.[5] Second, the teachers union, in the form of the Detroit Federation of Teachers (DFT), was beginning to feel its oats as a result of the 1965 passage of Public Act 379, which eliminated penalties for public employees who went on strike. Beginning in 1965 under the leadership of Mary Ellen Riordan, the DFT became a significant force in Detroit school politics. The union, emboldened by its new leverage, became an insistent and strong bargainer for higher salaries and smaller class sizes, putting further pressures on the district and its dwindling resources.

With little financial aid coming from the state, with the local revenue stream suffering from declining property values and consistent failures to pass operating millages, with the rising demands for improved programs and services for special populations, and with the persistent demands of an emergent teachers union, DPS was finding itself in ever deeper financial hot water. By 1967, Detroit faced a budget deficit of $12.3 million and prospects for a $32 million deficit by the end of the decade, with no resolution in sight. Perhaps the major factor that kept DPS solvent through the late 1960s and early 1970s, as Mirel (1993) suggests, was the influx of federal aid under ESEA (p. 314).

Court-Ordered Desegregation

In late 1969, in the middle of the black community's push for decentralization of the schools, the reform school board, mentioned earlier, took up the cause of desegregation with renewed vigor. In early 1970, the board, without much fanfare, developed a desegregation proposal for the city's high schools. The proposal, once it became public, was met with violent reaction from a good portion of the community. As Mirel (1993) well put it, "On Sunday, April 5, the *Free Press* and the *News* splashed the story of the board's 'sweeping integration plan' across the front pages and all hell broke loose" (p. 340). The months that followed were an imbroglio of charges and counter charges, of chaotic meetings of the school board, of state legislative action stripping statutory support for the plan, and of fast-moving and ultimately successful efforts to recall four members of the board who supported the desegregation plan.[6]

One outcome of all the uproar was the NAACP's decision finally to file a much broader desegregation suit aimed not only at DPS and its school board but also at the governor and the state attorney general. The case, *Milliken v. Bradley* (1974), went to trial in April of 1971. On hearing the case, the U.S. district court trial judge, Stephen J. Roth, issued one of the more sweeping desegregation orders that the nation had ever witnessed. Roth's order set forth a metropolitan busing plan calling for the integration of three-quarters of a million students across 44 school districts in the three counties—Wayne, Oakland, and Macomb—that made up the Detroit metropolitan area. Not surprisingly, the order was appealed—first to the U.S. circuit court where it was supported, and then to the U.S. Supreme Court where it was overturned and sent back to Judge Roth's district court. The high court ruled that a court-ordered school desegregation plan, absent segregative action on the part of outlying districts, could not cross school district lines in order to include the outlying districts. In short, in order for a multidistrict remedy to be ordered by a district court, the local governments of outlying school districts must have committed segregative acts, and in this case they had not. The court ruled, in effect, that the problems facing Detroit and other urban school districts serving large concentrations of low-income minority children were the responsibility of the cities, not the broader metropolitan community.

But Detroit was not off the hook. In remanding the case to the district court, the high court directed it to formulate a Detroit-only remedy. The district court's newly fashioned remedy consisted of a Detroit-only pupil assignment plan and four remedial programs: 1) remedial reading, 2) in-service teacher training, 3) student testing, and 4) counseling. Detroit Public Schools would bear one-half the cost, and the state of Michigan would bear the other half. While the state did challenge the district court's authority to order remedial programs, and its power to allocate one-half the financial burden to the state, it lost its challenge. The high court, in *Milliken* (1977), ruled that as part of a desegregation decree, a district court can order remedial education and supportive programs for children who have been subjected to segregation in the past; and the high court further ruled that DPS could constitutionally require that the state of Michigan pay one-half of the cost of such remedial programs. The bad news was that DPS, already saddled with the twin bugaboos of declining revenues and increasing demands, now had the burden of even further demands being placed upon it. The good news, at the least, was that the state of Michigan would have to pick up one-half of the tab.

One now might ask what good has come of all of this. By 1980, only some 26,000 white students remained in the city's public schools out of a total enrollment count of 214,736. By 1984, the count of white students was below 19,000, down to less than 10 percent of the district's total enrollment. Now that the student population in DPS is upward of 95 percent African American, one would have to conclude that the all-consuming question of school integration in Detroit has passed its time—the issue is now moot.

Return to a Centralized System

The era of decentralization (1971–81) was a stormy and sometimes violent period for Detroit and its school district, marked principally by disputes and clashes between the boards—both decentralized and central—and the teachers union. While salaries and class size continued to be major bones of contention, a new set of issues began to command center stage in negotiations with the union. In particular, questions of accountability and residency became paramount. Among the members of the regional boards—as well as local community members, and particularly members of the black community—there was a strong feeling that some students, particularly low-income and African American students, were being educationally shortchanged and that teachers needed to be held accountable for the academic achievement of all students in the schools. If the achievement was not forthcoming, then the responsible teachers should be replaced by the school principal, and all union contracts should contain such provisions. Given equal importance was the question of teacher residency. The regional boards, and the central board, were demanding that a Detroit residency requirement be included in all union contracts. Some saw this demand as a black–white issue. Most of the 5,000 (out of more than 20,000) Detroit classroom teachers who lived outside of the city were white. Still, one has to wonder, for the Detroit teaching force at the time was 47 percent black. Not surprisingly, the teachers union strongly denounced both demands—for teacher accountability and for a residency requirement. The confrontation finally culminated with the DFT calling a 43-day strike in September of 1973, a strike that Mirel (1993) describes as " . . . the longest and most bitterly divisive strike in the history of the school system" (p. 363).

The strike was finally broken in November by virtue of Governor William Milliken, in effect, taking the accountability issue "off the table" with his offer to the board and the union to establish a statewide panel that would study the accountability issue and develop a set of guidelines for teacher evaluation. Both parties also agreed to submit the other two issues—salaries and class size—to binding arbitration. The strike was ended but the issues remained unresolved (Mirel 1993, p. 364). Moreover, the rancor and violence continued.

As far as decentralization was concerned, it was quickly nearing an end. Disfavor and disappointment with the decentralized system were rampant throughout the city—among the media, among the several Detroit civic and business groups, among the black community, among the teachers and the DFT, among the trade and industrial unions, and among almost everyone including members of the state legislature. Finally, in mid-1981, the legislature passed and the governor signed into law PA 96, which put the future of decentralization to a vote of the citizens of Detroit. The vote turned out to be overwhelmingly in favor of jettisoning decentralization and returning DPS to a school system of centralized power and governance. Thus, in late 1981, DPS was forced to turn its attention to the arduous task of recentralizing the school system, one that for many at the time seemed to be broken.

A Cautionary Note

In our brief recounting of a series of significant events that took place and circumstances that prevailed in the 17-year period from 1964 through 1981, it is tempting to treat these as isolated incidents rather than what they were, namely, a series of closely related if not interrelated incidents and circumstances. It was not as if DPS and the school board could address themselves to the resolution of one problem and then move on to the next problem; all their problems were intertwined—often leading to disruptive situations that would try the substantial skills of all participants involved in the ongoing political process in which the schools were enmeshed. And the participants were, and continued to be, abundant—board members, administrators, union executives, teacher leaders, business leaders, community leaders, parent association leaders, and a host of other players in the process. In many ways, the state of affairs in the district involved levels of anger, turf battles, and, indeed, internecine warfare that would try the skills and patience of a saint—or a bevy of saints. As the reader will see, the problems didn't to go away as the years went by; if anything, they grew even larger and became even more intractable.

CONTINUING WHITE FLIGHT AND CALLS FOR REFORM: THE 1980s AND 1990s

At its peak in 1950, Detroit boasted nearly 1.9 million residents. Over the next 40 years, as we noted earlier, the city lost nearly half its population, falling to just over 1 million inhabitants by 1990. As Mirel (1998, p. 253) observes, "Due to the almost unrelenting exodus of whites since the 1950s, by 1990 over three-quarters of Detroit's inhabitants were African American, most of whom lived in racially isolated neighborhoods. According to sociologists Reynolds Farley and William Frey (1994), in 1990 Detroit ranked as 'the most segregated' of the forty-seven cities [metropolises] in the United States with populations of a million or more."

The city was also becoming extremely poor, with unemployment exceeding 15 percent in 1992, more than twice the national average. And, as one would expect, poverty's burden weighed heavily on the lives of Detroit's children. According to a study by the Children's Defense Fund, in 1990 over 46 percent of Detroit's children were living in poverty, one of the highest rates in the nation. This flight of white, middle-class families was prompted in large part by the aforementioned 1974 U.S. Supreme Court decision in *Milliken v. Bradley* (1974). In this decision, the court once again ruled that communities neighboring Detroit had no obligation to participate in an interdistrict desegregation plan aimed at improving educational opportunities for the city's overwhelmingly low-income minority student population. For Detroit, this ruling accelerated the ongoing student exodus. After peaking at nearly 300,000 students in 1966, with about equal numbers of blacks and whites, district enrollment fell to about 170,000 by 1990, with about 90 percent African Americans. And more than two-thirds of these children came from families living in poverty (Mirel 1998, p. 242).[7]

The flight of middle-class families from Detroit markedly increased the challenge of improving student achievement in DPS. While elementary schools showed some improvement on the California Achievement Test and Michigan's assessments (MEAP), high school outcomes were generally dismal.[8] For example, in 1987, the average ACT score in Detroit was about 14, more than four points below the national average and a *Detroit News* survey found that Detroit high school students had the lowest average ACT and SAT scores of the 10 largest school districts in the nation (Mirel 1998, p. 242).[9] Detroit's high schools were also beset with ongoing problems of student discipline and declining academic standards. Regarding Detroit's declining academic standards, Mirel observes:

> Declining academic standards had become a chronic problem since the end of World War II as increasing numbers of white working class and black high school students in Detroit were routinely and disproportionately placed in the general track and fed a steady diet of watered-down academic and personal development courses. This pattern did not change when the school system became majority black in the 1960s. As the nation began to raise graduation requirements in the late 1970s, Detroit followed suit, increasing the total credit hours for graduation from 160 to 200 and increasing the number of academic courses needed to graduate . . . At the same time, however, school leaders doubled the credit hours granted for a host of non-academic courses which to some extent neutralized the impact of the increases in academic subjects. Moreover, the system created a number of new "academic" courses that focused mainly on very basic skills and knowledge . . . In 1983, the system did put into place a basic skills competency test which when passed allowed students to graduate with an "endorsed," but not a regular, high school diploma. (p. 243)

The Erosion of Financial Control and Public Trust

While problems with student discipline, school safety, and academic standards concerned parents and educators, the district's deepening financial crisis commanded the attention of press and public. As a property-poor school district, DPS was heavily reliant on state aid for its operating revenue. Michigan's general aid system, a so-called guaranteed tax base formula adopted in 1973–74, served Detroit and other districts with low or declining property values well for six years as the state enjoyed generally robust economic health. This prosperity, however, came to an abrupt halt in the spring of 1980, when the nation plunged into recession. State aid fell sharply in 1980–81 and declined further the following year as the state remained in the grip of what was then the deepest and most persistent recession since the Great Depression.[10]

State aid rebounded in 1983–84 with the largest annual increase to date, due to economic recovery and a substantial albeit temporary increase in Michigan's personal income tax rate.[11] Nevertheless, despite the fact that Detroit voters substantially increased the district's operating millage rate in a series of referenda stretching from 1977 to 1985, bringing in considerable state matching aid under the guaranteed tax base formula, the district's finances remained in disarray for the entire decade of the 1980s.[12] After balancing its 1977–78 operating budget, DPS closed its books the following year with a small deficit, about one-half of 1 percent of annual spending.

Incredibly, despite the sizable increases in operating millage rates and matching state aid of the mid-1980s, the district amassed 11 consecutive annual budget deficits, culminating in a $159 million shortfall in 1988–89, an astounding 21 percent of budget. In 1983–84, the district closed its fiscal year with a $49 million operating deficit, the sixth consecutive annual deficit and the district's largest since 1973. In November 1984, Detroit voters approved a four-mill increase for school operations, the third increase in seven years. This local tax increase, which brought the district about three dollars in matching state aid for each local tax dollar, could have easily eliminated the district's deficit and created a fund balance for the district to protect against, and perhaps help to stem, continuing student exodus. The DPS school board, however, granted teachers a 10 percent raise for 1985–86 and 7 percent the next year. Consequently, the district ended its 1986–87 fiscal year with a $26 million deficit. When the board proposed no pay raise for 1987–88, the teachers walked out. The strike lasted three weeks, ending with a contract giving teachers a 6.5 percent raise that year and 7 percent the next. Predictably, the district's budget deficit exploded, reaching nearly $160 million by the close of 1988–89 and forcing the district to sell deficit bonds in 1990. As a result, Detroit taxpayers were strapped with 13 additional mills over 10 years to service that debt. Moreover, unlike the operating millage that entitled the district to generous matching state aid, these debt mills raised only local tax dollars. Once again, the interests of the powerful teachers union prevailed and the taxpayers paid the price.

How did all of this happen? In large part, the chronic budget deficits of the 1980s reflected a failure of the school board, the administration, and the teachers union to place the public interest before their own. Each party needed to sacrifice in order to contain costs and improve school quality. Failure to sign affordable collective bargaining agreements and build fund equity to protect the school system's financial future undoubtedly fueled the continuing exodus of those families who could afford to leave. The teachers union would not hesitate to order a walkout, local voters would approve millage increases, and the school board would yield to union demands that, despite the millage increases, exceeded the district's ability to pay. Throughout this period, the state essentially stayed on the sidelines.

It was not until 1990 that the legislature passed the Local Government Fiscal Responsibility Act (PA 72 of 1990). This legislation explicitly empowered the state to declare a financial emergency in any unit of local government, including school districts. Evidence of such an emergency, as enumerated in the new law, includes the failure of the local government to eliminate an existing deficit in any fund within two years or the projection of a local government's general fund in excess of 10 percent. If the superintendent of public instruction determines that a school district has a financial emergency, the governor appoints an emergency financial manager, with the advice and consent of the senate. The manager's powers are broad and substantial, including authority to renegotiate existing labor contracts. Sec. 43 of PA 72 reads, in part: "The school board shall comply with orders issued by the emergency financial manager . . . " No longer would the state tolerate a local school board's chronic budget deficits.

HOPE: The Rise and Fall of Grassroots Reform

The district's chronic inability or unwillingness to balance its budget despite substantial millage increases approved by district voters gave rise to a very promising but ultimately unsuccessful reform movement: the HOPE campaign to wrest control of the school board from the bungling incumbents. This reform group of board candidates included Frank Hayden, an African American city employee who chaired the School-Community Relations Organization; David Olmstead, a white Harvard Law graduate and former member of the Michigan School Finance Commission; Larry Patrick, an African American attorney who cochaired the Group of Organized Detroiters for Quality Education (GOOD); and Joseph Blanding, an African American who worked as an international representative of the United Auto Workers. This reform group enjoyed broad support, with backers including the Greater Detroit Chamber of Commerce, the Metropolitan Detroit AFL-CIO, the DFT, New Detroit, Inc., both major daily newspapers in the city, and all other major news outlets. Mirel (1998) succinctly summarizes their broad reform goals and vision: " . . . the themes the HOPE candidates stressed in their campaign echoed those that dominated Progressive politics in Detroit in the 1910s and 1920s—the moral integrity of the reformers, their desire to restore public confidence in the school board through their commitment to the wise stewardship of funds, their ability to get the school system's fiscal house in order, their promise to run the schools more efficiently and effectively, and their plans to introduce corporate structural and management innovations" (p. 249).

The 1988 election, one of the most highly publicized in Detroit history, was a resounding victory for all four HOPE candidates and a stinging repudiation of both the incumbents and their so-called financial rescue plan, a proposed 6-mill tax hike and $160 million bond issue. Upon taking office, the new board was faced with state demands to eliminate the district's chronic budget deficit and hire a superintendent as a condition of continuing the state loan. In August 1989, the board appointed John Porter as interim superintendent. The highly regarded Porter had served as president of Eastern Michigan University and state superintendent of public instruction, the first African American to hold that post. Porter soon presented his financial plan for the district: a 6-mill increase for school operations and a $150 million bond issue, requiring an additional 1.5 mills for debt service. Although nearly identical to the former board's financial plan, which had been opposed by major Detroit organizations and repudiated by voters, Porter's plan was endorsed by the Greater Detroit Chamber of Commerce, the Detroit Association of

Black Organizations, Black Parents for Quality Education, and New Detroit, Inc., and both requests were approved by more than 60 percent of the voters. The 6-mill operating increase was particularly important, generating a 3-to-1 state aid match for the local property tax revenue and allowing the district to close a budget deficit that had persisted for 11 years.

The HOPE Team's Reform Agenda

Beyond the financial rescue, the HOPE reformers pressed for two major reforms: empowered schools and schools of choice. Both initiatives were bold and controversial, but the former proved far more combustible, precipitating the downfall of the HOPE team. The history and details of these proposals and the controversy surrounding them have been fully chronicled by Mirel (1998). This brief summary of the pivotal school empowerment controversy draws from Mirel's account.

In their 1988 campaign literature, the HOPE team characterized empowered schools as exercising "greater decision-making authority through a process in which the principal establishes regular and meaningful opportunities for representatives of students, parents, community administrators, instructional and noninstructional staff to have input into the selection of areas and/or problems which are addressed and to suggest the solutions and strategies to be used." The process was voluntary, requiring the support of the principal, 75 percent of the teachers, 55 percent of the support staff, 55 percent of the parents, and 55 percent of the students voting in favor of their school becoming "empowered." Following such a vote, the board allocated 92 percent of the district's per-pupil allocation to the school to be spent at their discretion. Nonempowered schools received only about 70 percent of their per-pupil allocation. Each empowered school would be run by an elected council of educators and parents. The council's authority would extend to virtually all aspects of school operations, including faculty assignments, class scheduling, curriculum, and length of school year. Further, empowered schools were free to purchase supplies and services from any vendor, not just DPS central administration. Central office would require all DPS schools to maintain balanced operating budgets and meet the district's student achievement standards, but empowered schools would decide how best to accomplish those basic goals. This arrangement, the HOPE team contended, would improve decision making and performance not only at each school, but in central office as well, as the DPS bureaucracy would have to compete with private vendors for school contracts (Hula, Jelier, and Schauer 1997).

Following a promising start with 15 empowered schools, the board sought to expand the prerogatives of these schools, including the right to unilaterally waive provisions of the union contract and allow the schools to select their own teachers and pay higher salaries to "lead teachers." At this point, union opposition to school empowerment rose precipitously, and on August 31, 1992, just before the scheduled school start, the teachers walked out. Detroit Federation of Teachers President John Elliot argued that the waivers demanded by the board would negate collective bargaining rights at those schools, including teacher tenure, and were unacceptable. The teachers' union was joined in this opposition to empowerment by the Organization of School Administrators and Supervisors, which viewed the principals' new managerial discretion as a distraction from their role as educational leaders.

The strike lasted 27 days, with recriminations escalating after the board went to court for a back-to-work order that the union ignored (Bradley 1992). The new contract allowed the board to increase the number of empowered schools but greatly reduced their discretion. Moreover, the agreement included salary increases over the next two years that threatened to return the district to a deficit position despite the substantial millage hike approved by the voters just two years earlier. By 1995–96, the district's fund balance would be essentially depleted and turn negative the following year.

The 1992 election and HOPE's demise

Lingering bitterness over school empowerment led the DFT and the Detroit AFL-CIO to actively campaign against the four HOPE team members' reelection bid in 1992. Union opposition proved critical in the campaign. Despite an impressive record, including improved standardized test scores and a remarkable financial turnaround that included the closure of a $160 million budget deficit in 1989 and a modest but rising surplus in their three ensuing years, only one of the four members, Republican Larry Patrick, was retained by the voters. In October 1993, Deborah McGriff, hired as superintendent by the reform board in 1991 to implement the HOPE policy agenda, announced her resignation following a brief but tumultuous tenure. David Snead, principal of Cass Tech and a longtime DPS educator, was hired to replace her. Many DPS observers interpreted Snead's appointment as the effective end of the HOPE grassroots reform effort and a return to the heavily union-influenced status quo (see Hula, Jelier, and Schauer 1997).

Why did HOPE fail? The demise of the HOPE team so soon after their stunning electoral victory signaled to many observers, including some powerful state leaders, the impossibility of meaningful DPS reform from within and a likely return to the chronic budget deficits and poor academic outcomes of the pre-HOPE era. Mirel (1998) observes,

> . . . the HOPE reformers drew some of their inspiration for empowered schools from the decentralization and school-based management experiments in Chicago, Miami, and Rochester. But the HOPE initiative differed from these experiments in one very important way—unlike them it did not draw its power or authority from a stable, dependable base. The Chicago reforms were "top down," mandated by the state legislature, while those in Miami and Rochester were "bottom-up," initiated mainly by the union. The Detroit reformers, on the other hand, had drawn their power and authority from more volatile sources, namely the coalition that supported them in the 1988 election, and the voters who put them in office. (p. 260)

Mirel asserts that the HOPE team misinterpreted its electoral mandate. Voters elected the team to rescue the district from its chronic budget deficits and, in the process, punish the incumbent board members for their profligate spending on out-of-state travel, chauffer-driven cars, and other indulgences that infuriated many Detroiters. Voters were not particularly interested in empowered schools or schools of choice. More importantly, the HOPE team underestimated both the power of the DFT and its resistance to change. The union understood the HOPE team's electoral appeal and their potential to sell a substantial millage increase to the voters. Beyond the financial rescue, however, the DFT leaders had little interest in the team's education reforms.

One participant has characterized this impasse and subsequent fight to the finish between the union and the reform board as the inevitable consequence of the city's "dysfunctional civic structure." He observes, "People don't know how to talk with one another on the basis of the problem . . . the civic language of Detroit is the old style of labor negotiations. I mean in your face, side deals, don't trust anybody, you know, what can I get for myself, and the only way I can get for myself is by pushing somebody else down—very, very win-lose, very dysfunctional" (Hula, Jelier, and Schauer 1997). It was precisely this unwillingness of Detroit's educational "cartel," including longtime board members, union leaders, school administrators, and school activists, to change the organizational culture and policies of the district, combined with the city's waning influence in the state legislature, that was to give rise in the decade of the 1990s to the state's assertion of its constitutional power over public schools, with DPS its principal target.[13]

The Waning of Local Control

In the 1990 gubernatorial campaign, Republican candidate (and later three-term governor) John Engler promised property tax relief and education reform if elected. Once elected, Governor Engler and the Republican-controlled Senate made a substantial property tax cut their top legislative priority. Aided by a dramatic tax cut proposal from State Senator Debbie Stabenow, herself a Democratic gubernatorial candidate at the time, Governor Engler and the legislature enacted Public Act 145 of 1993, Michigan's historic measure that eliminated entirely local property taxes for school operations. With nearly two-thirds of Michigan's public school funding wiped out—some $6.5 billion in total—the governor and legislature set for itself a deadline of December 31, 1993, to rebuild the finances of Michigan's public schools. And they fully intended to reform education policy and governance as well.

When Engler signed the property tax cut into law in August of 1993, he predicted "stunning improvements" in public education resulting from the forthcoming school finance and education policy reforms. His prediction, of course, was based on an ideology that favored educational choice and school competition. Little reliable social science research evidence existed at that time to either support or refute his claim. His subsequent recommendations, refined and passed with bipartisan legislative support, included the replacement of Michigan's 20-year-old guaranteed tax base general aid formula and numerous categorical grants with a foundation grant system, an expansive charter school program, and, in 1996, interdistrict public school choice. Clearly, state political leaders were intent on reforming more than the school funding system; they sought an alignment of school finance and education policy that would raise achievement levels across the state. With the state now financing 80 percent of school operating costs, setting school operating millage rates for every district, and giving families new school choices, local control of the public schools was clearly on the wane.

The assertion of greater state leadership in K–12 public education had begun in earnest in 1990, when the legislature enacted a set of systemic education reforms. Public Act 25 of 1990 called on all Michigan schools to undertake a formal school improvement process, initiate an accreditation process for each school building, provide the public with a yearly status report on local education performance levels and reform efforts, and provide a core curriculum for all students. The centerpiece of these reforms was the core curriculum. The new law directed the SBE to promulgate a *model* core curriculum, and the school aid appropriation provided a small fiscal incentive for local districts to adopt one core curricular area each year.[14]

By taking control of school tax and spending decisions, setting school curriculum standards, and opening avenues to school choice beyond local district boundaries, the state began exercising powers it had long held, but little used, as a matter of constitutional law. The courts have consistently held that authority over education resides with state government. The pervasiveness of this power is made clear by a Michigan decision that states "[t]he legislature has entire control over the schools of the state . . . The division of the territory of the state into districts, the conduct of the schools, the qualifications of teachers, the subjects to be taught therein, are all within its (the state's) control" (*Child Welfare Society of Flint v. Kennedy School District* 1922).

Alexander and Alexander (2005), in their authoritative volume *American Public School Law*, observe, "In holding that education is a state function, the courts maintain that the state's authority over education is not a distributive one to be exercised by local government, but is a central power residing in the state. The legislature has the prerogative to prescribe the methods of education, and the courts will not intervene unless the legislation is contrary to constitutional provisions.

Michigan's assertion of state authority over the public schools in the early 1990s would impact DPS even more dramatically later in the decade. Gone were the laissez-faire days of the late 1970s and the

1980s, when DPS concluded 11 consecutive fiscal years with budget deficits and the state just watched. For the new Republican leadership in Lansing, such local independence was seen as intransigence and irresponsibility, and given Detroit's waning political influence in the legislature, it would no longer be tolerated.

Prelude to the 1999 State Takeover

In the late 1980s, state officials had threatened the DPS board with a takeover if they could not resolve the district's financial problems. In 1989 Mayor Coleman Young called for the abolition of the elected board and direct mayoral control as a means of stabilizing the district's finances (Mirel 1998). Nevertheless, the district did manage to end its 1989–90 fiscal year with a small fund balance and maintain small balances through 1993–94. While Proposal A of 1994 shifted the bulk of K–12 finance from the local property tax to state tax revenue, still DPS, which had little property wealth itself and had long been reliant on the state for most of its operating revenue, depleted its fund balance in 1994–95 and actually fell into deficit the following year.

The district fund balance recovered in 1996–97 and grew over the next two fiscal years, peaking in 1998–99 at $115 million, or about 9 percent of operating expenditures. Nevertheless, despite the district's relatively strong balance sheet and the solvency of the great majority of Michigan's school districts, Governor Engler, in his January 1999 State of the State address, renewed an earlier call for a state takeover of academically failing school districts. Citing Illinois legislative action giving Chicago Mayor Richard Daley authority to appoint the city's school board and chief executive, Engler proposed that the legislature give Michigan's mayors authority over schools (Franklin 2003). Although the initial takeover bill allowed for the "reconstitution" of any district that fell short of specific academic and fiscal standards, subsequent amendments created a Detroit-only bill, a result then DPS Superintendent Eddie Green attributed to anti-Detroit politics (Green 1999). The DPS board also pushed back, accusing the governor of concealing his real motive. Detroit School Board President Darryl Redmond charged that Engler's real purpose for urging the takeover was not improved student achievement but control of the district's $1.5 billion school bond referendum approved by district voters in 1994 (*Detroit News* 1999).

Redmond's charge was considered outlandish or dismissed as political hyperbole by most observers in Lansing and around the state, but his remarks reflected the deep distrust of state Republican leadership on the part of many Detroiters.

The Senate bill introduced by Republican Majority Leader Dan DeGrow and three colleagues, two Republicans and a Democrat, would amend the state school code but apply only to Detroit. The bill empowered mayors in cities with school districts enrolling at least 100,000 students (a convention used elsewhere in the school code to single out DPS for special treatment) to appoint a five-member reform school board, each of whom would serve a four-year term. The board would hire a CEO. The duties and powers of the elected school board would be suspended. The new governance system would remain in effect for five years. At that point Detroit voters could petition for a referendum on the continuation of the mayoral appointed board or a return to an elected board (Michigan Senate 1999).

A racial divide

A 1999 poll published in the *Detroit News* showed a majority of Detroiters believed the public schools were in need of reform, but sentiment over the proposed takeover legislation split along racial lines. About three-fourths of white respondents backed the proposal while more than half of African Americans polled opposed the legislation (Franklin 2003, p. 102). A reluctant Dennis Archer, the city's second African American mayor, came to support the takeover bill following a bipartisan deal negotiated by Senator Virgil Smith, the only African American member of the Detroit legislative delegation supporting the takeover, which would boost the district's annual state aid by $15 million (McConnell and Christoff 1999).

The Republican-majority House passed its own takeover bill with bipartisan support. Under this plan the governor would appoint a monitor to run the schools while retaining the elected Detroit Board of Education in an advisory role. The monitor's term would expire in 2003, when new board elections would be held and the local board's authority would be restored. The six Detroit Democrats who supported the House bill claimed that it, unlike the Senate version, protected the voting rights of Detroiters and placed responsibility for reform clearly on the governor (Franklin 2003).

Franklin (2003) asserts that this support of the House bill also stemmed from the House Democrats' dislike and distrust of Mayor Archer. One caucus member, Representative Lamar Lemmons, in an interview with the *Detroit Free Press*, explained his preference for Governor Engler over Mayor Archer as takeover leader: "If you want a plantation analogy, it's African Americans' experience that overseers are often worse than dealing with the master" (Bell 1999). The House bill was also a tactical response to the Senate version. The minority Floor Leader of the House Democrats, Detroiter Kwame Kilpatrick, called the bill a "strategic move" to frame negotiations with the Republicans (McConnell 1999).

The legislative compromise

In response to the House version, the Senate amended its own bill. The proposed school board was increased to seven members, with six appointed by Mayor Archer and the seventh seat given to state school superintendent Art Ellis or his designee, representing the governor. The board would hire the CEO, but the governor's representative was given unique veto authority over this crucial appointment.[15] The elected Board of Education would serve in an advisory capacity (Bell and Christoff 1999). The bill passed in both the Senate and the House with immediate effect, despite the opposition of all 13 House members from Detroit. Governor Engler quickly signed the bill, and Mayor Archer appointed Detroit's school superintendent, Eddie Green, as acting CEO until the new reform board selected a permanent chief executive.

Policy or Politics?

What prompted the singling out of DPS for takeover? Was it the low academic achievement of the students, the concern raised most often by proponents of the move and cited in the statute? As correctly noted by the opposition, DPS students were outperforming students in a number of other urban districts. If Detroit's achievement levels were so unacceptable to political leaders in Lansing as to prompt the takeover legislation, why were districts with lower achievement scores, including Inkster, Benton Harbor, Highland Park, Grand Rapids, Pontiac, Flint, and Muskegon not also targeted?

Was state concern over the district's finances behind the state's action? In fact, the district's financial position appeared to be steadily improving over the three years preceding the takeover. After closing the 1995–96 fiscal year (the first year under Proposal A) with a $2.7 million deficit, the district's year-ending fund balance rose steadily over the next three fiscal years, peaking at $115 million at the close of 1998–99.[16] The takeover was justified by political leaders on academic grounds, but passage of the Detroit-only measure clearly reflected the city's declining political influence in Lansing. Franklin (2003) notes,

> Between 1950 and 1990 Detroit's population fell from about 1.8 million to just over 1 million. As a result, the city has lost membership in the state House of Representatives from thirty seats in 1950 to twenty in 1970, to thirteen in 1999. Declining population had also affected Detroit's voting power. In the 1958 gubernatorial election, about 25 percent of the votes came from Detroit. In 1978, the city accounted for 11.5 percent of the votes, and in the 1998 election for 7.5 percent of the votes. And recently passed term limit legislation would soon force the most senior members of the Detroit legislative delegation, whose tenure and experience provided them with the greatest influence, to leave office. (pp. 110–111)

In political terms, the takeover did more than reflect Detroit's weakened position in Lansing. It also exposed a fissure in the city's Democratic power structure between Mayor Archer and his critics in the Michigan House, who felt he was too conciliatory toward Governor Engler during the takeover negotiations. Did Archer concede too much to Engler in this process, or did he correctly assess what was a political *fait accompli* given the votes in the legislature and then successfully back the amended Senate bill that empowered him, not the House bill that would have frozen him out? The latter seems more plausible. Archer viewed his power to appoint the school board members as an opportunity to improve school policy and administration while, at the same time, burnishing his resume as a future contender for statewide political office. Archer's decisions in the takeover process made sense as good policy and good politics.

The Appointed Board

The appointed board's first major task was appointing the CEO, a position empowered by the takeover law, Michigan Public Law 10, to fire teachers and principals, waive provisions of union contracts, and reorganize failing schools.[17] When the board could not agree on a candidate acceptable to the governor's designee, they appointed former Wayne State University president David Adamany as interim CEO. Although the takeover legislation was ostensibly motivated by concerns over students' academic achievement, district finances always remained a focus of the debate. Early in his tenure, Adamany ordered a financial audit of the district. This audit, the first such examination in a dozen years, uncovered widespread shoddy accounting practices, and charges of embezzlement were brought against three former bookkeepers. Further, 15 high school principals were cited for missing funds, unrecorded ticket revenue, and the use of school funds for personal expenses (Harmon 2000).

On January 18, 2000, the governor's designee, state Treasurer Mark Murray, who had replaced Ellis as the governor's representative, and the board's only white member, exercised his unique veto power to block the appointment of John Thompson, superintendent of the Tulsa, Oklahoma, schools, to succeed Adamany as the permanent CEO of DPS (Piliawsky 2003).[18] On May 4, 2000, the reform board selected Detroit native Kenneth Burnley, then superintendent of Colorado Springs Public Schools, as the district's first permanent CEO. The appointment was time limited. A sunset clause in the takeover statute required that Detroit voters decide in 2005 whether to continue mayoral control of DPS or return to the elected board. Public debate of the governance issue never subsided. New mayor Kwame Kilpatrick, elected in 2001, campaigned to continue the mayor's authority to select the CEO and establish an elected but advisory board of education. Kilpatrick, a former middle school teacher in Detroit and later Democratic state representative and minority leader of the Michigan House, became, at age 31, one of the nation's youngest mayors. While he was House minority leader, Kilpatrick opposed the idea of an appointed board (Mirel 2004). But he also opposed a return to the pretakeover system, a position he articulated to the *American School Board Journal* in 2004: "A return to the old board system runs the very high risk of undoing the progress that's been made, condemning ourselves to repeat the mistakes of the past, and forcing future generations to pay the price. That cannot happen" (Cook 2004).

Detroiters go to the polls (Proposal E of 2005)

Following the legislature's rejection of a Kilpatrick plan for continuing mayoral control of the public schools, the mayor decided to place the question before the Detroit voters in the November 2005 election. City leadership was divided on the issue. Supporters included the Detroit Chamber of Commerce, the Detroit Urban League, and the Black Slate, the political arm of the church Shrine of the Black Madonna. The opposition included the Detroit branch of the National Association for the Advancement of Colored People, the American Federation of State, County, and Municipal Employees, Keep the Vote, and a group called the Coalition to Defend Affirmative Action, Integration Rights and Fight for Equality by Any Means Necessary (Rich 2009, p. 158).

Kilpatrick, whose political career would be derailed three years later in a notorious text-message scandal and related perjury conviction, found himself embroiled in controversy during his November 2005 campaign for Proposal E and his own reelection.[19] Controversy arose over the lifestyle of the "hip-hop mayor," focused on the lease of a sport utility vehicle for his family. Kilpatrick won reelection, but Detroit voters hammered Proposal E by a 65 to 35 percent margin and approved the reinstitution of an elected school board. In 2005 Governor Granholm signed legislation rescinding the 1999 DPS takeover.

ASSESSING THE TAKEOVER YEARS

Governor Engler signed the original takeover bill in March of 1999. Mayor Archer appointed then Superintendent Eddie Green as acting CEO, and the new reform board selected David Adamany interim CEO in the fall of that year. In May 2000, the board selected Kenneth Burnley as the permanent CEO. During the first two years of the takeover, DPS enjoyed some measure of success in terms of both district management and student achievement.[20] For example, Adamany launched a successful building repair program and initiated the installation of an upgraded payroll management system. Both initiatives were applauded by labor and management alike. Another important reform, however, drew labor's wrath. Acting at Adamany's behest, the Republican-controlled legislature passed a law prohibiting principals and assistant principals from joining unions. The new law, which made principals middle managers and applied only to DPS, was unsuccessfully challenged by the DFT in federal court.

Year one of the takeover was marred, however, by an ominous sign: the loss of more than 6,000 students. Although DPS enrollment had declined in each of the three previous years, the loss sustained in 1999–2000, precipitated by a teacher strike voted by the union on August 30, dramatically accelerated the downward trend. The student losses continued to mount the following year, Burnley's first full academic year, with a drop of nearly 5,000 in the fall pupil count. District enrollment was relatively stable over the next two years, with a net loss of about 800 students, but the worst was yet to come.

Burnley's tenure

During his five-year tenure, Burnley made district finances and the capital program top priorities. Inheriting a massive $1.5 billion bond program approved by Detroit voters in 1994, Burnley directed the construction of 21 new schools and the renovation of many others. Other accomplishments included the installation of the new payroll system, outsourcing the management of the food service and school maintenance programs, and the purchase of 400 new school buses. And better yet, student achievement rose, with 4th grade reading scores reaching 70 percent proficiency on the MEAP (Rich 2009, p. 156).

The district's financial position, however, began to deteriorate by Burnley's third year, largely the result of collapsing enrollment. The fall 2003 pupil count plummeted a stunning 11,503 students from the prior year, and another 10,577 were lost the following year. These losses, the first of a longer-term collapse of DPS enrollments that has continued unabated to the present day, drastically reduced the district's operating revenue. Unable to reduce spending commensurately, the district spent its fund balance, which fell from $104 million at the close of 2001–02 to a deficit of $49 million in 2003–04 and a mere $4.7 million balance at the 2004–05 book closing.

The difficulties in managing such a decline in enrollment and revenue cannot be overstated. Noninstructional spending can be lowered through privatization, competitive bidding, and generally improved management. But eventually the classroom can no longer be protected. When the takeover commenced in 1999, DPS employed just over 8,000 classroom teachers. By the fall of 2005, at the takeover's end, the district's teaching force had dwindled to just over 4,600 (Michigan Department of Education n.d.). Due to seniority privileges in the DFT collective bargaining agreement, however, the teacher layoffs were aimed at the newer, lower-salaried teachers. As a result, the average teacher salary in the district rose from $42,774 in 1999–2000 to $69,379 in 2004–05. At the same time, the district's per pupil operational spending soared from $8,269 to $10,957.

Nevertheless, despite the severe financial problems triggered by plummeting enrollments and exacerbated by collective bargaining constraints on his management options, Burnley deserves generally high marks for his financial stewardship of DPS, particularly over his first three years as he rebuilt the district's crumbling infrastructure, shored up management controls, and maintained a respectable fund balance. Certainly, the problems multiplied during his last two years as students fled the district at an increasing rate. Still, Burnley managed to rebuild a modest fund balance during his final year, and while that year was a difficult one, the district's problems only accelerated following his departure.

An Elected Board Returns and the Decline Accelerates

In 2005, the newly elected board extended the appointment of William F. Coleman, a former deputy superintendent in Dallas, Texas, as DPS superintendent. On August 28, 2006, a little over one year into Coleman's tenure, the teachers' union voted to strike. This walkout lasted two weeks and proved a political and financial disaster for the district. With charter schools and schools of choice options available to Detroit families, DPS enrollment plummeted to 117,568, a staggering loss of more than 14,000 students. After two weeks, the parties agreed to a one-year pay freeze with small increases in the following two years. Four months later, Virginia Cantrell defeated Janna Garrison, leader of the ill-fated strike, for the presidency of the DFT (Rich 2009, p. 160).

The 2006 strike contributed to the superintendent's demise as well. Following a dispute between Coleman and board members over financial irregularities, on March 8, 2007, the board terminated Coleman's contract and appointed the district's chief labor relations officer, Lamont Satchel, interim superintendent.

Following a hurried search that attracted a weak applicant pool, the board appointed Connie Calloway, then superintendent of the 5,700-student school district in Normandy, Missouri, to be the new DPS superintendent. Calloway took office on July 1, 2007, the district's sixth superintendent in 14 years. On that date, the district began its 2007 fiscal year with a miniscule but positive fund balance of just over $7 million. Calloway and her administration sought to shore up the district's balance sheet, proposing a central office reorganization that would purportedly save nearly $1 million annually and inviting outside auditors to examine the district's finances. The reorganization plan, which called for a smaller central office staff, was approved by the board in October 2007.

The report of the outside auditors, however, was not embraced by the board. The report was highly critical of past district leadership, citing decades-old management problems, including deficits masked for years by short-term borrowing and interfund transfers. The auditors also found more than 600 teachers on the payroll but not in the budget. This report embarrassed board members, and relations between Calloway and the board were further strained by very public confusion over the district's financial status, with a report by Calloway and district CFO Joan McCray of a projected FY 2009 budget surplus, followed quickly by a revised projection of a $408 million deficit. This alarming projection prompted State Superintendent Mike Flanagan to recommend to Governor Granholm that she appoint a review team to examine the district's finances under the authority of Public Act 72 of 1990, the state's Local Government Fiscal Responsibility Act. The review team, which by law consists of the state superintendent, state treasurer, state budget director, and nominees of the speaker of the Michigan House and the senate majority leader, has 30 days to examine the district's finances and report its findings to the governor as to whether a financial emergency exists in the district.

Meanwhile, the student exodus continued unabated, with the fall 2007 count showing a loss of about 11,400 pupils from the prior year, followed by the loss of about 10,800 the next year (see Figure 7.1). The associated revenue losses proved disastrous, with the district closing the 2007–08 fiscal year with a $140 million deficit and the 2008–09 balance sheet with $219 million in red ink (see Figure 7.2). The inability of Calloway's administration to come to grips with the district's deteriorating finances, combined with board sensitivity over the public airing of the district's financial laundry, proved her downfall. Calloway was fired by the board on December 15, 2008, two months after Flanagan's triggering of the Public Act 72 review process and less than 18 months after taking office. District General Counsel Teresa Gueyser was appointed chief administrator pending the appointment of an interim superintendent. The district now had its 10th chief executive in 20 years, going back to John Porter's appointment in 1989.

The Financial Emergency

By early 2009, with the review team's report in hand, State Superintendent Flanagan and Governor Granholm had determined that a financial emergency did indeed exist in DPS. On January 26, 2009, Granholm, under authority of Public Act 72 and with the advice and consent of the state senate, appointed Robert C. Bobb Emergency Financial Manager for the district. He brought to the job an impressive resume, including service as the president of the Washington, DC, Board of Education, an elected position, and city manager and deputy mayor of the district. He had also served as city manager for Oakland, California; Richmond, Virginia; and Kalamazoo, Michigan; among other posts. His one-year appointment in Detroit commenced on March 2, but would be extended an additional year, to March 1, 2011.

The Freefall Continues

The Michigan statute governing the appointment of an emergency financial manager, providing as it does for a one-year appointment, suggests the emergency manager's role is not unlike that of an EMS team director at a disaster site. The carnage, one hopes, is mostly concluded, and the team's task is to staunch the bleeding and treat the injured. But in DPS, the carnage was far from over when Bobb assumed the financial reins. In the very short run, he was unable to halt the exodus of students from DPS or cut spending at a pace to offset revenue

Figure 7.1 DPS Enrollments, 1970 through 2009: Fall Counts

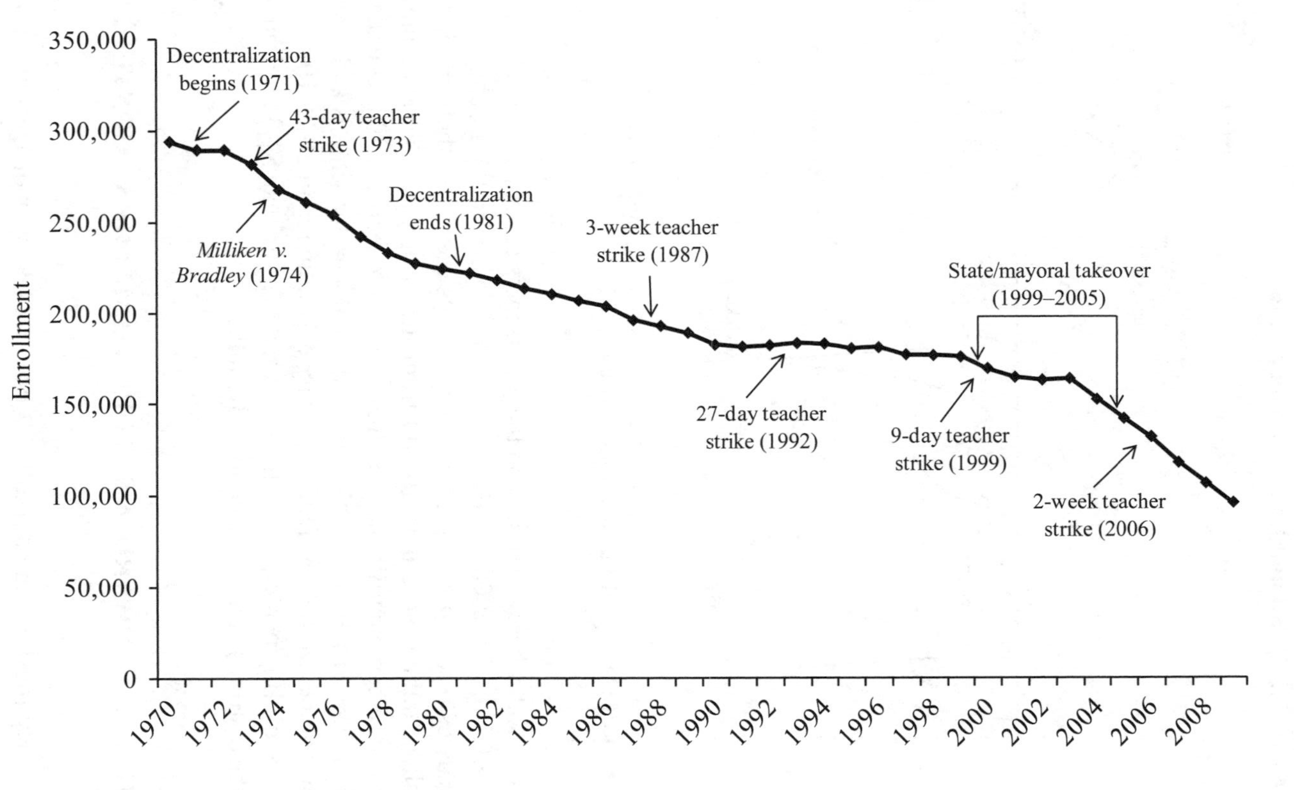

SOURCE: MDE Bulletin 1011, various years.

Figure 7.2 DPS Fund Balance History, 1970–2009

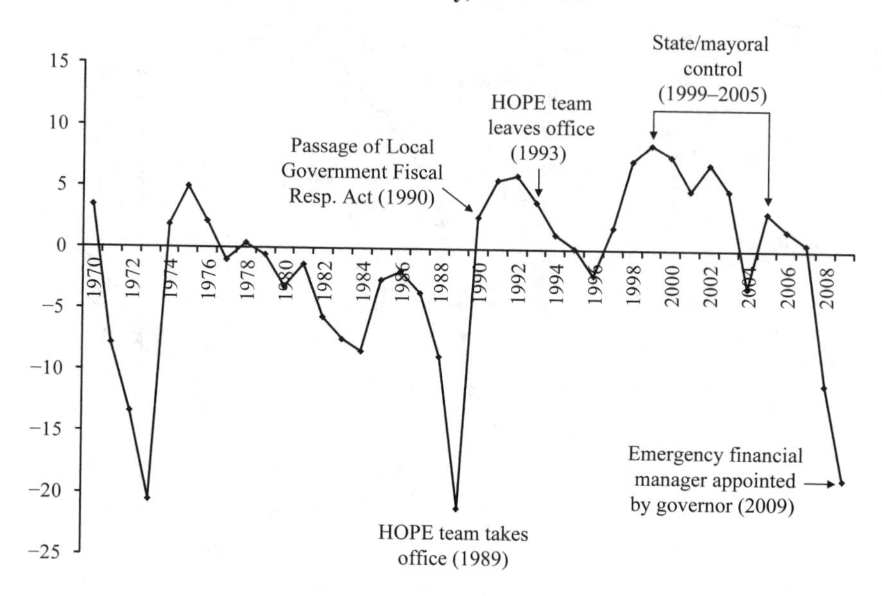

NOTE: Fund balance is a percentage of current operating expenditures.
SOURCE: MDE Bulletin 1011, various years.

losses. After three months on the job, Bobb's administration closed the books on the 2008–09 fiscal year with a $219 million deficit. When classes resumed in September, enrollments continued their precipitous slide, falling more than 10,000 from the prior year. The appointment of an emergency financial manager failed to boost public confidence in DPS and stem the outflow of students to charter schools and schools of choice. Moreover, DPS operating expenditures in 2009–10 actually rose by 10.3 percent from the prior year, to more than $1.34 billion, and the district's deficit soared to $332 million.[21]

GOING FORWARD: A RETURN TO MAYORAL CONTROL?

By most accounts, the 1999 mayoral takeover of DPS was a failure, but not entirely of the district's making. With the state's launch of aggressive charter schools and schools of choice programs, DPS enrollments plunged and finances deteriorated. Most important, student achievement stagnated after an early bounce and high school graduation rates remained alarmingly low. Further, the five years of mayoral control did not establish a foundation for the successful return to an elected board. To the contrary, the district's academic performance and financial condition have worsened significantly since the restoration of the elected board. Indeed, by any valid measure of district performance, DPS is in a more perilous position today than it was in 1999. However, while an argument on the merits for mayoral control may be persuasively made in 2010, the issue has become politicized in the extreme. Opponents of the 1999 takeover, including union leaders, elected board members, school administrators, and local school activists, managed to deflect attention away from the district's academic and financial deficiencies and, instead, portray DPS as the victim of an undemocratic state usurpation of local autonomy and voting rights. Nevertheless, the perilous condition of DPS, the embarrassing escapades of the elected board, and the imminent departure of the emergency financial manager well before the emergency is over have led some state and local leaders to call for an advisory vote of the city's electorate on the mayoral control question. Such a move has enjoyed a measure of success in other U.S. cities.

Mayoral Control in Urban Districts

The notion of running urban school districts out of city hall has gained popular support in recent years. In the 2006 Gallup poll, 29 percent of respondents favored mayoral control. By 2007, this figure had risen to 39 percent, and to 42 percent among parents. By 2008, nearly two-thirds of the states had passed legislation authorizing either the city or the state to govern and manage school districts that are underperforming (Wong 2009, p. 64). Wong et al. (2007) analyze 104 big-city school systems across 40 states and standardized achievement data from thousands of schools, comparing districts run by elected boards with those under mayoral control. They find that mayoral control has a statistically significant, positive effect on student achievement and also improves school district management and financial administration. However, city hall has generally not succeeded in narrowing the achievement gap between the highest—and lowest—performing schools (Wong 2009, p. 65).

At the same time, while the researchers found that city hall makes a difference, they offer two important caveats: first, a mayoral takeover may require a couple of years for improvement in districtwide achievement results, and second, the absence of any restrictions on whom the mayor appoints to the school board seems to dampen student achievement. Accordingly, Wong recommends that a system of mayoral control include a nominating committee that provides the mayor with a slate of candidates from which to select board members. He also cautions that evaluations of these systems allow at least two years for improvements in districtwide achievement results (Wong 2009, pp. 69–70).

Structure and context matter

While research tells us that mayoral control can boost school performance, it is no panacea. Previous district achievement remains strongly predictive of current achievement in takeover districts, and achievement gaps between high- and low-performing schools remain exceedingly difficult to close, at least in the short run. Indeed, the evidence suggests that takeover mayors have worked to maintain "lighthouse" schools to anchor middle-class neighborhoods in their cities. In this way, mayoral control has actually been associated with *greater* achievement stratification, as the lowest performing schools do not improve as much as some of the highest performers. As the mayors see it, their cities need to maintain a strong, middle-class population, and lighthouse schools are necessary to attract and keep those families in the city.

In keeping with a vast amount of previous research evidence, Wong and colleagues find a significant and negative correlation between a school's percentage of low-income, Hispanic, and African American students and academic achievement, particularly among high schools. The researchers conclude that "while mayors can produce significant, positive change at the high school level, it is evident that deeper challenges remain for a school system hoping to overcome underperformance" (Wong 2009, p. 83).

Financial management

Mayor-led districts do not spend more than board-led districts but they spend differently, outsourcing noninstructional services such as transportation, food service, safety services, and information technologies, and reallocating resources to instruction and instructional support. Most notably, mayors have been more able than elected boards to control labor costs, effectively leveraging cooperation and, on occasion, concessions from school employee unions. Such success in controlling labor costs, sometimes abetted by the enabling legislation granting mayoral control, has resulted in higher school district bond ratings and improved public satisfaction with the schools. Chicago is a notable example. The 1995 legislation barred any teacher strike during the first 18 months of mayoral control, contributing to both labor peace and a balanced district budget. This led, in turn, to an improved district bond rating from Standard & Poor's, enabling the appointed board to raise billions to finance districtwide capital improvements (Wong 2009, p. 83).

Mayoral control: Why it works

On the basis of their extensive research, Wong and colleagues find that mayoral control has generally raised student achievement and improved program administration and financial management. Why this success? The researchers see the mayors assuming a stronger mandate to improve school district outcomes than do elected school boards. The mayor's office has more juice than the board office. Wong (2009) observes,

> As an institution, the office of the mayor can play an instrumental role in improving district performance. The institutional form of charisma does not depend on a charismatic person for its foundation. Instead, "corporate bodies—secular, economic, governmental, military, and political—come to possess charismatic qualities simply by virtue of the tremendous power concentrated in them" (Shils 1965, p. 207). Because the office of the mayor carries stature and respect independent of the particular person who occupies the position, mayoral involvement can add substantial value to the school reform process. (p. 85)

WHAT'S NEXT FOR DPS?

While the emergency financial manager's appointment expired on March 1, 2011, the district's financial emergency most assuredly did not. The superintendent of public instruction, as expected, called for the appointment of a new emergency manager, this time by a new governor. Beyond that, little is certain. The elected board, which reportedly prepared to resume control of the district upon Robert Bobb's departure, is now reduced to the role of onlooker. A return to mayoral control of DPS is unlikely in the foreseeable future given the present dearth of political support.

So what is more likely to happen with DPS in the near term? The district has lost its status as Michigan's only Class 1 school district as a consequence of falling enrollment, thereby losing statutory protection against the opening of community college–authorized charter schools within its borders. Detroit Public Schools enrollments will continue to decline, perhaps at an accelerating rate, while charter school enrollments continue to climb. This trend will result in a hybrid system of public education in the city, comprised of traditional, DPS schools and charter public schools, some run by the district and a majority managed by private companies, including for-profit firms. And DPS will continue to lose children through schools of choice. This evolving system of public education will continue to provide parents with choices, and school leaders will be expected to open new schools and close those that fall short of achievement goals set by government. The system will be both market driven and government regulated, with all schools subject to increasingly stringent state and federal achievement standards.

These market and regulatory structures, of course, are driven more by politics and ideology than by solid evidence, and their success is far from assured. Indeed, the history of DPS presented here is marked by general socioeconomic decline; unproductive and, at times, destructive political conflict; financial mismanagement; revolving-door leadership; and educational silver bullets that have missed the mark. Can the long-awaited educational renaissance often promised but never delivered come to pass? Possibly, but much more than educational reform will be required. The essential building blocks of real and lasting improvement for schools and students remain unchanged: socially and economically stable families; strong and consistent leadership for the schools; and the capacity and willingness of government, business, and community leaders to cooperatively shape and support the city's evolving educational system.

Notes

1. Detroit was one of the 18 large urban school districts participating in the 2009 testing program as part of the NAEP's Trial Urban District Assessment. The district's participation was recommended by both national education experts and DPS officials to better evaluate the district's academic programs and student achievement on a national level (Bouffard 2010).
2. Richard Kahlenberg, "Ocean-Hill Brownsville at 40," *Taking Note, A Century Foundation Group Blog*, April 21, 2008. http://takingnote.tcf.org/2008/09/ocean-hill-brow.html (accessed July 21, 2011).
3. Mirel (1993) offers a telling quote from one survey respondent: "The teachers don't teach a damn thing . . . They don't give a damn if you don't learn or nothing, you know . . . Man, I didn't learn —— until I hit the 12th grade" (p. 312).
4. Coleman Young, at the time, was the leader of the black delegation in Lansing, and later was to become the elected mayor of the city of Detroit.
5. For a more broad perspective on the changing characteristics of public school children in large U.S. cities during the 1960s and the educational policies and programs designed to serve them, see Nelson (2005).
6. For the reader interested in a more detailed account of these happenings, we suggest a full reading of pp. 338–345 in Mirel (1993).
7. Mirel (1998) notes that the court-ordered busing program, which expired in 1989, was not the sole reason for the student exodus from Detroit. The perceived poor quality of education in most of the city schools also played a role. A 1990 survey conducted by the *Detroit Free Press* found that 14 percent of all African Americans in the city (and 25 percent of blacks with incomes over $20,000) sent their children to private or parochial schools. The figure was 43 percent for white Detroiters (Gilchrest 1990).
8. For more discussion of academic outcomes in Detroit schools during this period, see Mirel (1998, p. 242).
9. The ACT/SAT survey data are reported in Snider (1989).
10. For a discussion of Michigan school finance during this period, see Phelps and Addonizio (1983).
11. This tax increase, passed by the legislature and signed by Governor Blanchard in 1983, triggered the recall of two Democratic senators and a shift to a Republican majority in the Senate, elevating then little-known Senator John Engler to Senate Majority Leader. Seven years later, Engler would narrowly upset Blanchard in his quest for a third term.
12. Detroit voters were very generous toward their public schools during this time. Between September 1977 and November 1985, voters approved eight of nine tax

renewals or increases. The only defeat, an August 1980 rejection of a 3.5 mill increase, was reversed by voters three months later (Mirel 1998, p. 245).

13. The phrase *public school cartel* was coined by Wilbur Rich in Henig and Rich (2004).
14. The legislature refrained from mandating the core curriculum because of a provision in Michigan's 1978 constitutional tax limitation (Headlee) amendment, which requires the state to fully fund all new mandates imposed on local governments.
15. As the *Detroit News* put it, the "lawmakers handed [Governor Engler] a trump card over Mayor Archer in the selection of Detroit's school reform czar" (Piliawsky 2003).
16. Had the district failed to balance its operating budget in consecutive years, the state could have invoked the Local Government Fiscal Responsibility Act (Public Act 72 of 1990) and appointed an Emergency Financial Manager for DPS. That trigger, in fact, would be pulled 10 years later with the 2009 appointment of Robert Bobb as DPS financial czar.
17. Mayor Archer appointed Freeman Hendrix, his deputy mayor, as chair. Other mayoral appointees were New Detroit president Bill Beckham, Marygrove College president Glenda Price, community activist Marvis Coffield, Mexican Industries CEO Pam Aguirre, and Daimler Chrysler vice president Frank Fountain. State superintendent Art Ellis represented the governor.
18. The other board members supported Thompson's appointment by a five to zero vote, with one abstention (Piliawsky 2003).
19. Kilpatrick's primary opponent was Freeman Hendrix, former deputy mayor to Kilpatrick's predecessor, Mayor Dennis Archer, and Archer's selection to chair the appointed school board. Hendrix was not reappointed to the school board by Mayor Kilpatrick.
20. This brief summary draws from Rich (2009).
21. Detroit Public Schools FY 2010–11 Budget, adopted 6/30/10; available at http://detroitk12.org/data/finance/docs/FY 2011_Adopted_Budget.pdf.

8
Reflections on the Limits of Policy

As we neared the final chapter of this book, we began to reflect on our descriptions and discussions of the reforms, and attempts at reform, proposed and undertaken in Michigan over the past 40 years. We asked ourselves how we might make some coherent sense out of all of them. What framework or analytic schema might be helpful in organizing our reflections, might best serve to bring these endeavors together in reasoned and meaningful fashion? After some thought, we settled on a framework based on four predominant policy values that have long undergirded American education and certainly Michigan education: 1) equity, 2) adequacy, 3) efficiency, and 4) choice. Our initial question then became, to what extent have the policy reforms of the past 40 years, described in the preceding chapters, addressed these values and with what effect? And, ultimately, based on these reforms viewed in the light of these values, what have we learned and what might the future hold for Michigan public education?

First, a word about the four values. Equity is not necessarily equality, although sometimes it calls for equality. Equity is concerned with justice and fairness. It raises the question of whether the policy reforms have led to a system that is just and fair to the citizen taxpayers who have the responsibility of providing the resources necessary to develop and offer quality education programs in our public schools. It also raises the question of whether the policy reforms have been just and fair in their allocation of these resources among the more than 500 school districts, the more than 3,000 public schools, and the more than 1.5 million public school students in the state of Michigan. And, perhaps most importantly, equity raises the question of how just and fair the policy reforms have been in actually delivering a quality education to each and every child and young person who goes through our public school systems. In our descriptions and discussions in Chapters 2, 3, 4, and 7, we attempted to address each of these three questions.

The second value, adequacy, is a two-sided coin. The first side deals with the availability of resources and asks whether the revenue streams that the reform policies have put in place, principally state and local, are providing funds sufficient to deliver a quality education to each and every child and young person, and also asks the question whether these revenue streams are strong and stable enough to provide the necessary funds in both good and bad economic times. The second side of the adequacy coin raises the question of whether these same resources are sufficient to ensure that a quality academic program is offered in each and every public school and public school district. In short, adequacy concerns itself with the volume and stability of the revenue stream, as well as with the sufficiency of those revenues to the task of delivering a sound basic education from grades 1 to 12 to every public school student. In our discussions in Chapter 2, we addressed the first side of the adequacy coin, the question of the yield and stability of the state's revenue stream. In Chapter 4, which addressed the academic outcomes of schooling, we began to look at the other side of the adequacy coin, namely, whether the revenues are sufficient to provide a quality education, a sound basic academic education, to all the students in our public schools. In Chapter 7 we looked specifically at how DPS has fared, and is faring, in terms of the volume and stability of its revenue stream, as well as how successful the district has been in providing a quality education to its students.

Efficiency is a value near and dear to the hearts of most Americans and most Michiganders. It asks the question of whether the schools are making good use of the resources being provided them, whether we as citizens and taxpayers are getting "the best bang for the buck," whether money is making a difference, whether the schools are indeed being held accountable for student performance. We spoke to these questions initially in Chapter 2. In Chapter 3, we spent a good deal of time describing and commenting on past and particularly more recent efforts to develop a state accountability system for the schools of Michigan—so that citizens can be assured, in the words of the U.S. Congress and the U.S. Department of Education, that no child is being left behind, and that all children, all schools, and all school districts are making adequate yearly progress in bringing all students to acceptable levels of academic proficiency. In Chapter 4, we described at some length an important corollary to efficiency and accountability—the 40-year effort to develop and implement both a state assessment program and a national assessment program aimed at assessing the academic achievement levels of the students in our public schools, and then publicly reporting that information to the citizenry. In Chapter 7, we focused again on the dreadful failure of DPS to bring its students to acceptable levels of academic proficiency, as measured either by the MEAP or the NAEP.

Choice, the last of the four values, also has two dimensions. The first dimension, and the one that usually comes to mind, is choice of school for both students and parents. It is to this dimension that we devoted Chapters 5 and 6; in Chapter 7 we also turned the lens of choice on Detroit. Parental voice and parental choice, as well as student voice and student choice, became the *cause célèbre* of many national and state-level reform efforts beginning in the early 1990s. We have witnessed across the nation, and certainly here in Michigan, policymakers paying increasing attention to parents' and other citizens' power or right to choose the type and the setting of the schooling that will be provided to their children. In Michigan, this increasing attention led to the legislature's 1993 establishment and the rapid growth of charter schools, or public school academies (PSAs), as described and discussed at length in Chapter 5. The Michigan legislature in 1996 further enhanced parental and student choice in its adoption of the schools of choice program examined at length in Chapter 6.

The second dimension of choice, as applied to public education, usually goes by the name of local control—the extent to which educational decisions are left at the local school district level or centralized at the state level, or for that matter at the federal level. This dimension of educational choice is reflected in Richardson's (1976) comments, made some years ago but still relevant today: "The selective devolution of spending authority and of the responsibility of program planning and implementation can make American government more responsive and responsible to the American people . . . By moving authority and resources outward [maximizing choice at state and local levels], we can make more of American government accessible to public scrutiny and to public participation" (pp. 4–5).

In viewing policy reforms in public education of the past 10–20 years, one would have to conclude that the tide has turned and is now running strongly in the other direction. This, of course, raises the question of how much authority and decision making actually has moved upward and outward from the local district level to the state level and on to the federal level as a result of the education policy reforms and attempts at reform. While we do not address this dimension of choice directly in the preceding chapters, with the exception of the focus on Detroit in Chapter 7, our views are somewhat implicit, if not explicit, throughout our descriptions and discussions in all of our chapters. It would seem that there is no question but that recent years have seen an upward and centralizing movement of authority and decision making in American public education. Yet in Detroit, this movement has been something of a ping-pong phenomenon—first the decentralization effort of the 1970s, then the recentralization of the 1980s followed by the state takeover of the late 1990s and the early 2000s, then the return to an elected board in 2005 followed shortly after by the appointment of an emergency financial manager in 2009, and now the rising call beginning in 2011 for mayoral control of the schools.

A word of caution is in order for the reader. While we will attempt to proceed in orderly fashion and base our reflections on these four values, we will not necessarily succeed in treating them in sequential order; these values tend not only to be closely interrelated but they also compete with one another. As we have noted elsewhere:

> . . . the underlying values, demands and interests that drive public policy decisions are often mutually incompatible—in short, they compete with one another. These values, demands and interests—all vitally important to us as American citizens—include equity, adequacy, efficiency and choice . . . But when taken together, they all cannot be given equal weight. An answer to one will influence the answer to another. But that is inherent in the nature of the public policy process in our nation and state. Coming to an acceptable balance among these competing values, demands and interests is the continuing task before the citizens of the state and their elected representatives. (Kearney and Addonizio 2002, pp. 64–65)

EQUITY

Equity for Taxpayers

In reflecting on the policy reforms put in place in 1993–94 under Proposal A, one has to conclude that, with certain reservations, the reforms resulted in substantial improvement in equity for property taxpayers. Under Proposal A, total property taxes were reduced by about 26 percent. For homeowners the reduction was about 32 percent, and businesses enjoyed a cut of about 13 percent. In addition, homeowners who remain in their homes over a period of years benefit from Proposal A's introduction of a cap on annual increases in their residential property values. However, the cap is a mixed blessing—only homeowners who choose to stay in their homes over a long period of time actually benefit from the cap, since on resale the property is reassessed at 50 percent of market value, the normal assessment ratio. This circumstance has led over time to considerable disparities in assessed values among houses of comparable market value—resulting in significant differences in the property taxes paid by current owners of these houses. Yet both sets of owners enjoy the same level of school, municipal, and county services. This particular situation is neither fair nor just for the set of homeowners who are more mobile, who are less permanent in their primary residences.

The significant reduction in property taxes brought about by Proposal A also is a mixed blessing to the taxpayer in another way: it resulted in a significant reduction in property tax revenues, particularly in local tax revenues that had to be replaced through state taxing mechanisms. The revenue hole, in large part, was filled by an increase in the retail sales tax rate from 4 to 6 percent, rather than an increase in the personal income tax rate. Most would argue that the retail sales tax is, at the least, inherently but moderately regressive—that is, the lower the income of a family, the higher the percentage of its income that will go to pay the tax. This further reduces the equity characteristics of the overall tax structure that currently supports public education in Michigan. The retail sales tax also generally is a less stable tax, meaning its yield is more subject to fluctuations in the economy than is the property tax or the personal income tax.[1] We have more to say about this in our subsequent discussion of adequacy.

Before we leave our discussion of equity for taxpayers under the 1994 school finance reforms, we must note one problem that was completely ignored. Today in Michigan, no state school aid is provided for capital outlay financing. Local school districts are obliged to fund their capital needs from cash reserves, building and site sinking funds, or the sale of bonds. In the instance of both building and site sinking funds and bond sales, the local district must rely exclusively on its local taxpayers to provide the funds necessary to retire the debt. Since no equalization aid is provided by the state, considerable inequities accrue for both taxpayers and pupils due to the continuing large differences among school districts in their property tax bases. The sole assistance given by the state is through the School Bond Loan Program, wherein the local district can borrow from the state to help meet its annual principal and interest payments on its bonds. Again, we have a situation that is neither fair nor just for property taxpayers residing in property-poor school districts. Detroit, in particular, with its relatively low property tax base, suffers demonstrably from the lack of any state equalization aid for capital outlay financing. For example, when it comes to meeting capital outlay needs, Detroit would have to levy a property tax rate eight times the rate levied in neighboring Bloomfield Hills to generate the same amount of revenue for capital purposes.

While Michigan *property* taxpayers today are in a much more equitable situation than they were prior to the adoption of Proposal A, still, as *retail sales* taxpayers their situation has to be considered less equitable, particularly for those taxpayers in low-income households who feel the brunt of the tax's inherent regressivity.

In addition, the present precipitous downturn in the Michigan economy, coupled with rising rates of unemployment, has directly affected retail sales tax collections and contributed mightily to the current shortfall in state school aid revenues. What is the likelihood that Michigan citizens will see changes in the retail sales tax in the years to come, and subsequent improvements in the equity— as well as the adequacy—of the tax structure? If change is to come, what appears to be most advantageous is not a move away from the retail sales tax, but rather a move to broadening the base of the tax to services while at the same time moderately reducing its rate to, say, 5 percent or so. On the one hand, this would result in increased revenues, and on the other hand a lesser tax burden on lower income families.[2] But, as Ballard (2010) points out,

> The politics of sales-tax reform are very difficult. Lobbyists fight hard to maintain the privileged status of the services that currently get preferential treatment. And yet the *economics* of sales-tax reform are absolutely and completely solid. Extending the sales tax to services is a slam dunk, both in terms of fairness and in terms of economic efficiency. If we create a level playing field by taxing goods and services in the same way, our tax system will be

> both fairer and more efficient. If we continue with the current system, which taxes some activities at 6 percent while other activities get special treatment, the long-term effect will be the continued erosion of the tax base. This will perpetuate economic inefficiency and an unfair tax system, and it will damage our ability to pay for public services in Michigan. (pp. 184–185, emphasis in the original)

The foregoing discussion and comments on equity for taxpayers offer an ideal segue into a discussion of adequacy. But before we do that, we want to remain focused for a moment on notions of justice and fairness, and raise questions about the effects of Proposal A on equity for students.

Equity for Students

Did Proposal A lead to a more just and fair distribution of resources among the public school districts, public schools, and public school students of Michigan? When examining equity for students under the Proposal A reforms, it is useful to employ three definitions of equity. The first, which we call *horizontal equity*, calls for "equal treatment of equals," with the goal being to minimize the spread among districts in the distribution of basic programs and services or, as more often is the case, the spread in the distribution of dollars needed to pay for those basic programs and services. The second definition of equity, *fiscal neutrality*, calls for no variation among districts in basic or special programs and services as a result of factors considered suspect, such as local property tax wealth. The third, *vertical equity*, calls for "unequal treatment of unequals," with the goal being to provide for pupils with special needs, such as the handicapped or disadvantaged. Under this third definition, unequal dollars need to be made available for special programs and services for these pupils.[3]

At first blush, horizontal equity, a just and fair distribution of resources for all students, has improved appreciably as a result of the Proposal A reforms. Prior to the adoption of Proposal A, there were tremendous inequities in the distribution of basic program resources among Michigan's public school districts and public schools. In 1993–94, revenues per pupil, the usual measure employed in examinations of resource equity, ranged from a high of $10,377 per pupil in the Bloomfield Hills school district to a low of $3,261 per pupil in the Onaway school district—a difference of $7,116 per pupil! Even the doubters might agree that in this case money did indeed make a difference.

By school year 2000–01, the policy reforms enacted under Proposal A had changed Onaway's numbers significantly and Bloomfield Hills' numbers only moderately. Bloomfield Hills had grown slightly—some 10.4 percent over the seven years—to $11,854 per pupil. Onaway had grown significantly—some 48.5 percent over the same period—to $7,303 per pupil. While there still was a sizable difference, the difference had been reduced to $4,551 per pupil. In effect, very low revenue per pupil districts such as Onaway had been raised at a rapid rate over the period, while high revenue per pupil districts such as Bloomfield Hills had been held to lesser rates of increase over the same period. The goal wasn't equality, but rather equity, i.e., reducing the differences to what the legislature saw as just and fair given the circumstances; in effect, to put an acceptable foundation floor under each school district. By 2000–01 all Michigan school districts had been brought to at least that acceptable foundation floor and then were frozen in their relative positions, with each district increasing annually its revenue per pupil by identical amounts, and maintaining in the following years up to the present time the approximate $4,500 difference between the highest and lowest revenue per pupil districts. This leveling up process achieved what it was designed to do, i.e., narrow the gap between the high and low revenue districts. It certainly wasn't perfect equality, but it was a definite improvement in horizontal equity, fairness, and justice.

At first glance, it would appear that the 1993–94 reforms also brought about considerable improvement in *fiscal neutrality*. In past years, a district's property tax base—a suspect factor in terms of our definition of fiscal neutrality—was a major reason for the wide differences that existed among Michigan school districts in the dollars per pupil available to support basic programs and services. Under Proposal A's new foundation program, this strong connection was broken, at least in theory. Reliance on local property tax revenues has been reduced considerably; local revenues now account for only roughly 20 percent of total school revenues as opposed to their previous mark of better than 60 percent.

Still, vestiges of the past structure remain. In part, these are attributable to three decisions the legislature made in enacting the new foundation program. First, rather than move all districts in which the 1993–94 per pupil revenues were under $5,000 up to the $5,000 starting point immediately, the legislature chose to move these districts up gradually. Second, the legislature chose not to bring all remaining districts down to the $5,000 per pupil starting point in 1994–95. Rather, it chose to use each individual district's 1993–94 revenue per pupil level as the starting point and increase that level on a sliding scale, at least in the first year of the program. Third, the legislature chose not to "level down" but rather to "hold harmless" those districts in which 1993–94 per pupil revenue levels exceeded $6,500, as long as voters in those districts were willing to tax themselves at a commensurate rate in addition to the required 18 mill levy.

Because of these decisions, the past negative effects of large variances among school districts in their taxable property values per pupil remain to a considerable extent in the present arrangements. One might say they constitute *residual effects* that have yet to be removed. In fairness, the legislature may have had no other choice. To "level up" all districts would have placed an impossible demand on state revenue sources and undoubtedly was out of the question. To "level down" high spending districts very likely would have been politically impossible.

What of *vertical equity* under Proposal A's new school finance program? The answer to this question is much more difficult. On the one hand, we know that the legislature, in its finance reform package, increased substantially its commitment to funding programs for at-risk youngsters. A new categorical program provided some $230 million in additional funds in 1994–95 to school districts whose 1993–94 revenue per pupil was below $6,500 and that had a high incidence of children coming from poverty circumstances. This was accomplished by adding 11.5 percent (a 1.115 per pupil weighting) to the foundation allowance of those school districts that were eligible. Eligibility was determined on the basis of numbers of pupils eligible to receive free and reduced-price lunches in those districts whose 1993–94 per pupil revenues were below $6,500. This $230 million at-risk money was a part of the total of $1.3 billion that the legislature appropriated in 1994–95 for special and categorical programs. By 2002–03 funding for the at-risk program had risen to $314.2 million but has since leveled off and dropped a bit to $310 million in 2009–10. The federal government also provides another $1.5 billion earmarked for special needs. Undoubtedly, local school districts also direct some of their general fund dollars to support special needs programs. Thus, we can argue that all three levels—local, state, and federal—acknowledge and provide for "unequal treatment of unequals," that vertical equity is taken into account in Michigan's current public school finance arrangements.

On the other hand, we have no good way of determining whether these needs are being fully met. Furthermore, some contend that until we fully achieve horizontal equity and fiscal neutrality, our attempts to provide for vertical equity result largely in reducing differences in revenue per pupil caused by suspect factors rather than increasing, as they should, differences based on justifiable factors such as a high incidence of disadvantaged children. They argue, for example, that districts like Detroit or Grand Rapids, which have a high incidence of such pupils and do indeed receive substantial additional dollars per pupil under both the state "at risk" and other categorical and federal compensatory education programs, still lag far behind districts like Bloomfield Hills in total revenues per pupil. The attempt to address vertical equity concerns through categorical aid serves mainly to reduce somewhat the large initial gap in available revenues (and expenditures) per pupil between a Detroit or a Grand Rapids and a more revenue rich school district like Bloomfield Hills. In theory, if the system were working properly, and the three principles of horizontal equity, fiscal neutrality, and vertical equity all were coming fully into play, one would expect to find in Detroit or in Grand Rapids, when compared to Bloomfield Hills, a higher rather than lower level of total revenues per pupil and, subsequently, a higher rather than lower level of current operating expenditures per pupil. The reader might conclude that this is an interesting but undoubtedly impractical argument, at least for now.

ADEQUACY

The Strength and Stability of the Revenue Stream

We next turn our attention to a consideration of adequacy, and address first that side of the adequacy coin that deals with the strength and stability of the revenue stream. This, in our view, is the most pressing policy problem now facing Michigan public education. To put it bluntly, inadequacy is a better word to describe the current Michigan tax structure. For a number of reasons, the current tax structure is not delivering the revenues needed to adequately support essential public services, including but not limited to public education. Most observers argue that the Michigan tax structure is broken, well beyond short-term fixes, and now demands a substantial if not total restructuring. At the time of this writing, the state is facing a $1.6 billion shortfall in 2011–12, and the outlook for the next budget year is even more dire and very likely will extend into future budget years unless corrective action in the form of increased revenue, spending cuts, or a combination of the two is soon taken. Yet both houses of the legislature, as well as the governor, throughout the past several years continued to procrastinate, wrangling about short-term fixes rather than attending to the task of reforming the tax code and establishing new policies that would ensure the strong and stable revenue streams needed to support public education and other essential public services. In contrast, the new Republican administration and Republican legislature, voted into office in 2010, have moved rapidly to enact a new series of wide-ranging budgetary measures. Unfortunately, these measures do not bode well for the public schools, which now face further reductions in state aid and consequently further reductions in personnel and programs.

At the present time, sources of tax revenue for the state of Michigan include revenue from the state income tax, the sales and use taxes, the 6 mill state education property tax, the business tax, the transportation tax, the lottery, and miscellaneous other taxes, plus revenue from federal agencies. The Michigan Constitution has established a general fund plus several special funds to be used as depositories for these revenues, and from which the legislature draws as it annually appropriates dollars to the different units of state and local government. One of these special funds is called the School Aid Fund (SAF), to which the legislature turns for the dollars it appropriates to help support the annual operation of Michigan's public schools. The revenues in the SAF now come from a number of sources but principally from the retail sales tax, the biggest contributor to the SAF, and those revenues account for approximately 46 percent of the total funds in the SAF. On the passage of Proposal A, the retail sales tax increased from 4 percent to 6 percent, with the increased revenue earmarked entirely for the SAF. By prior action, the

Michigan Constitution already required that 60 percent of the revenue generated from the existing 4 percent retail sales tax rate be deposited in the SAF. Thus, 60 percent of the revenue generated from the first 4 percent tax on retail sales, plus 100 percent of the revenue from the additional 2 percent tax on retail sales, are constitutionally dedicated to the SAF. The retail sales tax revenue, while not the only factor, is clearly the most important factor in ensuring the adequacy and stability of the revenue stream going to support the public schools.

However, even though this is a sizable amount, it does not cover the entire sum needed by the legislature to fund the State School Aid Act. Consequently, other state revenue sources—or portions of them—also are earmarked for the SAF. Two other major contributors to the SAF are the personal income tax, which makes up about 19 percent of the SAF, and the 6 mill state education property tax at about 14 percent.[4] Thus, almost 80 percent of the funds in the SAF are dependent on tax revenues from three principal taxes: 1) the retail sales tax, 2) the personal income tax, and 3) the 6 mill state education property tax. A downturn in any one or all of these sources means trouble for the public schools. As we have noted elsewhere, the heavy dependence on the retail sales tax is particularly problematic:

> The substitution of sales tax revenue for property tax revenue is likely to impair the long-run stability of school revenue in Michigan. It is well established that sales tax revenue is more income-elastic than property tax revenue and thus more volatile over the economic cycle. As an illustration, during the 20 years from 1972 to 1992, property tax assessments in Michigan grew at an annual rate of 7.1 percent, while the replacement revenue sources, consisting largely of sales tax revenue, grew *only* 6.6 percent annually. Moreover, during the economic downturn from 1989 to 1992, property taxes rose 8 percent annually, while the replacement revenues increased a mere 3.6 percent annually. (Kearney and Addonizio 2002, p. 40)

From 2007–08 to 2008–09, earmarked revenues from the three main taxes that are the major contributors to the SAF dropped significantly. Retail sales tax revenues dedicated to the SAF declined from $4.9 billion in 2007–08 to $4.6 billion in 2008–09, a 6.1 percent decrease, followed by a slight uptick of $30 million in 2009–10—a total decrease over the three years of 5.5 percent. Personal income tax revenue dedicated to the SAF dropped by 6.7 percent in 2008–09 and another 2.5 percent in 2009–10—a total decrease of 9.1 percent over the three years. The 6 mill state education property tax was off by 2.5 percent in 2008–09, and dropped another 3.6 percent in 2009–10—a total decrease of 6.1 percent over the three-year period (Michigan Department of the Treasury 2009). All of this has led and will continue to lead to increasing shortfalls in state aid for Michigan public schools—shortfalls that can be made up only by reductions in educational programs and other operating expenditures, or by dipping into fund balances—a one-time only source of funds.

The reduction in educational programs has substantial implications for the other side of the adequacy coin, namely, the question of whether the level of resources, now and in future years, is sufficient to ensure a quality academic program for each and every student in each and every public school and public school district. However, before we turn to this question, we first offer a final thought on the inadequacy of the current tax structure. Whether the answers lie in extending the retail sales tax to services and reducing the rate, or increasing the rate of the personal income tax or moving to graduated rates, or increasing the 6 mill state education property tax to, say, 8 mills, or some combination of the foregoing, we leave to those with more expertise in tax policy. We argue simply that Michigan needs to restructure its tax system without delay. To do otherwise will have deleterious consequences for our public schools and the future of the state of Michigan. There is, of course, a complementary argument, that is, the need to also cut costs. However, in our view, the argument for further cost cutting needs to acknowledge the reality that a lot of cost cutting already has taken place, and that many districts are now "down to the bone."

Resources Sufficient to Support a Sound Basic Education

It is now widely believed that a school finance system should provide all local districts a level of revenue adequate to allow all students to achieve high standards of academic performance, generally measured by state assessments of student achievement. This belief leads to two interrelated questions: What is an adequate educational program, and what does it cost? In Chapter 2 we noted that the focus of recent school finance litigation has moved from equity to adequacy, from concerns about relative property wealth per pupil and spending levels per pupil to the more fundamental matter of student achievement. One of the more recent writers in this area, Michael Rebell, an ardent advocate of litigation in support of achieving "educational adequacy," offers the following observation:

> I think the term 'sound basic education' is the best phrase available for the concept that often is described as 'educational adequacy.' Sound basic education connotes that students need a core, fundamental level of education in order to succeed in the contemporary world and that to be sound this basic level of education must allow them *to function competently as citizens and to compete effectively in the modern economy* [emphasis added]. (Rebell 2009, p. 21)

The question remains, of course, what are the components that should constitute "a core, fundamental level of education"? In Chapter 3 we noted that there were substantial disagreements back in the 1950s and 1960s among the many voices calling for the reform of the American high school. On the one side were those who subscribed, and still do, to the views expressed by James B. Conant, who strongly favored strengthening the comprehensive high school and its central theme of curricular differentiation, providing students of differing abilities with a wide range of courses and programs attuned to their interests and abilities. On the other side was a sizable group of advocates who championed the views of Arthur Bestor, who called for more rigor and academic focus in the schools and more demanding curricular requirements in the academic subjects. Bestor's view has prevailed of late. Reading, writing, and mathematics, along with science and moderate social studies, have become the central focus of state assessment programs such as the MEAP and certainly the NAEP. However, there already is some evidence that nationwide the pendulum may be moving back toward Conant's (1959b) view. In Chapter 3, we cited the recent advocacy of campaigns such as A Broader, Bolder Approach to Education (2011), championed by a group of education notables who suggest that we should begin to move beyond attention "not only to basic academic skills and cognitive growth narrowly defined, but to development of the whole person, including physical health, character, social development and non-academic skills . . ." (p. 2).

How will these competing arguments likely play out? And how will they contribute to fashioning clear statements of what Michigan, or any other state for that matter, ought to set forth as the components of a sound basic education? A few short months ago, the powers that be in Michigan might have responded that this already had been done, that a clear statement of what constitutes a sound basic education is set forth in the standards of academic performance on which the MEAP is based. In effect, they might argue that those standards, along with their accompanying subject matter and grade level expectations, quite clearly defined what constitutes an adequate education—a sound basic education—in Michigan. And under the MEAP and the Michigan Merit Exam (MME) we now have extensive information on how Michigan schools and students are doing vis-à-vis these academic standards and grade level expectations. In Chapter 4, we discussed at some length current statewide results on the MEAP and the MME, laying out the percentage of students achieving proficiency in a range of subject matter areas and at different grade levels. And we contrasted these results with similar results on the NAEP, noting very large differences between the two sets of results.

Judging Michigan schools only on the basis of their MEAP scores paints a much rosier picture than judging them on the basis of their NAEP scores. By Michigan standards, fully 74 percent of the state's combined 4th and 8th graders were proficient in reading in 2007; but when using NAEP standards that figure fell to 33 percent—a drop of over 40 percentage points. Almost identical differences were seen in combined 4th and 8th grade math scores. And perhaps more telling and greater cause for concern is Michigan students' decline over time in performance on the NAEP when compared with other states. As we noted in Chapter 4, Michigan's rank among participating states in 4th grade reading fell substantially from 1992 to 2007, as did its ranking in 8th grade mathematics over the same period. Particularly alarming was Michigan's decline in 8th grade math scores for African American students, with Michigan ranking next to last in 2007 among 41 reporting states. Even more alarming yet were the dreadfully low NAEP math, reading and science scores for 4th and 8th grade students in DPS.[5]

Why are there such differences between Michigan students' MEAP and NAEP performances? Has Michigan set the bar too low? Do the Michigan tests lack rigor? Has the NAEP set the bar too high? Are the NAEP tests too rigorous? And, at root, are the comparisons between the MEAP and the NAEP results truly valid comparisons? Many experts argue that it is with considerable risk that one undertakes comparisons of the MEAP and NAEP results, and that such comparisons at best should be used with extreme caution. Still, such comparisons, driven largely by NCLB, have become widespread and continue to be made, and public school personnel, as well as state and national policymakers, are forced to address them.

In Chapter 4 we noted that the SBE recently attempted to address this issue, at least in part, by taking action to raise the bar on the MEAP by setting the cut scores at higher levels. We also noted that some contend that even better answers lie in the nation's schools moving to a common set of content and performance standards, and a common set of achievement measures. And recently we have seen considerable movement toward developing a common set of nationwide content standards, as well as toward building a common set of nationwide achievement measures based on those standards (Cavanaugh 2009; Lewin 2010).

But even if the problems of comparability of standards and assessments are resolved, as well as the matter of clearly defining what actually constitutes a sound basic education, the question of what such an education would cost still remains. That is, what level of resources will it take annually to provide an education that will ensure all students have the opportunity to achieve at a high level of academic performance, to truly attain a sound basic education?

Very little has been done in Michigan to address this question. In effect, decisions about how much it will take to annually fund the public schools are often made, in Michigan and many other states, through what Rebell (2006, p. 467) has characterized as "ad hoc political dealmaking processes," rather than through a rational decision-making process. Accordingly, in our judgment, Michigan should give serious consideration to undertaking an education adequacy study, or what is commonly called a "cost study." There is an argument that the SBE is the proper body, and has the responsibility, to undertake such a study. Under Article VIII, Section 3 of the Michigan Constitution, the SBE is charged with "leadership and general supervision over all public education." In that same section, the board is also charged with a responsibility to "advise the legislature as to the financial requirements in connection therewith."

While the SBE annually may well offer the legislature its advice on the education budget and state aid to the schools, to our knowledge, with one exception, more than 40 years ago, it has never undertaken a comprehensive study of the costs of an adequate public education in Michigan, nor offered advice to the legislature based on such a study.[6] We suggest that such an effort by the SBE is long overdue. We are not suggesting that Michigan's relative decline in NAEP performance or the achievement shortcomings of individual districts, schools, or student groups are primarily attributable to insufficient funding. We do assert, however, that school resources do matter and that Michigan's education leaders and policymakers should more carefully assess these resource needs, particularly in light of the declining resources sustained by most Michigan districts over the past six or seven years.[7]

EFFICIENCY

Efficiency as Accountability

In Chapter 3, we described and discussed state accountability systems and equated the term efficiency with the term accountability—holding that in many ways they were interchangeable terms. In fact, we argued that perhaps a better and more publicly accepted understanding of the term accountability, particularly as it is applied to public education, comes from educational historian Raymond Callahan's linking of accountability and efficiency (Callahan 1964, p. 234). Efficiency asks whether the schools are being held accountable, whether they are making good use of the resources provided to them, whether we as citizens and taxpayers are getting "the biggest bang for the buck," whether money is making a difference. Callahan identifies efficiency as the maxim often claimed to be the basic premise of American manufacturing, namely, "the finest product at the lowest cost." A state accountability system, at root, is designed to demonstrate whether the public school system is turning out "the finest product," whether all students are achieving expected or desired levels of proficiency in the several academic subjects being offered, and whether the schools themselves are performing adequately when it comes to such measures as the employment of highly qualified teachers, student retention rates, and high school graduation rates.

We also traced in Chapter 3 the long history of accountability systems, or parts of such systems, particularly in Michigan. This history began with the University of Michigan's Secondary School Accreditation Program instituted in 1871, moved on to John Porter's Six-Step Accountability Program of the early 1970s, then to the legislature's accountability framework enacted under Act 25 of 1990, and more recently to Tom Watkins's EducationYes! adopted in 2002. We described this last program at length, along with the proposed revisions of that program, namely, MI-SAS and MI-SAAS—the latter slated to be implemented in school year 2011–12, and most recently the new legislated requirement for the evaluation of teachers and administrators—with individual teacher evaluations linked to student academic performance.

While few appear to be opposed to accountability as such, many appear to question the design and implementation of the state accountability systems established under the requirements of NCLB.[8] In Michigan we find considerable concern, if not outright skepticism, about the requirements of EducationYes! as well as the requirements being proposed under MI-SAS and MI-SAAS. Not the least of these concerns, as we pointed out in Chapter 3, is what will happen in 2013–14—the school year the final bill comes due—if Michigan has failed to meet the NCLB and AYP goal of 100 percent proficiency based on its own standards, i.e., those measured by the MEAP, and, even more likely, those measured by the NAEP.[9]

Much uncertainty remains in fashioning answers to these questions, which is considerably exacerbated by the fact that NCLB itself may be subject to major revisions depending on what the Congress may or may not do in the pending reauthorization of the Elementary and Secondary Education Act and its component Title I and NCLB programs. Whatever may come out of the reauthorization, we can be fairly certain that any significant changes in the law and its requirements will be largely driven by the Obama Administration's education agenda as articulated by Arne Duncan, the current U.S. Secretary of Education (see, for example, Dillon [2011a]).While it may be naïve, if not foolish, to predict what the likely outcome of the Congressional reauthorization effort will produce, particularly in light of the substantive changes in the U.S. House of Representatives resulting from the 2010 midterm elections, it seems we can be somewhat assured that it will contain the four key elements in the Secretary's Race to the Top program. These include an emphasis on charter schools, the use of achievement test scores based on so-called value-added approaches in teacher evaluation, merit pay systems based on these results, and encouragement of local districts to dismiss entire staffs of failing schools. The last three of the four fall neatly into our category of policies strongly oriented toward the value of efficiency or accountability. Judging from all of this, it probably is quite safe to say that state and federally mandated school and school district accountability systems are here to stay. What remains are the questions of what likely will be the shape, content, and emphases of these systems. At this point in time, we do not know (see, for example, Jennings [2010/2011]). We choose only to repeat the questions offered at the conclusion of Chapter 3, namely, will existing or redesigned accountability systems truly lead to increased academic success for students? In the words of John Porter, do they hold promise of providing " . . . the guarantee that all students without respect to race, income, or social class will acquire the minimum school skills necessary to take full advantage of the choices that accrue upon successful completion of public schooling . . . " (Kearney 1971, p. 5)? Then, what happens, and where do we go, if we find that all this effort is for naught?

CHOICE

The first of the key elements in Secretary Duncan's Race to the Top program is an emphasis on charter schools, which offers a convenient segue into our fourth category of policies, namely those based on the value of choice.

Michigan parents and students today enjoy three choices in their selection of public schools. The first choice is to attend a traditional public school, the kind with which we all are familiar, and which by far enroll the vast majority of Michigan's public school pupils. For decades, this was Michiganders' only public choice, and for those living in poorly performing districts and unable to afford private school tuition or a residence in a more desirable school district, no choice at all. Accordingly, Michigan lawmakers created additional choices. Thus, the second choice is to attend a charter school, as described in Chapter

5. The third choice is to leave the home school district and to attend a traditional school in a neighboring district, an option provided under the schools of choice program summarized in Chapter 6.

Michigan's Charter Schools

We turn first to the second choice mentioned above and reflect on Michigan's charter schools, known administratively and legally as public school academies (PSAs). As we noted in Chapter 5, the initial advocates of charter schools argued that subjecting public schools to market forces would compel them to be more responsive to parents and students. The advocates viewed traditional public schools as non–market driven; the resources—including steady and increasing salaries—continue to flow irrespective of performance. In a market-driven school, on the other hand, they argued that the principal and the teachers would become accountable for the performance of the organization since the resources and reward structures would be tightly linked to performance. The bottom line would become "no performance, no resources." Thus, central to their idea of the market-driven school was the notion of competition, which, in turn, would ensure accountability and quality. In the long run, good schools would drive out bad schools. In order to continue to receive resources, schools would have to respond to the demands of the consumers.

For many of their early champions, charter schools represented a "silver bullet," not only to right what was wrong with public education, but also to provide the impetus for radical reform of the schools. Back in 1994–95, Governor John Engler, as well as the Republican Senate and many legislators of both parties, viewed the introduction of a market-driven mechanism into public education as the *sine qua non* of any meaningful reform—a view supported by many in the business community. Indeed, Governor Engler spoke of the creation of literally hundreds of charter schools. As he publicly stated, "With charter schools, I predict nothing less than a renaissance of public education in Michigan" (Kearney 1994). However, as we noted in Chapter 5, Michigan's charter school program has been neither an unqualified success nor a disaster. Some PSAs are excellent, many have waiting lists, some struggle with poor management and poor outcomes for students, and some have been closed. They neither have become as good as they were expected to be, nor as bad as their opponents claimed they would be.

In many ways, one might say they have proved to be *pareto superior*, that is, they have made some students better off without harming others. There is growing evidence that, when it comes to academic achievement on the MEAP, many PSA students are doing as well as, if not even a little better than, the regular public school students in their host districts in the elementary and middle school grades. Certainly when compared to all students across Michigan, we find a considerable lag in PSA achievement scores. But then we often find the same lag in the schools in the host districts. And, we would argue, the host districts provide the more valid basis for comparison as their students more closely match their PSA peers in important socioeconomic characteristics and community influences.

In Chapter 5, we also noted that there are two unresolved policy issues that serve to hinder the effectiveness if not the efficiency of charter schools in Michigan. The first centers on the lack of authority present statutes afford the superintendent of public instruction to effectively oversee the authorizers and call them to task on their responsibilities for overseeing the PSAs they charter. The second concerns the inability of the PSA boards to effectively oversee the educational management organizations they hire to help run their schools. Both of these issues, and a number of other related issues spelled out in Chapter 5, need to be resolved if the PSAs are to succeed over the long run. If that happens, and there is continuation of financial support, there is considerable hope that the PSAs will continue to mature and will become a fixture among Michigan public schools, that indeed they will come to represent a reasonable if not promising alternative to the traditional public school.[10]

As Weiss (1990) and Glenn (1989) have argued, there also are quite appropriate and compelling reasons for promoting parental choice, aside from or in addition to improved educational outcomes. One of these reasons centers on the long-cherished notion of the value of personal choice that " . . . each person ought to have the opportunity to control the conditions of his life, and in concert with others, the conditions of life in his or her community" (Richardson 1976, p. 5). Thus, one might well argue that the efficacy of PSAs and broadened educational choices in Michigan should not be judged exclusively on the question of whether they lead to improved academic achievement, or for that matter the achievement of other educational outcomes. It may be enough that PSAs will restore to parents and students, and perhaps to teachers, a legitimate role in deciding the nature and quality of public schooling in their immediate community.

Michigan's Schools of Choice

The third choice mentioned above provides Michigan parents and students an opportunity to attend school in a neighboring district, providing the neighboring district's school board has made the decision to accept nonresident students—and many of them have. Currently there are nearly 80,000 Michigan students participating in the schools of choice program. As we noted, this tends to be a winning situation for the student as well as for the nonresident or receiving district, and a losing situation—at least financially—for the sending district. For the student (and his or her parent), there are any number of positively perceived outcomes, including a broader if not richer educational program, particularly at the high school level, a more desirable if not more (or less) diverse mix of fellow students, and a more convenient location near the parent's place of work, to name a few. For the receiving district, assuming it has the seats available, the greatest boon is its receipt of a state foundation allowance for each incoming student with the accompanying likelihood of little or no additional cost or expenditure. Unfortunately, the sending district is left in the lurch. It loses receipt of the student's foundation allowance but with little or no lessening of its costs and expenditures. Thus we have a "win-win" situation for the parent and the student as well as for the nonresident or receiving district. For the sending district, it's clearly a "lose-lose" situation.[11]

But there is another concern that should receive continuing attention from the legislature—the possibility that social equity may be a problem, particularly if schools of choice leads in some situations to further segregation by race and class and unequal opportunities for students. In Chapter 6 we raised that possibility, noting instances of sorting that have occurred in some areas of Michigan where the schools of choice program is in effect. The most notable examples we offered were in Berrien County, where three neighboring school districts are involved—Benton Harbor, Coloma, and Eau Claire—and in Detroit, where their pupil losses have been particularly high. In Berrien County, there appears to be considerable movement of students from the Benton Harbor public schools to the public schools in Coloma and Eau Claire, with some considerable evidence that a "creaming" effect is taking place. The data suggest that the Benton Harbor public schools increasingly are becoming even more segregated on the basis of race and economic disadvantage, while the other two districts are becoming more diverse on both counts. In Detroit, between 2008 and 2010, its public schools have lost 8,500–9,000 students to surrounding suburban school districts. The question then becomes one of balancing the positive effects of a desirable policy—providing increased parental and student choice—against the negative social effects of the same policy.

The Upward and Centralizing Movement of Educational Decision Making

In our initial comments on the value of choice, we identified a second dimension of choice—the extent to which educational decisions are left at the local school district level or centralized at the state level, or for that matter at the federal level.

For a long run of years dating back to the 18th century, local control of the public schools was a cherished value. As Will (1962) puts it: "Centralizing tendencies in administration strike at the very roots of laissez-faire concepts that have led many persons to believe that the local governments and private entities permitted to function within a state under constitutional and statutory law can [and should] do as much as they please without interference from State administrative agencies . . . They see central administrative authority as the embodiment of all the 'isms' that are alien to democratic government."

The "folklore" of local control didn't die easily, but beginning in the 1960s it began to fade slowly away under a continuing onslaught of reform efforts initiated at the state level and national level. In Chapter 4, in our discussion of the early development of the MEAP, we discussed at some length the gauntlet of opposition this effort faced from administrators and teachers, as well as state legislators representing local constituencies. A similar experience faced the early developers of the NAEP—from both local educators and state officials. In Chapter 3, where we addressed state accountability systems, we traced the development of a multitude of policy reforms beginning in the 1970s, at both state and federal levels, all of which led not only to a further centralization of power at the state level but also and principally at the federal level. As of this writing, a new force has recently arrived on the scene, namely, the aforementioned federal Race to the Top program, funded at $3.5 billion. These funds, distributed under a competitive grant program, have gone to those states that agreed to undertake a series of tightly focused and federally mandated school reform initiatives. As noted earlier, successful competitors will be expected to increase the number of charter schools in their state, use standardized test scores in evaluating teachers, establish merit pay systems, and dismiss entire staffs of failing schools. We also noted that it is not just the actions of state and federal governments that are exercising pressures toward centralization; there also are forces for change emanating from nationwide or national nongovernmental sources. Witness the current efforts of the coalition of national organizations behind the push for common national standards, with the National Governors Association and the Council of Chief State School Officers overseeing the "common core" effort. And recently, we have the report of the Strategic Management of Human Capital project calling for states and school districts to overhaul how they recruit, prepare, evaluate, and compensate teachers (Odden 2011).

We now see ample evidence of the slow but steady movement of educational decision-making power and authority upward and outward away from the local level. However, as we noted earlier, Detroit seems to go back and forth on this issue—from decentralization in the 1970s, to recentralization in the 1980s, to state control in the late 1990s, back to local control in 2005, then on to the governor's appointment of an emergency financial manager in 2009, and now in 2011 to expanded powers for the emergency financial manager and rising calls for mayoral control of DPS. The question before us has become whether this increasing centralization and outward movement of educational decision making is a good thing or a bad thing. Will the concept, or folklore, of local control of educational decision making truly be put to rest? Should we accept the movement away from the highly decentralized system that characterized American public education in the 1950s and prior years, with the local school district reigning supreme, the state legislature funding the system but essentially adopting a hands-off posture, the state education agency following a low-key supervisory role, and the federal government remaining largely a nonplayer? Or do current times demand something quite different and closer to our present arrangements?

There is, of course, the old maxim of the golden rule: “He who gives the gold makes the rules.” We have seen that play out over the past 20 years, with the states increasingly taking on responsibility for a larger share of the costs of public education. Across the nation, the states on average currently are covering some 47.3 percent of the costs, the local level 43.7 percent, and the federal government 9 percent. This would seem to make a strong argument for more state control. But with the federal government now dangling another $3.5 billion in front of the states, the Golden Rule comes even more strongly into play, and increasingly favors the federal level.

At root this is a question about federalism. As we noted in Chapter 3, under the 10th Amendment to the U.S. Constitution education is a matter left to the states. Still the federal government appropriately gets into the mix on the basis of Article I, Section 8 of the U.S. Constitution—Congress’s authority and responsibility to “provide for the common Defence and general Welfare of the United States.” To what extent will citizens in the separate states accept, or even tolerate, further federal inroads into deciding what subjects and what content ought to be taught in our public schools? Are these properly decisions that should be reserved to the separate states, and to local school districts, respecting the long-held value of local control? Or is it more properly a matter of the nation’s general welfare, if not its common defense? We simply pose the questions; the answers will be fashioned within and among the nested tiers of the policy-making process as it operates at local, state, and federal levels.

THE LIMITS OF POLICY

The public policies that we have written about and reflect upon throughout this book address a broad range of educational issues—governmental, fiscal, administrative, organizational, instructional, professional and lay, parental and student, local and state, state and federal, and many more. But what is public policy and what are its limits? While there are any number of definitions of public policy, the one that appeals to us holds that public policy deals with "the authoritative implementation of scarce resources." This particular definition is further made clear in a metaphor fashioned some years ago by Thomas Green, a professor at Syracuse University. Green called it his *paradise metaphor*. In paradise, all values can be pursued simultaneously and without limit, but paradise is destroyed by either of two conditions: inadequate resources or irreconcilable interest or goals—that is, scarcity and conflict. Thus, the essential meaning of the term *policy* arises from its role in resolving these two fundamental human conditions of scarcity and conflict (Green 1994).

Green's metaphor makes abundantly clear that public policy—both in its development and in its implementation—is bounded by these two demanding constraints. First, policymakers most often must function in circumstances and settings marked by scarcity, whether it be scarcity of human resources, financial resources, or knowledge, including reliable evidence that particular policies will achieve stated goals. Second, policymakers also must function in circumstances and settings marked by the competing values, demands, and interests espoused by their constituencies, whether they be taxpayers, educators, school supporters, school critics, lay organizations, parents, or students. There is seldom consensus, at least initially, on how to build and maintain quality systems of public education, and seldom are there sufficient resources to achieve the desired ends. Policymakers are forced to operate continually in an environment marked by scarcity, uncertainty, and conflict. As a consequence, policy is often fueled more by ideology than evidence, and, on occasion, more by desperation than inspiration.

The fashioning and successful implementation of effective education policies necessitate that policymakers somehow accommodate the ongoing tensions arising from scarce resources and the irreconcilable interests and goals of their constituencies. This is no easy task. Further, policies adopted at the state or national level often fail to penetrate the "black box" of the classroom. That is, the crucial interaction between students and teachers is often unaffected by state or federal attempts at "remote control." There are indeed limits to policy, to what can be done, to what can be accomplished. In wrestling with this ever present conundrum, we would only hope that all those involved in the process be guided by the sentiments ascribed to a noted scholar in the early twentieth century: "What the best and wisest parent wants for his own child, that must the community want for all of its children. Any other ideal for our schools is narrow and unlovely; acted upon it destroys our democracy" (Dewey 1907, p. 19).

Notes

1. However, there is mounting evidence that property tax revenues also are experiencing a significant downturn as a result of the economic recession that began in 2008.
2. However, judging from the proposed budget and tax plan being offered by Republican Governor Rick Snyder, the likelihood of increasing and spreading the sales tax seems highly unlikely.
3. We are indebted to Berne and Stiefel (1984), for their clear exposition of many of the underlying concepts contained in this section.
4. The remainder is covered by a number of smaller taxes including the lottery transfer, the use tax, tobacco taxes, real estate transfer taxes, casinos tax, the liquor tax, a transfer from the general fund, and other miscellaneous taxes.
5. In December 2009, both Detroit newspapers made headlines with their reports that 69 percent and 77 percent of Detroit 4th and 8th graders, respectively, scored below basic on the NAEP math assessments, which is bad enough. As we noted in Chapter 4, the NAEP does not include the basic category in its definition of proficiency. Only the two top NAEP score categories, proficient and advanced, are included. Thus, by NAEP standards only 3 and 4 percent of Detroit's 4th and 8th graders, respectively, achieved proficiency in math. The later release of Detroit's 4th and 8th grade reading scores in early 2010 and science scores in early 2011 were no better.
6. The exception to this statement is that in the late 1960s the Michigan legislature appropriated funds to the MDE, at the behest of the SBE, to undertake a comprehensive study of elementary and secondary education in the state of Michigan. The department engaged J. Alan Thomas of the University of Chicago as executive director of the study. While not a "cost study" in the present sense of the term, the study certainly can be seen as a forerunner of the state cost studies that are becoming increasingly prevalent across the nation (see Thomas [1968]).
7. A two-stage remedy is one approach that has been suggested. In stage one, it would be the responsibility of the SBE to "cost out" an adequate education; in stage two, it would be the responsibility and obligation of the legislature to act on the board's advice, and determine from where the monies will come to "maintain and support an adequate education."
8. Interestingly this concern is now being raised at the federal level by none other than Arne Duncan, President Obama's Secretary of Education. On March 9, 2011, Secretary Duncan told the Congress that "more than 80,000 of the nation's

100,000 public schools could be labeled as failing under No Child Left Behind . . . This law is fundamentally broken, and we need to fix it this year" (see Dillon [2011a]).

9. The state is unquestionably destined to fail, given the State Board of Education's recent decision to raise the cut scores on the MEAP.
10. As reported in the *New York Times* (Winerip 2011), Robert Bobb, the emergency financial manager appointed by the governor to run DPS, is proposing to convert the entire district to charter schools. Is this is an attempt to provide a better education for Detroit students or to help resolve the district's $327 million deficit? In 2010, DPS lost 8,500 students to neighboring districts under the schools of choice program along with the $7,300 in State Foundation Aid that went with each student. As the *New York Times* article further notes, "Supporters say this [charter schools] could generate significant savings, since charters are typically non-union and can hire young teachers, pay them less and give them no pensions."
11. See note 10 above.

References

A Broader, Bolder Approach to Education. 2011. http://www.epi.org/files/2011/bold_approach_full_statement-3.pdf (accessed February 15, 2012).

Addonizio, Michael F. 1994. "School Choice: Economic and Fiscal Perspectives." Policy Report PR-B12. Bloomington, IN: Education Policy Center.

Addonizio, Michael F., and Doug Drake. 2005. *Revolution and Evolution: Michigan's Proposal A School Finance Reform, a Retrospective Analysis*. Okemos, MI: Michigan Prospect.

Addonizio, Michael F., C. Philip Kearney, and Henry J. Prince. 1995. "Michigan's High Wire Act." *Journal of Education Finance* 20(3): 235–269.

Alesina, Alberto, Reza Baqir, and Caroline Hoxby. 2000. "Political Jurisdictions in Heterogeneous Communities." NBER Working Paper No. 7859. Cambridge, MA: National Bureau of Economic Research.

Alexander, Kern, and M. David Alexander. 2005 *American Public School Law*. 5th ed. Belmont, CA: Wadsworth/Thomson Learning.

Angus, David L., and Jeffrey E. Mirel. 1999. *The Failed Promise of the American High School, 1890–1995*. New York: Teachers College Press.

Armor, David J., and Brett M. Peiser. 1998. "Interdistrict Choice in Massachusetts." In *Learning from School Choice,* Paul E. Peterson and Bryan C. Hassel, eds. Washington, DC: Brookings Institution Press, pp. 157–186.

Arsen, David, Tom Clay, Thomas Davis, Thomas Devaney, Rachel Fulcher-Dawson, and David N. Plank. 2005. *Adequacy, Equity, and Capital Spending in Michigan Schools: The Unfinished Business of Proposal A*. Lansing and East Lansing, MI: Citizens Research Council and the Education Policy Center at Michigan State University.

Arsen, David, David Plank, and Gary Sykes. 2000. *School Choice Policies in Michigan: The Rules Matter*. East Lansing, MI: Michigan State University Education Policy Center.

Ballard, Charles L. 2010. *Michigan's Economic Future: A New Look*. East Lansing, MI: Michigan State University Press.

Ballard, Jim. 2005. "How the MEAP Was Bleeped." *Michigan Lobbyist.* Spring: 49–51.

Beaton, Albert E., and Eugene G. Johnson. 2004. "Emerging Technical Innovations in NAEP." In *The Nation's Report Card—Evolution and Perspective,* Lyle V. Jones and Ingram Olkin, eds. Bloomington, IN: Phi Delta Kappa Educational Foundation, p. 463.

Belfield, Clive R., and Henry M. Levin. 2002. "The Effects of Competition on Educational Outcomes: A Review of the U.S. Evidence." *Review of Educational Research* 72(2): 279–341.

Bell, Dawson. 1999. "2 Competing Proposals Display Divided Loyalties and Capitol Confusion." *Detroit Free Press*, March 18, A:1, A:12.

Bell, Dawson, and Chris Christoff. 1999. "Senate Puts Schools on Archer's Chalkboard." *Detroit Free Press*, March 19, A:1, A:2.

Berne, Robert, and Leanna Stiefel. 1984. *The Measurement of Equity in School Finance*. Baltimore, MD: Johns Hopkins University Press.

Berry v. School District of the City of Benton Harbor. 515 F. Supp. 344 (1981).

Berry v. School District of the City of Benton Harbor. 195 F. Supp. 2d 971 (W.D. Mich. 2002).

Bestor, Arthur. 1985. *Educational Wastelands: The Retreat from Learning in our Public Schools*. Urbana, IL: University of Illinois Press.

Board of Education of Oklahoma v. Dowell. 498 U.S. 237 (1991).

Bouffard, Karen. 2010. "DPS Students at Bottom of National Reading Test Scores." *Detroit News*, May 20.

Bourge, Mary L. 2004. "History of the National Assessment Governing Board. In *The Nation's Report Card—Evolution and Perspective*, Lyle V. Jones and Ingram Olkin, eds. Bloomington, IN: Phi Delta Kappa Educational Foundation, pp. 211–218.

Bradley, Ann. 1992. "Detroit Teachers Defy Court's Back-to-Work Order." *Education Week* (September 30): 9.

Brictson, Paula T., and Edward D. Roeber. N.d. "Objective-Referenced Tests: An Alternative in a State Assessment Program." Unpublished manuscript.

Buckley, Jack, and Mark Schneider. 2007. *Charter Schools: Hope or Hype?* Princeton, NJ: Princeton University Press.

Budde, Ray. 1974. "Education by Charter." Paper presented to the Society for General Systems Research.

Bureau of Accreditation and School Improvement Studies. 1988. *Annual Report of the Bureau of Accreditation and School Improvement Studies 1987–88.* Ann Arbor: School of Education, University of Michigan.

Caesar, Gene, Robert N. McKerr, and James Phelps. 1978. *New Equity in Michigan School Finance: The Story of the Bursley Act*. Lansing, MI: Senate Committee on Education.

Callahan, Raymond E. 1964. *Education and the Cult of Efficiency*. Chicago: University of Chicago Press.

Campbell, Roald F., and Robert A. Bunnell. 1963. *Nationalizing Influences on Secondary Education*. Chicago: Midwest Administration Center, University of Chicago.

Carnoy, Martin, Rebecca Jacobsen, Lawrence Mishel, and Richard Rothstein. 2005. *The Charter School Dust-Up: Examining the Evidence on Enrollment and Achievement*. New York: Teachers College Press.

Cavanaugh, Sean. 2009. "Common Assessments Could Alter NAEP's Role." *Education Week* 29(12): 1, 11.

Center for Research on Education Outcomes (CREDO). 2009. *Multiple Choice: Charter School Performance in 16 States*. Stanford, CA: Stanford University.

Cherry Commission. 2004. *Final Report of the Lt. Governor's Commission on Higher Education and Economic Growth*. Prepared for Governor Jennifer M. Granholm. Lansing, MI: Cherry Commission. http://www.cherrycommission.org/docs/finalReport/CherryReport.pdf (accessed February 10, 2012).

Child Welfare Society of Flint v. Kennedy School District. 220 Mich. 290, 189 N.W. 1002 (1922).

Chubb, John E., and Terry M. Moe. 1990. *Politics, Markets, and America's Schools*. Washington DC: Brookings Institution.

Citizens Research Council of Michigan. 1992. "State Ballot Proposals A and C—Proposed Property Tax Amendments." Council Comments No. 1012. Detroit and Lansing, MI: Citizens Research Council of Michigan.

———. 2004. *Financing Michigan Retired Teacher Pension and Health Care Benefits*. Report No. 337. Detroit and Lansing, MI: Citizens Research Council of Michigan. http://www.crcmich.org/PUBLICAT/2000s/2004/rpt337.pdf (accessed May 11, 2011).

Clotfelter, Charles T. 1999. "Public School Segregation in Metropolitan Areas." *Land Economics* 75(4): 487–504.

Clotfelter, Charles T., Helen F. Ladd, and Jacob L. Vigdor. 2006. "Teacher–Student Matching and the Assessment of Teacher Effectiveness." NBER Working Paper No. 11936. Cambridge, MA: National Bureau of Economic Research.

Coleman, James S., Ernest Q. Campbell, Carol J. Hobson, James McPartland, Alexander M. Mood, Frederick D. Weinfield, and Robert L. York. 1966. *Equality of Educational Opportunity Study*. Report to the U.S. Department of Education. Ann Arbor, MI: Inter-university Consortium for Political and Social Research.

Conant, James B. 1959a. *The American High School Today: A First Report to Interested Citizens*. New York: McGraw-Hill.

———. 1959b. *The Revolutionary Transformation of the American High School*. Cambridge, MA: Harvard University Press.

———. 1961. *Slums and Suburbs: A Commentary on Schools in Metropolitan Areas*. New York: McGraw-Hill.

Cook, Glen. 2004. "Mayor May Take the Reins in Detroit." *American School Board Journal* 191(1): 4.

Council of Organizations and Others for Education about Parochiaid, Inc., et al. v. Engler, 455 Mich. 557 (1997).

Cullen, Julie Berry, Brian Jacob, and Steven D. Levitt. 2000. "The Impact of School Choice on Student Outcomes: An Analysis of the Chicago Public Schools." NBER Working Paper No. 7888. Cambridge, MA: National Bureau of Economic Research. http://papers.nber.org/papers/w7888 (accessed July 20, 2011).

———. 2003. "The Effect of School Choice on Student Outcomes: Evidence from Randomized Lotteries." NBER Working Paper No. 10113. Cambridge, MA: National Bureau of Economic Research. http://www.nber.org/papers/w10113 (accessed July 20, 2011).

Cullen, Julie Berry, and Susanna Loeb. 2003. "K–12 Education in Michigan." In *Michigan at the Millennium*, Charles Ballard, Paul N. Courant, Douglas C. Drake, Ronald Fischer, and Elisabeth R. Gerber, eds. East Lansing, MI: Michigan State University Press, pp. 299–321.

Darling-Hammond, Linda. 2000. "Teacher Quality and Student Achievement: A Review of State Policy Evidence." *Education Policy Analysis Archives* 8(1): 1–44.

Detroit News. 1999. "Schools Resist State Takeover." January 27.

Dewey, John. 1907. *The School and Society*. Chicago: University of Chicago Press.

Dillon, Sam. 2011a. "Most Public Schools May Miss Targets, Education Secretary Says." *New York Times*, March 10, A:16.

———. 2011b. "Bipartisan Group Backs Common Core Curriculum." *New York Times*, March 7, A:12.

Doyle, Dennis, and Daniel Levine. 1985. "Business and the Public Schools: Observations on the Policy Statement of the Committee for Economic Development." *Phi Delta Kappan* 67: 113–118.

Drake, Doug. 2002. *A Review and Analysis of Michigan Tax Policies Impacting K–12 Finances*. Lansing, MI: Michigan Association of School Administrators.

Duncombe, William, and Wen Wang. 2009. "School Facilities Funding and Capital-Outlay Distribution in the States." *Journal of Education Finance* 34(3): 324–350.

Durant et al. v. State of Michigan et al., 456 Mich. 144 (1997).

Eastman, J.C. 2007. "Reinterpreting the Education Clauses in State Constitutions." In *School Money Trials: The Legal Pursuit of Educational Adequacy*, Martin R. West and Paul E. Peterson, eds. Washington, DC: Brookings Institution Press, pp. 55–76.

Eberts, Randall, and Kevin Hollenbeck. 2001. "An Examination of Student Achievement in Michigan Charter Schools." Working Paper No. 01-68. Kalamazoo, MI: W.E. Upjohn Institute for Employment Research.

Education Policy Center. 2000. *Strengthening Accountability in Michigan Public Schools*. East Lansing, MI: Education and Policy Center, Michigan State University. http://www.educ.msu.edu/neweducator/fall00/epc3.htm (accessed May 12, 2011).

Educational Testing Service (ETS). 2009. "Addressing Achievement Gaps." *Policy Notes* 17(1): 1. http://www.ets.org/Media/Research/pdf/PICPN171.pdf (accessed November 28, 2011).

Education Week. 2009. "Quality Counts." 28(17): 39.

Ehrenberg, Ronald G., and Dominic J. Brewer. 1994. "Do School and Teacher Characteristics Matter? Evidence from High School and Beyond." *Economics of Education Review* 13(1): 1–17.

Elmore, Richard F. 1990. *Working Models of Choice in Public Education*. New Brunswick, NJ: Center for Policy Research in Education.

Epple, Dennis, and Richard Romano. 2000. "Neighborhood Schools, Choice, and the Distribution of Educational Benefits." *American Economic Review* 88(4): 33–62.

Executive Office of the President. 1990. *National Goals for Education*. Washington, DC: Executive Office of the President.

Farley, Reynolds, and William H. Frey. 1994. "Changes in the Segregation of Whites from Blacks during the 1980s; Small Steps toward a More Integrated Society." *American Sociological Review* 59(1): 23–45.

Ferguson, Ronald F., and Helen F. Ladd. 1996. "How and Why Money Matters: An Analysis of Alabama Schools." In *Holding Schools Accountable: Performance-Based Reform in Education*, Helen F. Ladd, ed. Washington, DC: Brookings Institution Press, pp. 265–298.

Finn, Chester E., Jr., and Herbert J. Walberg. 1994. *Radical Education Reforms*. Berkeley, CA: McCutchan Publishing Corporation.

Fiske, Edward B., and Helen F. Ladd. 2000. *When Schools Compete: A Cautionary Tale*. Washington, DC: Brookings Institution Press.

Flanagan, Michael P. 2010. Presentation on Changes to the Michigan School Accreditation and Accountability System. Memorandum to the State Board of Education, July 26, Lansing, MI. http://www.michigan.gov/documents/mde/MI-SAAS_Memo_330755_7.pdf (accessed May 12, 2011).

Franklin, Barry M. 2003. "Race, Restructuring, and Educational Reform: The Mayoral Takeover of the Detroit Public Schools." In *Reinterpreting Urban School Reform*, Louis F. Miro and Edward P. St. John, eds. Albany, NY: State University of New York Press, pp. 95–125.

Freeman v. Pitts. 503 U.S. 467 (1992).

Friedman, Milton. 1955. "The Role of Government in Education." In *Economics and the Public Interest*, Robert A. Solo, ed. Piscataway, NJ: Rutgers University Press, pp. 123–144.

Gawlik, Marytza A., Michael F. Addonizio, and C. Philip Kearney. 2010. "Evaluating Teacher Quality in Charter Schools: Evidence from the Detroit Metropolitan Region." Unpublished manuscript.

Gilchrest, Brenda. 1990. "A Choice That Is Academic: Education System's Curriculum Woes Drive Students Away." *Detroit Free Press*, December 17, A:1.

Gill, Brian, Michael Timpane, Karen E. Ross, and Dominic J. Brewer. 2001. *Rhetoric Versus Reality: What We Know and What We Need to Know about Vouchers and Charter Schools.* Santa Monica, CA: RAND.

Glenn, Charles L. 1989. *Choice of School in Six Nations*. Washington, DC: U.S. Department of Education, Office of Educational Research and Improvement.

Goldhaber, Dan D. 2007. "Can Teacher Quality Be Effectively Assessed? National Board Certification as a Signal of Effective Teaching." *Review of Economics and Statistics* 89(1): 134–151.

Goldhaber, Dan D., and Eric R. Eide. 2002. "What Do We Know (and Need to Know) about the Impact of School Choice on Disadvantaged Students?" *Harvard Educational Review* 72(2): 157–176.

Gongwer News Service. 2005. "Capital Notebook: Charter Bond Sales." 44(158): 8.

Green, E.L. 1999. "Why the Urgency to Take over Detroit Schools?" *Detroit News*, February 11, A:15.

Green, Thomas F. 1994. "Policy Questions: A Conceptual Study." *Education Policy Analysis Archives* 2(7): 1–14.

Greenwald, Rob, Larry V. Hedges, and Richard D. Laine. 1996. "The Effect of School Resources on Student Achievement." *Review of Educational Research* 66(3): 361–396.

Gross, Beatrice, and Ronald Gross. 1985. *The Great School Debate: Which Way for American Education?* New York: Simon & Schuster.

Grosse Pointe Public Schools. 1970. *The Michigan Assessment of Basic Skills: A Summary of Concerns*. Grosse Pointe, MI: Department of Instruction.

Grubb, W. Norton. 2009. *The Money Myth: School, Resources, Outcomes, and Equity*. New York: Russell Sage Foundation.

Hacsi, Timothy A. 2003. *Children as Pawns: The Politics of Educational Reform*. Cambridge, MA: Harvard University Press.

Hanushek, Eric A. 1981. "Throwing Money at Schools." *Journal of Policy Analysis and Management* 1(1): 19–41.

———. 1986. "The Economics of Schooling: Production and Efficiency in Public Schools." *Journal of Economic Literature* 24(3): 1141–1177.

———. 2007. "The Alchemy of 'Costing Out' Studies." In *School Money Trials: The Legal Pursuit of Educational Adequacy*, Martin R.West and Paul E. Peterson, eds. Washington, DC: Brookings Institution Press, pp. 77–101.

Harmon, B. 2000. "Detroit School Funds Misused." *Detroit News*, November 20.

Harris, Douglas N. 2009. "Would Accountability Based on Teacher Value Added Be Smart Policy? An Examination of the Statistical Properties and Policy Alternatives." *Education Finance and Policy* 4(4): 319–350.

Henig, Jeffrey, and Wilbur Rich. 2004. *Mayors in the Middle: Politics, Race, and Mayoral Control of Urban Schools*. Princeton, NJ: Princeton University Press.

Higgins, Lori. 2011a. "MEAP Will Be Tougher to Pass." *Detroit Free Press*, February 9, 2:A.

———. 2011b. "Site Lets You Size Up High Schools." *Detroit Free Press*, August 13, A:1.

———. 2011c. "1 in 5 Michigan Schools Falling Short." *Detroit Free Press*, August 16, A:1, B:10.

Ho, Andrew D., and Edward H. Haertel. 2007. "Apples to Apples? The Underlying Assumptions of State-NAEP Comparisons." CCSSO Policy Brief. Washington, DC: Council of Chief State School Officers.

Horn, Jerry, and Gary Miron. 2000. *An Evaluation of the Michigan Charter School Initiative: Performance, Accountability, and Impact.* Kalamazoo, MI: The Evaluation Center, Western Michigan University.

Hornbeck, Mark. 1999. "Engler Keeps Grip on Reform." *Detroit News*, March 26, A:1.

House, Ernest R., Wendell Rivers, and Daniel L. Stufflebeam. 1974. "An Assessment of the Michigan Accountability System." *Phi Delta Kappan* 55(10): 663–669.

Hoxby, Caroline M. 2000. "Does Competition among Public Schools Benefit Students and Taxpayers?" *American Economic Review* 90(5): 1209–1238.

———. 2002. "School Choice and School Productivity (Or Could School Choice Be a Tide That Lifts All Boats?)." NBER Working Paper No. 8873. Cambridge, MA: National Bureau of Economic Research.

———. 2004. *A Straightforward Comparison of Charter Schools and Regular Public Schools in the United States*. Cambridge, MA: Harvard University and National Bureau of Economic Research. http://www.tidioutecharter.com/pdf/charters_040909.pdf (accessed June 16, 2011).

Hula, Richard C., Richard W. Jelier, and Mark Schauer. 1997. "Making Educational Reform—Hard Times in Detroit 1988–1995." *Urban Education* 32(2): 202–232.

Jennings, Jack. 2010/2011. "The Policy and Politics of Rewriting the Nation's Main Education Law." *Kappan* 92(4): 44–49.

Johns, Roe L., Edgar L. Morphet, and Kern Alexander. 1983. *The Economics and Financing of Education*, 4th ed. Englewood Cliffs, NJ: Prentice-Hall, Inc.

Jones, Lyle V., and Ingram Olkin. 2004. *The Nation's Report Card—Evolution and Perspectives*. Bloomington, IN: Phi Delta Kappa Educational Foundation.

Kearney, C. Philip. 1970. "The Politics of Educational Assessment in Michigan." *Planning and Changing* 1: 71–82.

———. 1971. "Developing a New Role for the State Education Agency: The Michigan Experience." Presentation at the Institute for Chief State School Officers, San Diego, CA, August 5.

———. 1994. *A Primer on Michigan School Finance*. 3rd ed. Ann Arbor, MI: University of Michigan, School of Education, p. 49.

Kearney, C. Philip, and Michael F. Addonizio. 2002. *A Primer on Michigan School Finance*. 4th ed. Detroit: Wayne State University Press.

Kearney, C. Philip, Robert L. Crowson, and Thomas P. Wilbur. 1970. "The Michigan Assessment of Education." *Michigan Journal of Secondary Education* 11(2): 15–27.

Kearney, C. Philip, and Robert J. Huyser. 1973. "The Politics of Reporting Results." In *School Evaluation: The Politics and the Process*, Ernest R. House, ed. Berkeley, CA: McCutchan Publishing Company, pp. 47–59.

Kotlowitz, Alex. 1998. *The Other Side of the River*. New York: Doubleday.

Krueger, Alan B. 2003. "Inequality, Too Much of a Good Thing." In *Inequality in America: What Role for Human Capital Policies?* Benjamin M. Friedman, ed. Cambridge, MA: MIT Press, pp. 1–75.

Ladd, Helen F. 2002. "School Vouchers: A Critical View." *Journal of Economic Perspectives* 16(4): 3–24.

Lee, Valerie E., Robert G. Croninger, and Julia B. Smith. 1994. "Parental Choice of Schools and Social Stratification in Education: The Paradox of Detroit." *Educational Evaluation and Policy Analysis* 16(4): 438.

———. 1996. "Equity and Choice in Detroit." In *Who Chooses, Who Loses? Culture, Institutions, and the Unequal Effects of School Choice*, Bruce Fuller and Richard F. Elmore, eds. New York: Teachers' College Press, pp. 70–94.

Levin, Henry M. 1991. "The Economics of Educational Choice." *Economics of Education Review* 10(2): 137–158.

_______. 1998. "Educational Vouchers: Effectiveness, Choice, and Costs." *Journal of Policy Analysis and Management* 17(3): 373–392.

_______. 2000. "A Comprehensive Framework for Evaluating Educational Vouchers." Occasional Paper No. 5. New York: Columbia University, Teachers College.

Lewin, Tamar. 2010. "States Embrace Core Standards for the Schools." *New York Times*, July 21, A:1.

Linn, Robert L. 2004. "The Influence of External Evaluations." In *The Nation's*

Report Card—Evolution and Perspective, Lyle V. Jones and Ingram Olkin, eds. Bloomington, IN: Phi Delta Kappa Educational Foundation, pp. 303–305.

Martineau, Joseph A. 2007. "A Methodological Response to the June 7, 2007 NCES Report, *Mapping 2005 State Proficiency Standards onto the NAEP Scales*." Presentation to the National Association of State Assessment Directors, held in Nashville, TN, June.

McConnell, D. 1999. "Kilpatrick Suggests School Plan He'd Back." *Detroit Free Press,* March 20, A:10.

McConnell, D., and Chris Christoff. 1999. "School Deal Adds $15 Million." *Detroit Free Press*, A:1, A:3.

Michigan Department of Education (MDE). N.d. "Bulletin 1101." Various years. Lansing, MI: MDE. http://www.michigan.gov/mde/0,1607,7-140-6530_6605-21539--,00.html (accessed July 14, 2011).

———. 1970. *Levels of Educational Performance and Related Factors in Michigan.* Assessment Report No. 4. Lansing, MI: MDE.

———. 1971. *The Common Goals of Michigan Education.* Lansing, MI: MDE.

———. 2006a. "Michigan School Report Card." Summary Bulletin. Lansing, MI: MDE.

———. 2006b. *Public School Academies: Michigan Department of Education Report to the Legislature, 2005–06.* Lansing, MI: MDE.

———. 2007. *Public School Academies: Michigan Department of Education Report to the Legislature, 2006–07.* Lansing, MI: MDE.

———. 2008a. "Michigan School Report Card." Summary Bulletin. Lansing, MI: MDE.

———. 2008b. *Public School Academies: Michigan Department of Education Report to the Legislature, 2007–08.* Lansing, MI: MDE.

———. 2009. "Michigan's School Accreditation System: From EducationYES! to MI-SAS." Summary Bulletin. Lansing, MI: MDE.

———. 2011. "Governor, Detroit Public Schools Emergency Manager Jointly Unveil Dramatic Education Reform Plan to Restructure Failing Michigan Schools." Press release, Governor's Office. June 20. Lansing, MI: MDE. http://www.michigan.gov/mde/0,4615,7-140--258186--,00.html (accessed September 8, 2011).

Michigan Department of the Treasury, Office of Revenue and Tax Analysis. 2009. *Administration Estimates Michigan Economic and Revenue Outlook, FY 2008–09 and FY 2009–10.* January 9, Lansing, MI: Michigan Department of Treasury.

Michigan Senate. 1999. February 10, *Senate bill no. 10.*

Milliken v. Bradley, 418 U.S. 717 (1974).

Milliken v. Bradley, 433 U.S. 267, 287–88 (1977).
Milliken v. Green, 389 Mich. 1, 203 N.W. 2d 457 (1972); 232 N.W. 2d 711 (1973).
Mirel, Jeffrey. 1993. *The Rise and Fall of an Urban School System, Detroit, 1907–81*. Ann Arbor, MI: University of Michigan Press.
———. 1998. "After the Fall: Continuity and Change in Detroit, 1981–1995." *History of Education Quarterly* 38(3): 237–267.
———. 2004. "Detroit: There Is Still a Long Road to Travel, and Success Is Far from Assured." In *Mayors in the Middle: Politics, Race, and Mayoral Control of Urban Schools*, Jeffrey Henig and Wilbur Rich, eds. Princeton, NJ: Princeton University Press, pp. 120–158.
Missouri v. Jenkins, 515 U.S. 70 (1995).
Mt. Clemens-Macomb Daily. 1970. "Two School Districts Ban Questions." February, A:1.
Murnane, Richard J. 1988. "Education and the Productivity of the Workforce: Looking Ahead." In *American Living Standards: Threats and Challenges*, Robert E. Litan, Robert Z. Lawrence, and Charles L. Schultze, eds. Washington, DC: Brookings Institution Press, pp. 215–244.
Murnane, Richard J., and Jennifer L. Steele. 2007. "What Is the Problem? The Challenge of Providing Effective Teachers for All Children." *The Future of Children* 17(1): 15–43.
Murphy, Jerome T., and David K. Cohen. 1974. "Accountability in Education—The Michigan Experience." *The Public Interest* 36: 53–82.
National Center for Education Statistics, U.S. Department of Education (NCES). 2000. *Condition of America's Public School Facilities: 1999*. NCES Report No. 2000-032. Washington, DC: NCES.
———. 2007. *Mapping 2005 State Proficiency Standards onto the NAEP Scales*. NCES Report No. 2007-482. Washington, DC: NCES.
National Commission on Excellence in Education. 1983. *A Nation at Risk: The Imperative for Educational Reform. A Report to the Nation and the Secretary of Education*. Washington, DC: U.S. Department of Education, National Commission on Excellence in Education.
Nelson, Adam R. 2005. *The Elusive Ideal: Equal Educational Opportunity and the Federal Role in Boston's Public Schools, 1950–1985*. Chicago, IL: University of Chicago Press.
Nelson, F. Howard, Bella Rosenberg, and Nancy Van Meter. 2004. *Charter School Achievement on the 2003 National Assessment of Educational Progress*. Washington, DC: American Federation of Teachers. http://nepc.colorado.edu/files/EPRU-0408-63-OWI%5B1%5D.pdf (accessed June 16, 2011).
New York Times. 1989. "A Jeffersonian Compact: A Statement by the President and Governors." October 1, E:22.

———. 2010. "States Embrace Core Standards for the Schools." July 21, A:1.

North Central Association (NCA). 2009. "NCA CASI History." Alpharetta, GA: NCA. http://www.ncacasi.org/history/ (accessed February 13, 2009).

Obama '08. 2008. *Barack Obama's Plan for Lifetime Success through Education*. http://www.BarackObama.com (accessed February 18, 2009).

O'Conner, Brian J. 2009. "U.S. Rebound Will Leave Mich. in Dust." *Detroit News*, Oct.1, A:18.

Odden, Allan. 2011. *Strategic Management of Human Capital in Education: Improving Instructional Practice and Student Learning*. New York: Routledge.

Orfield, Gary, and Chungmei Lee. 2006. *Racial Transformation and the Changing Nature of Segregation*. Cambridge, MA: The Civil Rights Project, Harvard University.

Parents Involved in Community Schools Inc. v. Seattle School District, 426 F. 3d 1162 (2007).

Phelps, James L., and Michael F. Addonizio. 1983. "Michigan Public School Finance: The Last Ten Years." *Journal of Education Finance* 9(Summer): 3–16.

Piliawsky, Monte. 2003. "Educational Reform or Corporate Agenda? State Takeover of Detroit Public Schools." In *The Future of Educational Studies*, George Noblit and Beth Hatt-Echeverria, eds. New York: Peter Lang, pp. 265–283.

Plummer, E. 2006. "The Effects of State Funding on Property Tax Rates and School Construction." *Economics of Education Review* 25(5): 532–542.

Powell, Arthur G., Eleanor Farrar, and David K. Cohen. 1985. *The Shopping Mall High School*. Boston: Houghton-Mifflin.

Public Law 103-227, 103rd Congress. 1994. *Goals 2000: Educate America Act*.

Public Law 107-110, 107th Congress. 2002. *An Act to Close the Achievement Gap with Accountability, Flexibility, and Choice, So That No Child Is Left Behind*.

Public Sector Consultants. 1992. *Michigan in Brief: 1992–93 Issues Handbook*. Lansing, MI: Public Sector Consultants.

Ravitch, Diane. 1995a. *National Standards in American Education: A Citizen's Guide*. Washington, DC: Brookings Institution Press.

———. 1995b. *Debating the Future of American Education: Do We Need National Standards and Assessments*? Washington, DC: Brookings Institution Press.

Rebell, Michael A. 2006. "Adequacy Cost Studies: Perspectives on the State of the Art." *Education Finance and Policy* 1(4): 465–483.

———. 2009. *Courts and Kids: Pursuing Educational Equity through the State Courts*. Chicago: University of Chicago Press.

Rich, Wilbur C. 2009. "Who's Afraid of a Mayoral Takeover of Detroit Public Schools?" In *When Mayors Take Charge: School Governance in the City*, Joseph P. Viteritti, ed. Washington, DC: Brookings Institution Press, pp. 148–167.
Richardson, Elliot. 1976. "Dialogues on Decentralization: An Introduction." *Publius* 6(4): 1–6.
Ritter, Gary W., and Christopher J. Lucas. 2006. "Devil in the Details: Making Sensible Modifications to No Child Left Behind: A Policy Brief." *Education Finance & Policy* 1(2): 266–277.
Rivkin, Steven G., Eric A. Hanushek, and John F. Kain. 2005. "Teachers, Schools, and Academic Achievement." *Econometrica* 73(2): 417–458.
Rockoff, John E. 2004. "The Impact of Individual Teachers on Students' Achievement: Evidence from Panel Data." *American Economic Review* 94(2): 247–252.
Roeber, Edward D. 1986. *Michigan Educational Assessment Program—History and Development.* Report prepared for the U.S. Congress, Office of Technology Assessment, Congress of the United States. Washington, DC: U.S. Congress, Office of Technology Assessment.
Rose v. Council for Better Education, 790 S.W. 2d 186 (Ky. 1989).
Rothstein, Jesse M. 2006. "Good Principals or Good Peers? Parental Valuation of School Characteristics, Tiebout Equilibrium, and the Incentive Effects of Competition among Jurisdictions." *American Economic Review* 96(4): 1333–1350.
Roy, Joydeep, and Lawrence Mishel. 2004. "Advantage None: Re-Examining Hoxby's Finding of Charter School Benefits." Economic Policy Institute Briefing Paper. Washington, DC: Economic Policy Institute.
Sanders, William L., Arnold M. Saxton, and Sandra P. Horn. 1997. "The Tennessee Value-Added Accountability System: A Quantitative, Outcomes-Based Approach to Educational Assessment." In *Grading Teachers, Grading Schools: Is Student Achievement a Valid Evaluation Measure?* Jason Millman, ed. Thousand Oaks, CA: Corwin Press, pp. 137–162.
"Schools Resist State Takeover." 1999. *Detroit News*, January 27.
Schultz, Marisa. 2010. "Foes of Mayoral Control for Detroit Schools to Protest." *Detroit News*, June 13.
Sederburg, William A., and Herbert C. Rudman. 1984. "Educational Reform and Declining Test Scores." *Michigan School Board Journal* 30(24): 8–10, 24.
Serrano v. Priest, 96 Cal. Rptr. 601, 487 P. 2d 1241, 5 Cal. 3d 584 (1971).
Serrin, William. 1975. "The Detroit Disease: An American Infection." *Urban Review* 8(2): 153–154.
Shankar, Al. 1988a. "Address to the National Press Club." Washington, DC.
———. 1988b. "A Charter for Change." *New York Times*, July 10, E:7.

Shils, Edward. 1965. "Charisma, Order, and Status." *American Sociological Review* 30(2): 199–213.

Smith, Marshall S., and Jennifer O'Day. 1990. "Systemic School Reform." *Journal of Education Policy* 5(5): 223–267.

Snider, William. 1989. "In Backing Tax Proposals, Voters Endorse School Reforms." *Education Week* (September 20): 1, 12.

State Board of Education (SBE). 2003a. *Final Report and Recommendations of the Michigan Accreditation Advisory Committee to the State Board of Education*. Lansing, MI: Michigan State Board of Education.

———. 2003b. "Standards for Accreditation. EducationYES! A Yardstick for Excellent Schools." Summary Bulletin. Lansing, MI: Michigan State Board of Education.

Taylor, Frederick W. 1911. *The Principles of Scientific Management.* New York: Harper & Brothers.

Teske, Paul, Mark Schneider, Christine Roch, and Melissa Marschall. 1999. "Public School Choice: A Status Report." In *City Schools: Lessons from New York*, Diane Ravitch and Joseph Viteritti, eds. Baltimore, MD: Johns Hopkins University Press, pp. 313–338.

Thomas, J. Alan. 1968. *School Finance and Educational Opportunity in Michigan.* Lansing, MI: Michigan Department of Education.

Tirozzi, Gerald N. 2009. "Principals' Perspective—The Case for National Standards." *Education Week* 28(24): 21.

Toch, Thomas. 1991. *In the Name of Excellence*. New York: Oxford University Press.

United States. 1962. *Congressional Record: Proceedings and Debates of the 87th Congress*. Washington, DC: Supt. of Docs., Government Printing Office.

U.S. Department of Education. 2004. *America's Charter Schools: Results from the NAEP 2003 Pilot Study*. Washington, DC: National Center for Education Statistics.

———. 2006. *Digest of Education Statistics 2005.* Washington, DC: National Center for Education Statistics.

Urquiola, Miguel. 2005. "Does School Choice Lead to Sorting? Evidence from Tiebout Sorting." *American Economic Review* 95(4): 1310–1326.

Vergari, Sandra 2007. "The Politics of Charter Schools." *Educational Policy* 21(1): 15–39.

Vinovskis, Maris A. 1998. *Overseeing the Nation's Report Card: The Creation and Evolution of the National Assessment Governing Board.* Washington, DC: National Assessment Governing Board. http://www.nces.ed.gov/nationsreport card/about/naephistory.asp (accessed March 3, 2009).

———. 2009. *From a Nation at Risk to No Child Left Behind.* New York: Teachers College Press.

Wassmer, Robert W., and Ronald C. Fisher. 1996. “An Evaluation of the Recent Move to Centralize the Finance of Public Schools in Michigan.” *Public Finance and Budgeting* 16(3): 90–112.

Weiher, Gregory R., and Kent L. Tedin. 2002. “Does Choice Lead to Racially Distinctive Schools? Charter Schools and Household Preferences.” *Journal of Policy Analysis and Management* 21(1): 79–92.

Weiss, Janet A. 1990. *Comparing Market Incentives with Ideas as Instruments of Education Policy.* Ann Arbor, MI: Institute of Public Policy Studies, University of Michigan.

Will, Robert F. 1962. “State Administrative Rulemaking.” *School Life* 44(April): 19–21.

Williams, Brian A. 1998. *John Dewey at the University of Michigan.* Ann Arbor, MI: Bentley Historical Library, University of Michigan. http://www.soe.umich.edu/files/John_Dewey_Michigan.pdf (accessed August 31, 2011).

Winerip, Michael. 2011. “For the Detroit Schools, Hope for the Hopeless.” *New York Times,* March 14, A:13.

Witte, John F. 2000. *The Market Approach to Education: An Analysis of America's First Voucher Program.* Princeton, NJ: Princeton University Press.

Witte, John F., Deven E. Carlson, and Lesley Lavery. 2008. “Moving On: Why Students Move between Districts under Open Enrollment.” Occasional Paper No. 164. New York: National Center for the Study of Privatization in Education, Teachers College, Columbia University.

Wong, Kenneth K. 2009. “Does Mayoral Control Improve Performance in Urban Districts.” In *When Mayors Take Charge: School Governance in the City*, Joseph P. Viteritti, ed. Washington, DC: Brookings Institution Press, pp. 64–90.

Wong, Kenneth K., Francis X. Shen, Dorothea Anagnostopoulos, and Stacey Rutledge. 2007. *The Education Mayor: Improving America's Schools.* Washington, DC: Georgetown University Press.

Ypsilanti Press. 1970. “Slanted Pupil Tests—Who Checked, O.K.'d Them?” January 23.

Zelman v. Simmons-Harris, 536 U.S. 639 234 F. 3d 945 (reversed) (2002).

Authors

Michael F. Addonizio is a professor of education policy at the College of Education, Wayne State University, where he teaches graduate courses in public school finance, the economics of education, and education policy. His research interests include K–12 public school finance, teacher labor markets, and educational choice. He has taught at Wayne State since 1994.

Prior to joining Wayne State University, Addonizio served as assistant state superintendent for research and policy in the Michigan Department of Education and as education policy advisor to Governor John Engler. He has served as a consultant to the Michigan State Board of Education, the Michigan Superintendent of Public Instruction, the Office of the Michigan Attorney General, the U.S. Department of Education, and the Detroit Tigers Major League Baseball team. He also served as an appointed member of the Michigan Commission on Charter Schools in 2001–02. He holds an AB in English from Holy Cross College, an MA in public policy from the University of Michigan, and a PhD in economics from Michigan State University.

C. Philip Kearney is a professor emeritus at the University of Michigan, where he was a professor in the school of education from 1980 to 1998. From 1985 to 1992 he also was director of the Bureau of Accreditation and School Improvement Studies; from 1987 to 1989, associate dean of the school; and in 1988, interim dean. In late 1995, on leave from the university, Kearney joined the National Board for Professional Teaching Standards as senior program director.

Kearney has served as a consultant to Monash University and the Australian Council on Education in Victoria, South Australia, and New South Wales; the Ministry of Education and Research in Bucharest, Romania; the Education Development Center, Inc., in Boston, Massachusetts; the National Research Council in Washington, DC; the James B. Hunt, Jr. Institute for Educational Leadership and Policy in Chapel Hill, North Carolina; and Nova Southeastern University in Fort Lauderdale, Florida. From 2007 to 2010, he served as adjunct professor at Wayne State University.

Prior to coming to the University of Michigan, Kearney served as associate director and then deputy director of the Institute for Educational Leadership in Washington, DC. From 1968 to 1977, he was with the State of Michigan as an associate superintendent of public instruction. He also has been a classroom teacher, a guidance counselor, and a building and central office administrator in public schools in the states of Washington and Ohio.

Kearney is a former president of the American Education Finance Association, and served as one of seven public members of the U.S. Department of Education's National Advisory Council on Education Statistics and as presiding officer of that body. He is a veteran of four years service as an infantry officer in the United States Marine Corps. Kearney holds BA and MA degrees from the University of Portland in Oregon, and a PhD from the University of Chicago.

Index

The italic letters *f, n,* and *t* following a page number indicate that the subject information of the heading is within a figure, note, or table, respectively, on that page. Double italics indicate multiple but consecutive elements.

About the Institute

The W.E. Upjohn Institute for Employment Research is a nonprofit research organization devoted to finding and promoting solutions to employment-related problems at the national, state, and local levels. It is an activity of the W.E. Upjohn Unemployment Trustee Corporation, which was established in 1932 to administer a fund set aside by Dr. W.E. Upjohn, founder of The Upjohn Company, to seek ways to counteract the loss of employment income during economic downturns.

The Institute is funded largely by income from the W.E. Upjohn Unemployment Trust, supplemented by outside grants, contracts, and sales of publications. Activities of the Institute comprise the following elements: 1) a research program conducted by a resident staff of professional social scientists; 2) a competitive grant program, which expands and complements the internal research program by providing financial support to researchers outside the Institute; 3) a publications program, which provides the major vehicle for disseminating the research of staff and grantees, as well as other selected works in the field; and 4) an Employment Management Services division, which manages most of the publicly funded employment and training programs in the local area.

The broad objectives of the Institute's research, grant, and publication programs are to 1) promote scholarship and experimentation on issues of public and private employment and unemployment policy, and 2) make knowledge and scholarship relevant and useful to policymakers in their pursuit of solutions to employment and unemployment problems.

Current areas of concentration for these programs include causes, consequences, and measures to alleviate unemployment; social insurance and income maintenance programs; compensation; workforce quality; work arrangements; family labor issues; labor-management relations; and regional economic development and local labor markets.